PRAISE FOR
GIVING DONE RIGHT

"Phil Buchanan has dedicated his professional life to the question of what makes philanthropy most effective. Throughout, he has remained committed to the idea that nonprofits need a disciplined focus on results, while also keeping clear that nonprofits differ in significant ways from business. Anyone who seeks to achieve impactful philanthropy would do well to learn from his vast experience and deep wisdom."

—**Jim Collins**, author of *Good to Great*, coauthor of *Built to Last*

"Phil Buchanan is arguably the best informed and most insightful thought leader in philanthropy today, and this book shows him at his best: Like its author, *Giving Done Right* is grounded in data, animated by real stories well told, and provocative in ways that shed more light than heat. An essential and highly readable guide for foundations and donors ready to move beyond feeling good to doing good."

—**Richard Ober**, president and CEO, New Hampshire Charitable Foundation

"*Giving Done Right* punctures myths and provides helpful guidance about the complexities and joys of philanthropy. Buchanan makes a persuasive and always practical case for why nonprofits are not like businesses, why giving is not like investing, and how readers can find their own satisfying path to doing great good."

—**Rosabeth Moss Kanter**, Arbuckle Professor, Harvard Business School, founder of the Harvard University Advanced Leadership Initiative

"Giving is easy. Giving with real impact is anything but. In this go-to primer, Phil Buchanan offers invaluable insights about the art and practice of strategic philanthropy."

—**Stephen Heintz**, president, Rockefeller Brothers Fund

"*Giving Done Right* should be required reading for anyone looking to better understand how to achieve more effectiveness in their giving. Phil Buchanan's research, data, and storytelling make clear the challenges with bringing a business mindset to solving social problems. This book provides a thorough overview of the change in mindset necessary to attain more satisfaction with your giving."

—**Pamela Norley**, president, Fidelity Charitable

"The Center for Effective Philanthropy created the first-ever genuine accountability mechanism for determining the effectiveness of foundation performance. Phil Buchanan first articulated the obvious need, crafted a workable mechanism for measuring performance, and then succeeded in selling it to foundation officers and trustees. That Grantee Perception Report has now become the gold standard for foundations to assess the effectiveness of their giving on all important criteria. In *Giving Done Right*, Buchanan has widened his clear vision beyond foundations by providing a reliable guide for all donors—individuals, foundations, corporations, and indeed recipients of charitable dollars—who are determined to do their charitable giving and spending the right way. Anyone resolved to get the biggest and wisest bang for their charitable dollars need look no further for guidance now than this experience-filled, reader-friendly book."

—**Joel Fleishman**, director of the Duke University Center for Strategic Philanthropy, author of *Putting Wealth to Work: Philanthropy for Today or Investing for Tomorrow?*

"Phil Buchanan knows and celebrates the diversity of the nonprofit sector, from the smallest community-based organization to the largest university or museum; from the individual donor making small annual gifts to her favorite charities to the largest private foundation awarding hundreds of millions in grants. *Giving Done Right* is full of data, insights, and helpful suggestions for us all."

—**Carol Larson**, president and CEO, David and Lucile Packard Foundation

Giving
Done
Right

Giving Done Right

EFFECTIVE PHILANTHROPY AND MAKING EVERY DOLLAR COUNT

PHIL BUCHANAN

PUBLICAFFAIRS

New York

PublicAffairs
Hachette Book Group
1290 Avenue of the Americas, New York, NY 10104
www.publicaffairsbooks.com
@Public_Affairs

Printed in the United States of America

First Edition: April 2019

Published by PublicAffairs, an imprint of Perseus Books, LLC, a subsidiary of Hachette Book Group, Inc. The PublicAffairs name and logo is a trademark of the Hachette Book Group.

The Hachette Speakers Bureau provides a wide range of authors for speaking events. To find out more, go to www.hachettespeakersbureau.com or call (866) 376-6591.

The publisher is not responsible for websites (or their content) that are not owned by the publisher.

Print book interior design by Amy Quinn.

Library of Congress Cataloging-in-Publication Data has been applied for.

ISBNs: 978-1-5417-4225-3 (hardcover); 978-1-5417-4223-9 (ebook)

LSC-C

10 9 8 7 6 5 4 3 2 1

For Lara

CONTENTS

Author's Note ix
Foreword by Darren Walker xi

Introduction It's Not Your Business: Why Giving Is a
Challenge Like No Other 1

1 Nonprofits and Their Unsung American Heroes 11

2 So Many Ways to Give 35

3 A Tough Balance: Choosing Your Goals 63

4 Strategy Done Right: Achieving Your Goals 83

5 Essential Partners: Selecting and Working with Nonprofits 107

6 No Easy Answers: Assessing Performance 135

7 Deploying All the Tools 159

Conclusion A Virtuous Cycle of Good 185

Giving Resources 195
Acknowledgments 199
Notes 205
Index 219

AUTHOR'S NOTE

This book would not exist were it not for the support of the Board of Directors and staff of the Center for Effective Philanthropy (CEP), the nonprofit organization where I have worked for the past seventeen years. Although the views expressed in these pages are mine, I have drawn heavily on research and knowledge developed by CEP. I am grateful for all the support I have received in undertaking this project. Fifty percent of all royalties associated with the sale of this book for the first year following its publication will go to CEP to support its ongoing work.

FOREWORD

We live in a time of many urgent challenges. Inequality has widened the gap between the rich and the poor. In the United States, the free press is under attack, while mass incarceration tears at the fabric of our society. Racism and nationalism are on the rise around the world, while people find their opportunities inhibited by persistent injustices based on their gender, race, sexual orientation, ability, or citizenship status. Meanwhile, climate change threatens the planet and people everywhere. The list goes on.

These challenges seem daunting on their own. They might even appear insurmountable when we consider the finite resources we have to solve them. Yet what gives me hope is that people from every walk of life see those problems—in their local communities, nations, and world—and ask, How can I help?

For many people and through many decades, one answer to that question has been philanthropy. In fact, when Andrew Carnegie wrote his 1889 essay "Wealth," he envisioned philanthropy as a necessary and effective means of ameliorating the worst conditions the free market produced. The idea that the wealthy were obligated to give away money during their lifetime was radical at the time. Following the publication of Carnegie's essay, what we now know as the modern field of philanthropy emerged. As a result, millions of people have access to tools and resources with which to improve their lives.

In the 130 years since Carnegie's original essay—now known as the Gospel of Wealth—the number of people, foundations, and resources joining the field of philanthropy only continues to grow. At the same time, we have continued to learn, and we know more today than Carnegie could have imagined. We have gained experiences, understanding, and perspective from decades of success and failure. We have new technologies, data, research, and tools available to help us. We have learned more about how to be effective—how to understand the root causes of problems, build institutions, and partner with communities to ensure they have a voice in the decisions that affect them. We have new insights into how structural inequalities, unconscious biases, and systemic injustices have influenced what we've done wrong in the past and where we are today.

And yet, for as much as we've learned, understanding philanthropy's impact remains a challenge. For many of us who want to do good, there is always the question of how to do it right.

Of course, it's important to remember two things. First, money alone cannot solve problems.

Money can fund institutions that make lasting change by putting in work across generations. It can support individuals doing good work and help them realize their ideas. And the people who run these institutions, support these individuals, and scale these ideas—people throughout the nonprofit sector—are, as this book suggests, the unsung heroes of our society. At a moment when trust in so many institutions is in decline, civil society organizations such as these are fundamental—doing the work beyond the purview of government or business, work that our communities and society desperately need.

Now, more than ever before, many are looking to civil society to promote virtues of fairness and equality—to help shore up and save our democracy. And there is a crucial role that philanthropy can play in that effort. It can and should help restore the commitment to justice that drives our society to care for itself. Beyond engaging in charity, it can combat the underlying forces testing the heart of our democracy, whether it's the current assault on journalism, the curtailing of basic democratic rights such as voting, the ever-widening inequality gap, or systemic racism and discrimination. On top of these benefits, this sector has the ability to cross divides and build bridges, to connect and convene people interested in making this world better from every sector, and to restore empathy and remind people that we have more in common than we realize—in our hopes for the future, experience of the human condition, and desire for justice.

Which brings me to the second piece that's important to remember: Just as money alone does not solve problems, philanthropists are not alone in doing this work.

In my own career in philanthropy, I have been fortunate to call on Phil Buchanan for wisdom and counsel. Every time I have sought his help, Phil has cut through the noise and gotten to the root of the issue. He is a master problem solver, and he never fails to formulate solutions that incorporate the best methods and most potent thinking.

No one has a better view of the diversity of this sector, the range of organizations and needs, the emerging trends, and troublesome errors. He is a student of the field, a skilled researcher and author of numerous thoughtful reports. His unique perspective—as someone who has led a growing organization, advised countless others, and even given himself—has made him an invaluable thought partner and trusted advocate of the sector and its future.

Put simply, Phil has dedicated nearly two decades and this early part of the twenty-first century to improving philanthropy for decades to come.

What's more, as president and chief executive of the Center for Effective Philanthropy (CEP) for the past seventeen years, Phil has advised countless individual donors and foundations and built CEP into an indispensable resource for all those who hope to make a difference. Thanks to his leadership and stewardship, CEP has become an essential repository of insightful data and best practices.

This book is no different.

In these pages, Phil not only synthesizes the many lessons he's learned over the course of his time at CEP, but presents the wealth of knowledge he's acquired through his long career. He combines data and stories with practical advice for givers of every kind and category and helps all of us who want to help figure out how to do it most effectively.

Of course, Phil's leadership is not only defined by his brain or the extensive knowledge he brings to the table. It is also defined by his heart.

Phil models the kind of passionate advocacy for the individuals and organizations doing good that all funders and philanthropists should aspire to. He knows this work is done by people, for people, and that funding can only be effective if it acknowledges that. He understands, better than most, that the health of our civil society is inextricably linked to the health of our democracy.

Indeed, an active and effective civil society is crucial to the success of any democracy, especially one that draws its power and strength from "we the people." The organizations, institutions, foundations, and advocacy groups that compose this "third sector" of society give citizens the space to organize and make their voices heard, and serve and represent their needs and interests. So, when leaders like Phil work to strengthen civil society, they simultaneously strengthen the foundation of our democracy: the people.

That's why this work and this book are so important.

Whether you are the leader of a foundation or an individual with limited money to give, this book has something to offer you. If you are looking for on-the-ground, practical advice on how to execute effective philanthropy, regardless of the scale, it will undoubtedly leave you intrigued, informed, and, more than anything, inspired.

It does not matter what you do for a living or even how much money you have to contribute. This book is written for doers of all kinds. It's written for all those who desire to go a step beyond giving and learn how to give effectively.

As we envision the future of philanthropy for the twenty-first century, as we push this field beyond simple generosity, we can continue to make philanthropy a more precise, targeted, and effective tool for justice. This book helps us learn how.

I am so glad that if you are reading this book, you too can have this benefit my colleagues and I have long enjoyed—the wise counsel and big heart of Phil Buchanan—and take it with you as you give. Together, we can channel all of our resources, energies, and passion toward not just giving done right, but doing good—and doing justice—with our giving.

Darren Walker
President, Ford Foundation

Introduction

IT'S NOT YOUR BUSINESS

WHY GIVING IS A CHALLENGE LIKE NO OTHER

"I JUST WANT to know we made a difference," one multibillionaire philanthropist, in her sixties, told me.

Even those whose full-time job is giving get anxious about it. "I worry about whether we're doing all we can, as well as we can. I worry that we're not. I worry we don't even really know. I worry all the time," a foundation CEO shared.

Every week, I have conversations like these with people. They're allocating resources—a lot of resources—to address pressing social problems. It's a huge privilege, and indeed most people who meet them and learn what they do are rather jealous. But it's also an awesome responsibility, so they worry. Those who work at institutions where giving is their job and individual givers alike see the impact of their philanthropy as among their most important legacies (second only—and not always second—to their kids and grandkids), and they don't want to squander it.

This worry about maximizing the good of giving has been the recurring conversation for more than seventeen years of my professional life, as the founding chief executive of the Center for Effective Philanthropy (CEP). Research we've conducted on foundation CEOs reveals not only a widespread sense that philanthropy must do better, but also uncertainty about how. In analyzing results from a survey and in-depth interviews with these leaders, we found that the overwhelming majority believe foundations can make a significant difference in society, but few believe they're realizing their full potential.[1]

This uncertainty and concern aren't all that different from the anxiety of my friends and family members—people of more regular means—who wonder whether their own charitable contributions are making a difference. You've probably wondered the same thing as you've written a check, made a contribution online, or directed a gift from a donor-advised fund you hold at your local community foundation. After all, it's not nearly as easy to gauge the impact your giving has as it is to check the performance of your 401(k). That's because, while investments can be easily measured by their returns, the impact of giving is much more challenging to assess.

So Many Questions

This book is for givers at all levels who struggle with how to make the most difference. It's for the megadonors and the everyday givers—the overwhelming majority of American households that contribute to charitable organizations. They do so because their hearts compel them to; they want to make a difference when it comes to issues and causes they care deeply about. But, in their head, they ask:

Am I on the right track to make the impact I seek?

What do I need to understand about the nonprofit sector and philanthropy to give well?

Should I give when asked by someone knocking on my door, or by the cashier at the store, or in response to a natural disaster?

Am I focused on the right goals? Did I choose the right giving strategies to achieve them?

Is my money really going where I intend?

How will I gauge progress?

What resources can help me do my giving well?

It's overwhelming; I get it. And if there's anything I've learned during my time working on these issues and helping givers face these questions, it's that answers are elusive. But my hope is that, in the pages that follow, I'll help you understand the unique challenge of giving as well as the essential ingredients for effectiveness, so you can know that you've maximized your chances of contributing to real, lasting impact.

I also hope to help persuade you of philanthropy's great contributions—historical, present day, and potential future—to making the United States and this planet a better place. To be an effective giver, you need to learn from what's worked, or you'll be doomed to make the same, predictable mistakes many new givers make.

In the United States, giving has done more good than even many givers realize, and though many challenges remain, it has contributed to much of what makes this a great country. It has also contributed to global progress in improving the human condition; this is by any number of measures the best time in human history to be alive. That point feels especially important to underscore now, amid an increasing torrent of external criticism of philanthropy.

Giving and Nonprofits Aren't Like Business

Criticism of philanthropy, which has been on the upswing in recent years, comes especially from those who promote the idea that business or market-based approaches offer the answer to the giving challenge. I can't tell you how many times I've heard someone say that philanthropy isn't effective and that nonprofits and donors need to act more like businesses—although it isn't clear what that statement even means. This thinking has been going on for a while. I heard it nearly two decades ago while getting my MBA at Harvard, and it's only grown more intense since then.

Indeed, it seems that much, if not most, of what business school faculty, management consultants, Silicon Valley tech titans (or titan wannabes), and others have written about philanthropy in the past few decades takes the view that charitable giving and the nonprofit sector more broadly are broken and in need of an injection of "business thinking." People invoke that term as a synonym for "well-managed" or "effective." I worked as a strategy consultant in the business world, and I can tell you this: It's not. Moreover, this claim does a disservice to the incredible array of highly effective nonprofits and nonprofit leaders in the United States.

"We must reject the idea—well intentioned but dead wrong—that the primary path to greatness in the social sectors is to become 'more like a business,'" argues Jim Collins, one of the few prominent business thinkers who seems to understand philanthropy and nonprofits. "Most businesses—like most of anything else in life—fall somewhere between mediocre and good. . . . So then, why would we want to import the practices of mediocrity into the social sectors?"[2]

I agree with Collins, and I'm concerned that the constant critiques of nonprofits as "lesser than" are beginning to alter the public's and lawmakers' views, contributing to damaging policy changes such as the effective curtailment of the charitable deduction in the tax reform bill that took effect in 2018. (It's likely to significantly reduce the number of filers itemizing and therefore benefitting from the deduction.) I'm also concerned that the counsel to operate like a business is confusing and runs counter to achieving impact. Most nonprofits and nonprofit leaders I know are rigorous, data-driven, and fully aware of how different their work is than that of business—requiring different approaches to goal selection, strategy development, implementation, and performance assessment.

The most effective givers understand this difference, too. These philanthropists know that, while their business acumen (or that of their forebears) may have created their wealth, giving effectively requires a different set of skills. It necessitates a different level of collaboration and relationship-building, deep humility, and a recognition of how difficult it is to chart cause and effect. In each of these ways, and many others, it's different than what it takes to be effective in business. It is its own unique challenge, requiring its own unique discipline. That's what technology entrepreneur and investor Mario Morino found out after the business he helped build was acquired in 1995. Morino, a self-made multimillionaire who grew up in a working-class family in Cleveland, is now in his seventies, with two decades of giving behind him and many lessons learned.

"I probably did as much background research as anyone, and I'd argue I didn't do enough," he told me. "I was really arrogant." Morino said he was too quick to assume that what worked in his business experience would translate to his giving. Over the years, he has become one of the most thoughtful givers I know, and his influence has been significant. But, as he'd be the first to tell you, it hasn't been easy.

Givers are often seeking to address the most entrenched problems—the very ones that have defied market or government solutions. That intractability means success won't come quickly. While many givers are anxious about whether they're achieving results, as Morino and those who seek out CEP for counsel often are, others have the opposite problem. They think they've accomplished a great deal when they haven't. "Everyone's puking on the sidewalk while this guy is taking a bow," Morino explained in his characteristically blunt way.[3]

Morino would agree that we need to be on the lookout for innovative and creative approaches that will work better than the old ones. But he'd also say that he's learned that there are few easy answers and no quick fixes.

Giving Has Been a Powerful Force for Good

We tend to focus on the challenges and problems we see. After all, there are many today, including disturbing threats to our democratic institutions, growing inequality, and a rising tide of racism. But it's also important to remember the progress we've made. As *New York Times* columnist Nicholas Kristof put it, 2017 was "probably the very best year in the long history of humanity." On metrics from the number of people in poverty, to illiteracy, to childhood mortality, to disfigurement from disease, to blindness, there has been enormous progress.[4] Givers have contributed to this progress and much else: supporting the research that led to commercial aviation and the Internet, combatting environmental degradation and cleaning up rivers and lakes, ensuring that poor children have somewhere safe to go after school or helping them progress academically, curing disease, and caring for the sick and dying.

Giving has made a huge difference in all of our lives. Look at the work of foundations and nonprofits to combat tuberculosis in the United States one hundred years ago.[5] Or the work of the Robert Wood Johnson Foundation and many others to reduce the rates of smoking in the United States between 1990 and 2010.[6] Or, more recently, the work of the Civil Marriage Collaborative, a consortium of givers that pooled their resources and strategically aligned their grantmaking over eleven years and to the tune of $153 million. They achieved results beyond what anyone would have pre-dicted when the US Supreme Court ruled that the right to marry is constitu-tionally guaranteed to same-sex couples in 2015.[7]

Despite the real challenges around us—such as poverty, the threat of terrorism, or the treatment of military veterans—we cannot deny the prog-ress that has been made on many fronts.

Giving—your giving—can make a difference.

I'll aim to equip you with the facts and insights that will allow you to do just that. This book will describe and refute the most common and dam-aging myths. It will help you learn from what has worked and build on that success. It will help you understand that you're not alone in the realization that it's hard to do good well—much harder, in fact, than building wealth, as Andrew Carnegie famously observed.[8]

Effective Giving Essentials

In the pages that follow, I'll lay out what we know about what it takes to be an effective giver. In Chapter 1, I'll offer a high-altitude look at the US non-profit sector in all its vastness and diversity, arguing that it plays a distinc-tive and important role in our society—one that touches all our lives for the better. Then, in Chapter 2, I'll discuss the giving landscape and the myriad ways to give in pursuit of impact.

In Chapters 3 through 6, I'll turn to the particulars of what it takes to be effective, which I believe are universally applicable to individual and institutional givers who are dedicated to doing their giving well. It's about thoughtful goal selection, the identification of smart strategies, great rela-tionships with those you support, and assessment of progress. In Chapter 7, I'll discuss additional tools that you might employ to pursue your goals. Finally, in the Conclusion, I'll bring you back to why it all matters.

In addressing each of these areas, I'll draw on the extensive research CEP has conducted since I was hired as its first staff member in 2001. I'll also draw on what my colleagues and I have seen up close from our work with hundreds of foundation clients, including most of the world's largest foundations, as well as the individual donors and families affiliated with those institutions. Whenever possible, I'll tell you the stories—of givers, nonprofits, and those who benefit from their work—that bring effective philanthropy to life. I'll sort through the hype about "new" approaches, weeding out the fads from the promising innovations and refuting the most destructive myths. I use examples from both individual givers and institutional ones because I think, regardless of whether you're giving your own money or you work at a foundation as a program officer, the principles of effective giving apply. I think givers can learn from a broad range of examples. There are lessons for all of us in the giving of John D. Rockefeller and Bill Gates, just as there are lessons for tech titans in the giving of those with more-limited resources.

In the final pages of the book, I'll introduce you to two people whose lives have been transformed by giving and who have been inspired by the experience to give back themselves. That's the nature of giving done right: It sparks a virtuous cycle. Like the famous concept of the butterfly effect, which argues that a single butterfly can change weather patterns, effective giving ripples inward and outward, with far reaching positive consequences for givers and recipients. So, too, can ineffective giving reap far-reaching negative effects, resulting in tornadoes that inflict damage that was never intended.

Developing the Skills for Impact

There are some crucial insights and lessons to be learned by those who want to make a positive difference with their giving: the everyday check writers; the holders of donor-advised funds; the individual donors and families establishing or considering establishing foundations; those who advise donors establishing foundations; family offices of the wealthy and those who staff them; and the staff and boards of foundations and other grantmaking institutions. Whatever your motivation for giving—whether it comes from your religious beliefs, your concern about injustices, values passed along by your parents or family, or your personal experience with a problem or a disease—I hope this book helps you do your giving more effectively. I hope this book is also of interest to those curious about the role of giving in American society, including the growing number of students and academics studying the nonprofit sector and all those who raise money from, and interact with, individual and institutional givers.

I have drawn on a variety of sources to inform the perspectives I share in the pages that follow: CEP's extensive research, almost all of which has been led by my colleague Ellie Buteau, PhD, CEP's vice president for research; our experience working with hundreds of foundation and major donor clients, which my colleague Kevin Bolduc, CEP's vice president for assessment and advisory services, has overseen; insights of members of CEP's extraordinary board of directors as well as our more than forty staff members in our Cambridge, Massachusetts, and San Francisco offices; writing and analysis of others whose work I respect; and personal observation based on my interactions with thousands of givers as well as many nonprofit leaders.

I should note that many of the givers I discuss, especially the institutional ones, are clients of CEP, and many also provide some grant support to the organization. Some of the stories I tell focus on people with whom I've worked closely, including current and former members of our board of directors. I seek always to bring sober eyes to my discussions of their work. When describing donors and foundations, I relate only publicly available data or information from direct interviews with those involved. In several instances, I describe client engagements or conversations using pseudonyms instead of real names, and I've taken pains to ensure those examples aren't identifiable.

I focus primarily on the US context simply because it's what I know best. I don't claim to have all the answers, but I believe there are certain practices, principles, and approaches that will help you achieve greater success in your giving. In many—maybe even most—cases, the tenets of giving effectiveness run directly counter to conventional wisdom and to what you may have heard or read.

I believe givers can play a role in our society that other actors can't or won't, and that when they do it well the impact is profound. I'm inspired by many of those with whom I've had the privilege of working and from whom I have learned much. I hope, over the pages that follow, to inspire you to do the hard work required to be effective.

The fundamentals of effectiveness in giving are timeless and difficult to master. Just as there's no shortcut for the aspiring young soccer player through the painstaking process of developing her foot skills—juggling the ball for hours on end—so, too, the effective giver must learn and practice to become good. The effective giver must develop the skills and techniques that separate the philanthropic stars from the also-rans.

And just as skills for soccer differ from those required for success in basketball, what's needed to be effective in your giving is different from what's needed in business. It's not easy. It takes a lot of work, deep thought, humility, and a willingness to grapple with difficult-to-answer questions. But it pays off in greater progress toward your giving goals, whatever they may be.

It's worth the effort.

⪢ 1 ⪡

NONPROFITS AND THEIR UNSUNG AMERICAN HEROES

TIFFANY COOPER GUEYE grew up in the 1980s in the predominantly poor, African American Boston neighborhood of Dorchester, raised by her grandmother, who received food stamps. Gueye attended public school in an almost exclusively white, affluent suburb through a busing program intended to desegregate Boston-area schools. It was in that elementary school that she learned firsthand of the dramatic differences in opportunity determined by the neighborhood in which you happen to grow up.

The affluent Boston suburb was also where Gueye experienced racism. She recalls the third grade when, for weeks and weeks, she had tried and failed to play on the tire swing in the schoolyard. Every day, she was too late—her classmates beat her in a race to get to the swing first. By the time it was her turn, recess was over.

One day, Gueye finally was the first to reach the swing. But a classmate grabbed the swing from the other side and tried to stop her from using it. Gueye explained to the girl that she was there first so it was her turn.

The girl stared at Gueye and said, "Well, at least I'm not black."

At that moment, it sank in that she was one of only a few African Americans bused to an overwhelmingly white school that was swimming in resources—in sharp contrast to the school near her grandmother's Dorchester apartment. Her white classmates walked to school through their leafy neighborhoods, on streets lined with massive houses, or took a short bus ride. Gueye's day began before 6:00 a.m. and included hours on the bus. This incident became the defining one in Gueye's decision to spend her career working to close the gap between minority kids from low-income families and their better-off peers.

Motivated by this experience, Gueye went to Boston College, where she majored in psychology. Following her third-grade dream, she began working at a national nonprofit called BELL, which stands for Building Educated Leaders for Life. Gueye earned a PhD in educational research, evaluation, and measurement, also from Boston College, while working full-time at BELL. She was named CEO when she was just twenty-nine.

BELL helps inner-city kids succeed academically by countering "summer learning loss" via rigorous summer programs. (Summer learning loss—or academic backsliding during the summer vacation—occurs for all students but is much more pronounced among those in lower socioeconomic strata.) With funding from foundations, BELL has gone through the most rigorous possible evaluations—randomized control trials (RCTs) that compare the results for the kids in their programs with those for identical populations that didn't go through their programs. Think of clinical trials for drugs applied to social programs—one population gets the program, one doesn't, and the results are compared.

The RCTs, conducted by third parties, showed BELL's programs to be effective. They found statistically meaningful differences in academic performance between those who participated and those who didn't. BELL now has a budget of $20 million and is widely considered a model program. It reaches more than 16,000 students annually and is working with the YMCA to scale up dramatically to reach tens of thousands, maybe eventually hundreds of thousands, more young people.

Gueye, now in her late thirties, served for nine years as CEO until she stepped down in the summer of 2017. That spring, Boston College awarded her an honorary degree in recognition of her extraordinary leadership.[1]

"You Can Read a Balance Sheet?!"

Despite her achievements, you've probably never heard of Gueye until now, and if you're like many, you may not recognize just how talented nonprofit leaders often are. Look at the way people write about nonprofits: "The nonprofit model is broken," Ryan Seashore, founder and CEO of CodeNow, declared on TechCrunch.com. "Unless you're part of a unicorn nonprofit . . . then your organization likely has too much overhead, too much bureaucracy, and a lack of focus on impact. Everything feels slow," he continued, and "not enough like a for-profit startup."[2] This is a widely held view in the technology startup world. Reddit cofounder Alexis Ohanian uses almost identical language to Seashore's, writing in *Wired*: "Let's be real: The nonprofit model is broken. The twentieth-century way of guilting people into giving to an opaque, inefficient organization with massive overhead is no longer a viable model."[3]

Despite their impressive accomplishments, Gueye and other nonprofit leaders don't get the respect they deserve. They're idealists, they're passionate, and they're hard working. The best of them are, like Gueye, also amazing managers and leaders, brilliant strategists, and both finance- and data-savvy. They need to possess all the skills of a business CEO and many, many more. That may not be the stereotype about nonprofit leaders—but it's the truth.

Gueye told me how an MBA student in a class where she was a guest speaker was surprised when he learned about all that Gueye needed to do in her role, including ensuring quality programs, raising money, overseeing rigorous evaluations, and managing the financial and operational sides of the organization.

"It's amazing," the student said, astonishment in his voice. "You really understand finances, too, and how to talk about your income statement and balance sheet."

"Why would you expect anything else?" Gueye said. "I run a $20 million organization."[4]

The student had assumed that because she ran a nonprofit, she was "soft," not a numbers person. Maybe a visionary and a "do-gooder," but not a strong manager. His tone was patronizing.

But Gueye's role required her to do everything a CEO of a business does, including understanding the financials, and a lot more. It's in many ways a harder job than the jobs of her for-profit counterparts, not an easier one. Nonprofit leaders are a little like Ginger Rogers, who—as a cartoon famously described her—did everything Fred Astaire did, but backwards and in high heels.

Understanding the unique role of the nonprofit sector as well as the distinct challenges nonprofit leaders face is essential to being an effective giver. Too many givers fail to take the time to really gain this understanding. This chapter provides an overview of the lay of the land—an orientation to the terrain you'll need to understand and navigate to be effective.

No Respect

Misconceptions about nonprofits are common, and not just among MBA students. I know many givers who have a dim view of nonprofit leaders. But, to be effective, you need to reject the stereotypes and understand the unique challenges of running a nonprofit and what nonprofits most need from their funders. After all, you are dependent on the nonprofits you fund to deliver results.

The nonprofit sector, in all its vastness and diversity, is the "people's sector." It is a distinct part of the American fabric, with its history in the religious freedom the early European settlers sought.

Alexis de Tocqueville famously remarked on Americans' tendency to come together in pursuit of various causes in the 1830s:

> Americans of all ages, all stations of life, and all types of disposi-
> tion are forever forming associations. Americans combine to give fêtes,
> found seminaries, build churches, distribute books, and send mis-
> sionaries to the antipodes. Hospitals, prisons, and schools take shape
> in that way. Finally, if they want to proclaim a truth or propagate
> some feeling by the encouragement of a great example, they form an
> association.[5]

One hundred and fifty years later, John Gardner—founder of Common Cause and secretary of Health, Education, and Welfare under President Lyndon Johnson—described the sector as one

> in which we are committed to alleviate misery and redress grievances, to give rein to the mind's curiosity and the soul's longing, to seek beauty and defend truth where we must, to honor the worthy and smite the rascals with everyone free to define worthiness and rascality, to find cures and to console the incurable, to deal with the ancient impulse to hate and fear the tribe in the next valley, to prepare for tomorrow's crisis and preserve yesterday's wisdom, and to pursue the questions others won't pursue because they are too busy or too lazy or too fearful or too jaded.[6]

The nonprofit sector plays a distinct role, as Gardner so beautifully described. And individual nonprofits play many different roles: advocate, provider of aid to those in need, watchdog, educator, association.

The sector's role is distinct from government and business. Indeed, nonprofits are often a counterweight to both. As Rockefeller Brothers Fund president Stephen Heintz often says, the sector plays a kind of "checks and balances role" relative to business and government. Its existence contributes to a dynamic tension that is in some ways analogous to the three branches of the US government. By playing this role, former Connecticut College president Claire Gaudiani argued that philanthropy has "saved capitalism over many decades, like a smart, kind friend watches out for a somewhat intemperate but gifted colleague, advising him throughout his life on the need for self-restraint and better judgment."

Gaudiani offered up numerous examples, such as the campaigns by the nonprofit Environmental Defense Fund and others to ban DDT, convince McDonald's to stop using Styrofoam containers, and help phase out the use of lead in gasoline.[7]

"A Wonder of the World"

There is a tremendous diversity of nonprofit missions and approaches. Contrary to a widespread misconception, nonprofits aren't just about helping people out of poverty—although that, too, is a role many nonprofits play. As Duke University's Joel Fleishman has noted, "poverty is a problem that, ultimately, only government itself can completely remedy."[8] So aside from poverty alleviation, there are nonprofit research institutes, nonprofit associations, nonprofit museums, and nonprofit policy think tanks. Fleishman, who himself worked for years as a leader at a multibillion-dollar foundation, the Atlantic Philanthropies, wrote that the American civic sector "is a wonder of the world and an unprecedented social phenomenon—not unlike America itself, which, with all its shortcomings, is arguably the most dynamic, inclusive, and democratic society the world has ever seen."[9] The fact that this stirring description of our country feels perhaps less apt today than when Fleishman penned it a little over a decade ago only underscores the importance of this ideal, and of the role of nonprofits and philanthropy in helping America to be its best.

Nonprofits are also a much bigger part of our economy than most people realize. The nonprofit sector makes up almost one-tenth of US gross domestic product (GDP) in terms of total revenue. Employees of nonprofits make up more than one-tenth of the labor force. Millions volunteer.[10] And when it comes to writing checks, the people's sector engages most Americans. The majority of Americans are givers and, while there are some signs the proportion of households giving may have declined between 2000 and 2014 (even as total dollars raised reached record highs), philanthropy remains a great American tradition.[11] As Patrick Rooney of Indiana University's Lilly Family School of Philanthropy often notes, more Americans give to charity than vote in presidential elections.[12]

Historian Olivier Zunz described the nonprofit world as an expression of our democracy that has engaged wealthy donors, like Andrew Carnegie and Bill Gates, and ordinary citizens, like those who bought Christmas seals to fight tuberculosis or wear pink ribbons to support the battle against breast cancer. Zunz argued that giving is "a quintessential part of being American and another means of achieving major objectives."[13]

A powerful contemporary articulation of the role of nonprofits comes from Vu Le, executive director of Seattle-based nonprofit Rainier Valley Corps, which "promotes social justice by cultivating leaders of color, strengthening organizations led by communities of color, and fostering collaboration between diverse communities." On his blog, *Nonprofit AF*, Le wrote that nonprofits and philanthropy are responsible for many things we take for granted in everyday life. "If you feel safe walking down the street, it's probably because there are nonprofits working on neighborhood safety," he wrote. "If you appreciate all the free art and music around you, it is probably because there are nonprofits supporting kickass artists and musicians." He goes on to point out many results of nonprofits' work that are enjoyed every day, such as parks and clean air, organic food, cures for illnesses, the freedom to use a public bathroom or drink at a water fountain—the list goes on and on.[14]

Interestingly, many in the general public seem to understand this fact. The nonprofit sector has historically been the most trusted in the United States, with citizens placing more faith in it than in either business or government, according to respected measures like the Edelman Trust Barometer. Now, trust in all our institutions is declining rapidly—and that includes trust in nonprofits, which appears to have declined significantly in 2018.[15] Whether that's a temporary blip—perhaps related to the swirl of controversy and scandal surrounding the foundations affiliated with the 2016 presidential candidates—or a permanent decline remains to be seen. My hope is that trust rebounds, and more and more people come to see that, the inevitable bad actors notwithstanding, the nonprofit sector deserves the public's trust.

As a giver, it's important to understand the sector's power and breadth—as well as some essential truths about it. So, let's dip to a lower altitude now and look more closely at the crucial features of the landscape.

From Harvard to the Homeless Shelter

Ask people about the nonprofit sector and many conjure up images of soup kitchens or the Red Cross providing supplies after hurricanes. But the sector is more vast and diverse than that. Harvard University, with an endowment of just under $40 billion, is a nonprofit.[16] So is the homeless shelter with a few hundred thousand dollars in revenue. So, in all likelihood, is your town's youth soccer association. Many nonprofits charge fees, of course—indeed, fees make up a larger proportion of total nonprofit revenue than charitable contributions—but they also rely on donations to cover their costs. (More on that in a moment.)

Just as the corner dry cleaner has little in common with Google beyond both being for-profit enterprises, nonprofits are a widely diverse set of organizations. Nonprofits in the United States have in common a tax-exempt status. This status requires 501(c)(3) organizations, which are the vast majority of nonprofits, to focus on providing public benefit and to avoid direct political activity. They also are required to reinvest their surpluses rather than paying them out to shareholders or owners. These organizations vary from those working to help people in need, to those working to protect wildlife and the environment, to those seeking to address the underlying causes of problems such as climate change or poverty.

This diversity matters because it means that most general statements about nonprofits are, almost by definition, wrong. So, I recommend that you seek to understand the particular characteristic of the nonprofits working on the issues you care about rather than falling victim to sweeping generalizations or stereotypes about the sector.

Small and Mighty

Though the nonprofit sector is huge, most of the organizations that constitute it are small. Three-quarters of nonprofits have annual budgets of less than $500,000.[17] Even the foundation-funded nonprofits that CEP surveys regularly—tens of thousands in the past fifteen years—tend to be small. The median budget is just $1.4 million.

The large number of small nonprofits is often lamented, taken as a sign of inefficiency and waste. Sometimes that's true. Sometimes a nonprofit should expand to serve more people. You might look, as has the New York–based Edna McConnell Clark Foundation, which has $1 billion in assets, to help highly effective nonprofits like BELL "scale" to expand their programs across the country or around the world.

But bigger isn't always better. You might also look to strengthen small, local organizations and encourage learning about what works among the nonprofits you fund (your "grantees")—because sometimes that's the best way to reach your goals. That's what founder, president, and sole funder

Rose Letwin and the ten staff members at Seattle-based environmental funder Wilburforce Foundation do.

Wilburforce has $100 million in assets, supplemented with generous annual contributions from Letwin, and makes $15 million in grants each year. To meet its goal of protecting natural habitats, it must work with local, often small, organizations. These nonprofits receive grants from Wilburforce because they're best situated to make a difference on the issues the foundation seeks to address. "We need place-based organizations that understand the local context and have the relationships," said Executive Director Paul Beaudet. For Wilburforce, then, "scale" is more about an approach than the growth of the specific organizations it supports. "We are not looking for the splashy big bet," he explained.[18]

To protect forests in Alaska, for example, Wilburforce makes grants to the Sitka Conservation Society, which had a budget of only $150,000 when the funding relationship started. Why? Because that local organization and its local staff, who know the area and the community, are best positioned to do certain aspects of the work, including mobilizing local citizens, that need to be done to safeguard that environment. Wilburforce helps connect local organizations facing similar challenges, so that they can learn from each other, and it offers other assistance to help those organizations become more effective. But it isn't looking for those organizations to grow dramatically.

So, it's important to remember that bigger isn't always better. Depending on your goals, strategies, and particular context, you may want to support small nonprofits, large ones, or a mix. It all depends.

Whatever your strategy, you should keep in mind the budget and staff size of the organizations you fund when you set your expectations in areas such as reporting and data collection. Sitka Conservation Society, with its small staff, doesn't have the same capacity for interaction with its donors and funders as larger environmental organizations. But that doesn't mean it's not the best organization to focus on its specific mission.

Not Just Donations

How do nonprofits cover their costs? Many people are surprised to learn that the biggest source of revenue isn't charitable contributions. The majority of nonprofits' revenues comes from fees paid for services or goods that they provide.[19] People often discuss earned revenue for nonprofits as though it's a new concept, especially those who don't understand the sector well. But earned revenue is as old as the nonprofit form—think of Goodwill or Girl Scouts (and their cookies) or the nonprofit museum that gets a mix of admission revenue and philanthropic support.

In recent decades, earned (or fee-for-service) revenue has comprised about 70 percent of total nonprofit revenue. That proportion has remained relatively flat.[20] Much of this earned revenue comes in the form of payments from government, which is contracting with nonprofits to provide crucial services to citizens. These services include hospitals and human services organizations helping vulnerable citizens from military veterans to foster children. But much also comes from fees. Think of tuition, for example, or dues to a membership association.

Yet even though fee-for-service is the majority of their revenue, US nonprofits raise a tremendous amount of money from charitable contributions—more than $400 billion in 2017, a record.[21] And, of course, there are many individual nonprofits that are entirely supported by charitable contributions. The level of giving in this country, consistently about 2 percent of GDP, is an incredible achievement and the envy of the world. The United States is ranked among the most charitable nations in the world.[22]

What is the right revenue mix for nonprofits? Again, there is no one correct answer. It depends. Nonprofits shouldn't chase earned revenues—they should pursue earned revenue when doing so is consistent with the achievement of their mission. Are there earned revenue opportunities that are aligned with the aims a nonprofit seeks to achieve? If so, as in the case of Girl Scouts teaching young girls about entrepreneurship while also raising money for programs through cookie sales, for example, then nonprofits should go for it. If, on the other hand, pursuing earned revenue would distract from their mission, then nonprofits should pursue only philanthropic support.

People frequently discuss the "sustainability" of nonprofits. Often, the assumption is that earned revenue is more sustainable than contributed revenue. But that's not necessarily the case. A loyal base of individual and institutional donors may be as or more dependable than an earned revenue stream. So, you shouldn't assume that the absence of an earned revenue stream is a problem. The right revenue mix will vary depending on a nonprofit's goals and context. Givers should understand how an organization is funded, what the mix of revenue streams is, and why that funding strategy makes sense for that organization. If earned revenue makes up a significant proportion of an organization's overall revenue and is being generated in a way that's consistent with mission, that's great—and then its growth becomes a key metric to monitor to understand how the organization is doing.

From Dependency to Dependability

A related myth is that it's bad for nonprofits to be "dependent" on giving. Why?

It's time to reframe how we think about dependency. Let's focus on the positive connotations of being dependable, as in, "She's a dependable friend." Because many nonprofits—even when they have a healthy earned revenue stream—still require philanthropic support. And as long as they're delivering results, that shouldn't be a problem. Nonprofits that deliver results should be able to count on dependable philanthropic support year after year after year. Results are the best yardstick.

After all, what's the alternative to a mix of philanthropic and government support for, say, Horizons for Homeless Children, which provides high-quality preschool for homeless kids in Massachusetts? Ask the four-year-olds to start a moneymaking "social enterprise" and cover their own costs?

Horizons for Homeless Children needs ongoing private giving. Even my then-eleven-year-old daughter, Ava, saw that when we visited one of its preschools. She understood that, unlike in her family, these children didn't have anyone to write a check for tuition. "This place feels exactly like the preschool I went to," Ava said as we left.

That's the point! And philanthropy—people giving money to help kids because their parents can't pay and because they deserve a fair chance in life that education can help provide—is what allows the kids to attend.

And while government programs help with some of the cost, they don't cover all of it.

Yet so-called dependency remains a fear in philanthropy. Grant proposal forms from foundations frequently ask nonprofits to explain how they will be sustainable beyond the support they receive from their donors. Foundation CEOs and trustees, as well as individual givers, frequently ask me how they can avoid nonprofits becoming dependent on them and what the exit strategy is.

Short of the problem being permanently solved or the government stepping in, there often is no exit strategy. Until homelessness is ended and there are no homeless kids, or the government decides to provide universal pre-K education, there will be a need for Horizons for Homeless Children to do its work. Givers shouldn't expect Horizons to find some new revenue source beyond the support it receives from the government and individual and foundation donors.

Furthermore, I don't see a lot of evidence that there's a real risk of dependence by nonprofits on a single funder. My answer to the question of how to avoid dependency is this: "Don't try." The reality is very few nonprofits can count many—or any—funders that have been consistently supportive over decades. Funders come and go, and revenue streams change and evolve. There is no dependency problem in the nonprofit sector. If we care about results, what we need is more consistent giving to high-performing organizations, not less.

After all, if you're clear on your goals as a giver, and if you have confidence that a nonprofit you support is delivering results that relate to the achievement of your goals, what's the problem? Givers shouldn't hesitate to support high-performing organizations that are working on important issues for the long haul.

Donors' Overhead Obsession

I'm sure you've heard the question before: "But how much of the donation will really go to the cause and how much will go to overhead?" Maybe you've asked it yourself.

It's a question that comes from a good place—no one wants their money wasted. But it's the wrong question. It's like judging a baseball team by their uniforms rather than their wins and losses. What matters are results. To achieve results, nonprofits need flexible support that allows them to make investments in getting better—in technology, performance management systems, or professional development, for example. They should make these investments regardless of whether those budget items are considered to be for "overhead" on the one hand or for the "program" or "cause" on the other.

With a few exceptions, it *all* goes to support the cause.

A soup kitchen pays for rent, staff salaries, the computers and technology to track its inventory, and whatever food it serves that isn't directly donated. Many givers would consider only the latter to be program and the rest overhead. But does it make sense for a giver to say they only want their dollars to support the food, when all these other expenses are also necessary for the soup kitchen to feed the hungry?

For too long, funders and watchdog charity-rating organizations have emphasized overhead ratios and sought to judge nonprofits on the basis of the proportion of dollars being spent on program. For decades, nonprofit leaders have protested this focus on how a budget is allocated over what really matters—results achieved—and then played along by emphasizing their low overhead to donors. Nonprofits are generally afraid *not* to play the game.

The problem is compounded by the fact that definitions are fuzzy, and one organization's overhead is another's program spending. The way they allocate their budget shouldn't matter if they can demonstrate results. What should matter, as UK philanthropy consultant Caroline Fiennes and others have pointed out, is the effectiveness and impact of nonprofits.[23]

To be sure, there are exceptions. Givers have a legitimate interest in understanding what proportion of their dollars ends up in the hands of for-profit fundraising professionals, for example. A widely discussed 2013 investigative report by the *Tampa Bay Times* and the Center for Investigative Reporting identified "America's Worst Charities" on the basis of the proportion of funds raised that were paid to for-profit solicitors. Topping the list was the Kids Wish Network, which raised nearly $128 million over a decade—$110 million of which went straight to the solicitors they hired to raise money. Some of these organizations seem to exist as little more than shells for for-profit fundraisers.[24]

"More Damage Than Good"

In general, however, overhead is a "poor measure of a charity's performance," as GuideStar CEO Jacob Harold, former Charity Navigator president and CEO Ken Berger, and BBB Wise Giving Alliance president and CEO Art Taylor wrote in a 2013 open letter to donors. The letter was remarkable because Berger and Taylor ran organizations that historically had relied on overhead ratios to evaluate nonprofits. They reconsidered and asked givers to consider not just overhead, but "transparency, governance, leadership, and results." I agree that these are helpful broad categories, and we'll get to more specifics of how givers can screen nonprofits in Chapter 6. Yes, budget allocation is relevant; for example, in the case of the kinds of abuses I mentioned above. However, as these three leaders of organizations that seek to evaluate nonprofits wrote, "Focusing on overhead without considering other critical dimensions of a charity's financial and organizational performance does more damage than good."[25]

Their effort has started to shift the discussion on this topic. Many foundations, including the Ford Foundation, Bill & Melinda Gates Foundation, and others, have revised or are beginning to reexamine their restrictions on overhead. More important, several major foundations—including Ford, again, as well as Citi Foundation and the Chicago Community Trust—have announced their intention to provide more *unrestricted* support to organizations whose goals overlap with their own. They're supporting organizations with flexible grants that the organizations may use however they deem fit to execute against their missions! They join others that have for years provided unrestricted support to a significant proportion of the nonprofits they fund. They get how important this is.

Many individual givers, like Paul Shoemaker, who made his money as an executive at Microsoft, get it, too. Shoemaker was founding president of Social Venture Partners—a network of giving circles across the globe with its headquarters in Seattle. He put it this way: "If we want to make sure that funds go toward an intended social outcome, we must make an agreement on the mutual outcome and let grantees decide how to best spend the funds (the means) to achieve that goal (the end). . . . If you're worried that grantees might misspend funds, and if you can't trust them, don't make the grant in the first place."[26]

While there are signs of change, with more individual givers and foundations recognizing the importance of flexible funding, unrestricted support from the big foundations remains pretty flat, at about 20 percent of grant dollars and between 20 and 25 percent of grants made.[27] And too many individual givers still obsess about overhead. To be effective, nonprofits need flexible support.

One reason is to pay competitive salaries. No one enters the nonprofit sector to get filthy rich, nor should they, but neither should they need to take a vow of poverty. It's a competitive job market like anywhere else. For nonprofits to attract and retain the talent they need to achieve the results they seek, they must be able to pay at a level that realistically accounts for the competing opportunities talented people have.

At CEP, for example, we hire top students from colleges across the country to work as data analysts in our Cambridge, Massachusetts, and San Francisco offices. Total compensation in the first year is about $70,000 to $80,000. This is less than the six figures a candidate would make at, say, McKinsey or Facebook in a similar role—because our budget is limited and because we know people value our mission, culture, and the chance to work at a small organization with a lot of opportunity for advancement—but it's enough for us to attract the right candidates. Sadly, it's also significantly more than many nonprofit executive directors are paid.

Where the Action Is

In recent years, there's been considerable discussion of for-profit companies and hybrid "social purpose" for-profits (also referred to as low-profit liability companies [L3Cs] or B corps) displacing nonprofits. These include companies like outdoor clothing and gear outfitter Patagonia and online prescription glasses retailer Warby Parker, whose investors are willing to accept a lower financial return because they're also looking for a social one. There also has been much related discussion about the "blurring boundaries" between the business and nonprofit sectors.

Antoine Didienne, the founder of Vavavida, a fair trade and ecofriendly accessories company, wrote that "the social enterprise movement has passed beyond being a trend and is a mainstay of business, which is good news for the world. It is the new normal and is only getting bigger." He pronounced it "the future of commerce."[28] Another proponent of for-profit hybrid enterprises, Heerad Sabeti, declared in *Harvard Business Review* that "we are in a new era" in which what he dubs the "fourth sector" will increasingly be where the action is.[29] Many proponents of L3Cs and B corps suggest that nonprofits are, essentially, yesterday's news.

The data tell a different story.

There are roughly 1,600 L3Cs in the United States and 2,600 B corps worldwide.[30] Relative to the more than one million nonprofits in the United States alone, their numbers are insignificant. With revenues that exceed $1.7 trillion (US GDP is about $18 trillion), the nonprofit sector is large— and very much where the real action remains for addressing many of our most vexing challenges.[31]

Indeed, there are few significant operating hybrid models or for-profit "social enterprises" that can credibly claim that they're doing meaningful work to achieve important social goals. Perhaps that's because there are only a limited number of areas in which it's possible to achieve crucial goals related to addressing tough social problems while simultaneously generating a profit. There may be a happy alignment of profit and positive social impact for a solar energy company, for example, but it's tough to imagine how profits and social impact align when we're seeking to address homelessness or help foster youth achieve better outcomes. Nonprofits frequently address the very challenges that can't be addressed while pursuing profits.

Look, I'm happy that companies like the ones I mentioned earlier exist, and I'm always pleased to buy their products. But they remain the exception. Moreover, there's much they simply cannot affect related to their social impact goals. I'd urge givers to approach companies that claim to be making a significant positive impact with a healthy skepticism, and not to confuse buying a nice new Patagonia jacket with philanthropy.

The bottom line is that giving to nonprofits will continue to be the most important and effective tool—despite other worthy ones—in the toolkit of the effective philanthropist. The biggest variable in determining your impact as a giver is how you approach giving away your money—whether you're writing checks from your checkbook or making grants through a donor-advised fund or a foundation, whether you're the donor or a staff member of a foundation. To be sure, there are other useful tools—from influencing policy to impact investing—and we will discuss them. But giving money wisely to the right nonprofit organizations to address your chosen giving goals is central.

Tricky to Measure

The most crucial distinction between the sectors is the challenge of measuring performance. For the for-profit sector, the ultimate performance measures are universal and relatively easy to gauge—stock price or profit, for example. For the nonprofit, the financial statements are important, but they don't tell you about its effectiveness in reaching its goals.

There is simply no universal performance measure for nonprofits—no way to directly compare, say, the results of an environmental advocacy organization to those of a mentoring program. This is why there will never be an analog to a stock exchange, in which nonprofits are compared across universal measures, and "investors" can decide which ones to support. The idea has been endlessly discussed and never fulfilled because it makes no sense.

It's not just that there will never be a universal metric. It's also that our values come into play when comparing nonprofits. If you care more about climate change and I care more about mentoring at-risk youth, we will evaluate outcomes achieved in these areas very differently.

The complexity of assessing nonprofit performance doesn't make performance assessment any less important; quite the opposite. It's crucial that nonprofits decide on the key measures that they will monitor to gauge progress against their goals. A good performance management system informs course corrections and allows for continuous improvement. For an organization like BELL, a randomized control trial—the most extensive, expensive, and rigorous measurement approach—was crucial to demonstrating the efficacy of its programs. (BELL also tracks a series of more-timely indicators of its performance on a regular basis.) For other organizations, different approaches will make sense.

Unfortunately, it's too easy for nonprofits to be deemed "high impact" or "high performance" when they're not. Some of the same organizations that have been most celebrated and supported because of their performance have actually produced mixed results. These organizations include big-name, respected nonprofits like Teach for America (TFA).

TFA, a teacher training and placement program headquartered in New York, may be impressive on any number of dimensions and was for many years a media darling—the subject of numerous fawning articles. But it's tough to argue based on the available evidence that it has significantly influenced educational outcomes in a way that comes close to the early hype. Yet it has been for many years among the most significant recipients of foundation support among all education-focused nonprofits.[32]

TFA was famously founded by Wendy Kopp, who proposed the idea of a teacher corps in her 1989 Princeton University senior thesis. The idea was to recruit the best students from the best colleges and universities and place them in struggling schools for a two-year commitment, and the theory was this would lead to better results. "The group has, on the one hand, attracted a generation of smart individuals who might not otherwise have considered going into teaching," observed *Education Week*. "But it has also been accused of 'deprofessionalizing' teaching, by bypassing established channels for preparing teachers and tolerating generally high rates of turnover by virtue of its two-year-commitment standard."[33] While TFA has passionate advocates and detractors, it's difficult to understand what justifies the level of philanthropic giving it has received in light of its results over the past three decades.

Meanwhile, many nonprofits with great results labor in virtual anonymity and struggle to raise money. As a giver, you need to know how to sort through and figure out which is which.

Most nonprofit leaders that CEP has surveyed—those that receive some foundation support—care deeply about performance assessment and work hard to get it right. Our research is clear on that point.[34] Too often, however, nonprofits don't get the support they need from givers to do this important work. In our surveys, we see that two-thirds of nonprofits don't get any help from their foundation funders—financial or nonfinancial—when it comes to assessment. And too often, givers don't pay heed to nonprofits on this issue, imposing their demands for "evidence" instead of asking nonprofits what would be most useful. Nonprofit CEOs say they feel they're being asked for information that givers want, not necessarily what would help them to manage more effectively as leaders of their organizations.[35]

Saving Lives

It's a difficult terrain, the nonprofit world, with diverse challenges that are distinctly different from business challenges for-profit leaders face. Yet many leaders thrive and are passionate about their work and the missions of their organizations. I think of another such leader, Gregg Croteau, who runs UTEC, a nonprofit in the old mill town of Lowell, Massachusetts, a small city thirty miles northwest of Boston with a population of 108,000.

If not for his work clothes, you'd almost mistake Croteau for one of the young people he seeks to help: He is boyish looking, with a strong build that likely helps the mostly young men he's trying to reach take him seriously. He projects confidence and street smarts. Croteau, who is in his late forties, grew up just north of Boston in Revere—"you can identify us by our gold chains," he jokes—and lives and breathes his work. A group of teen leaders formed UTEC in 1999 in response to rampant gang violence. The organization hired Croteau in 2000, when a $40,000 grant from the city was secured to get the organization off the ground. He responded to a small ad in the help wanted section of the local newspaper that read, "EXCITING OPPORTUNITY. Teen Center needs Executive Director to create structure, dev. capacity, win sustaining funds, coordinate programs."

Croteau knew this was the job for him. The son of a schoolteacher and a municipal employee, he had worked with young people since he was an undergraduate and knew he wanted to continue to work in service of something bigger than himself. In the early days at UTEC, he was learning on the job. "A good day was breaking up a fight," he recalled.

Today, UTEC, which aims to "nurture the ambition of proven-risk youth to trade violence and poverty for social and economic success" in Lowell and the neighboring cities of Lawrence and Haverhill, is literally saving lives. UTEC has been held up as a model by both the current and former governors of Massachusetts and is nationally recognized for its results. It has a staff of forty-five and a budget of more than $6 million as it seeks to reach the members of the more than forty active gang sets operating in the region, as well as those young adults currently incarcerated. UTEC serves 800 to 900 young people each year, working intensively with about 160 to get them out of criminal activity and into a productive job.

Any given day finds Croteau and UTEC's "street workers" sitting at a bedside in a hospital after a shooting, visiting a gang member in prison, or attending a funeral. These are the places where UTEC staff find they can best begin the process of recruiting a young person to leave street life behind.

Alternatively, you might find Croteau working with staff who help UTEC's participants study for their GED. Or you might find him at one of UTEC's several social enterprises—including a mattress-recycling facility, a catering outfit, a café, and a woodworking shop that sells its cutting boards to Whole Foods—that bring in a million dollars in annual revenues and give its clients their first foothold in the working world. Or you might find him negotiating to secure a contract to supply almond and honey nut butter to grocery stores in the Northeast through UTEC's new commercial kitchen, which will employ another sixteen former gang members. Or you might find him raising money from business leaders or foundations. Or you might find him meeting with legislators to convince them to reform our criminal justice system.

You might find him on the phone with city leaders, trying to identify a new, larger facility for UTEC's mattress-recycling operation, as he was one day when I visited with him in late 2017. Hearing young people outside his office dropping F-bombs as he talked, he paused for a moment, put his hand over the phone, said, "Language!" and went back to discussing real estate and options for the recycling facility, without missing a beat.

"Sorry!" one of the teens said back.

Unsung American Heroes

Croteau is an educator, mentor, counselor, spiritual advisor, manager, businessman, fundraiser, policy advocate, mediator, and peacemaker all wrapped up into one. His job is infinitely more complicated and difficult than running an equivalent-size business—and yet his salary is just a fraction of what he could make elsewhere. He's passionate about what he does and totally focused on results—judging success by an array of metrics that include declining numbers of shootings and arrests. The overwhelming majority of young people who enter UTEC's programs stay out of jail and remain employed. UTEC's recidivism rate (those getting rearraigned after returning from incarceration within one year) is 10 percent, compared to the state average of more than 50 percent.

Although Croteau has won the support of some major foundations, he spends much more time than he'd like raising money—and too much of the agency's support comes in restricted grants that deny him the flexibility to allocate resources where he thinks they'll do the most good or to pay the salaries he believes his staff deserve. "Project funding seems great, but you're expanding your projects without expanding the engine of the organization," he explained. He also often faces unrealistic demands in terms of performance assessment. To qualify for funding, some foundations expect UTEC to undertake the same kind of randomized control trial (RCT) that BELL underwent—with some young people receiving UTEC's services and others serving as a control group that receives no intervention.

But unlike BELL, which couldn't possibly reach all the kids in its target population, UTEC is focused on a small enough population that the staff *can* reach all the young people who return from corrections or are gang involved in their geographic area. So, when it comes to an RCT, "I can't do it, ethically," Croteau explained, because it would mean putting lives at risk. He's not interested in expanding to other geographies. His vision of scale is "digging deeper to be more effective" with the population UTEC currently serves.

Croteau works nonstop—he's not home until 9:00 p.m. most nights and he bought himself a treadmill desk so he could get a workout during meetings in his office. Then he bought an exercise bike for those he's meeting with so they can exercise, too. He's quick to emphasize that he used his money, not UTEC's, for these indulgences—lest anyone think he isn't a good steward of philanthropic resources.

He told me he has never given thought to doing anything other than what he does, working with the highest-risk young adults. His passion is contagious. "We can't let this violence ever be seen as normal," he told a group of new UTEC employees at an orientation session I visited. "Because it's not. It's not normal."[36]

The people leading nonprofits like UTEC or BELL are talented individuals and leaders, grappling with a unique set of challenges. Understanding and respecting how difficult their roles are is crucial to being an effective giver. To spend time with Gregg Croteau or Tiffany Cooper Gueye—or the legions of other talented nonprofit leaders—is to be reminded that it's people like them who make our country better. They never give up on anyone and employ the best methods to help them.

They are unsung American heroes.

Givers do best when they recognize, respect, and get behind leaders whose goals overlap with their own and who are delivering results—leaders of organizations like these. Givers do best when they generously support these leaders and their organizations, empowering them to help strengthen our society and improve lives.

Because America's nonprofit sector is a defining strength of our country.

❖❖❖❖❖

Chapter 1 Review: Giving Guidance

1. **Leading a nonprofit is uniquely challenging because of the tricky terrain and because nonprofits are working on the toughest challenges.** Nonprofit leaders should be understood and

respected for the remarkable work they do each day. Look for leaders with humility, knowledge of their area of work and of nonprofits, "hard" and "soft" skills, and an ability to explain what they're seeking to achieve and how they measure performance.

2. **Sometimes bigger is better, sometimes not.** Seek to understand what makes sense, in terms of the size of organizations you will support, given your goals. Maybe you're seeking to help proven models grow, or maybe you're looking to support small, local efforts to deal with local challenges. The right answer to whether to give to large or small organizations depends on your goals and context. If you're funding small nonprofits, then make sure you're realistic in your expectations of them.

3. **Know your nonprofit economics.** Givers need to know how the organizations they support pay their bills. Whenever possible, provide unrestricted funding to organizations you trust and whose goals overlap with yours. That's the most valuable kind of contribution.

4. **Don't buy into the overhead myth—and seek real performance metrics.** Nonprofits should be judged on their results, not how they allocate their budgets. Of course, judging performance of nonprofits can be difficult because it isn't about the financial measures. You'll need to dive in to understand a nonprofit's goals and how it seeks to gauge progress against those goals.

❧ 2 ❧

SO MANY WAYS TO GIVE

O NCE YOU UNDERSTAND the nonprofit sector, you're well-positioned to be-gin thinking about how to do your giving. You now know that nonprofits are unique entities, frequently dealing with the problems that have defied market solutions. Their performance is judged not by financial indicators but by impact, which isn't nearly as easy to measure as profit or return on investment. If nonprofits aren't like businesses, then it stands to reason that giving isn't like investing.

But unfortunately and unhelpfully, many insist otherwise—that invest-ing is a useful analogy for giving. One of my business school professors at Harvard was an early and prominent promoter of this misguided analogy. He coauthored an article in *Harvard Business Review* (*HBR*) in 1997 that suggested that givers, and especially foundations, should act like venture capitalists.[1]

I remember sitting in his second-year elective course as an MBA stu-dent nearly two decades ago, listening to a guest lecturer describe how the "venture philanthropy" organization where she worked was applying the "principles of venture capital investing" to its work. She heaped disdain on what she called "traditional philanthropy," which, she argued, hadn't achieved results. She described nonprofit leaders as inept and in need of aggressive "investors" to hold them to account.

The students, most of whom knew little about philanthropy or nonprofits, nodded, save for a handful of us with experience in philanthropy and nonprofits. Because we knew she didn't get it.

Philanthropy has achieved a great deal in this country; it's been crucial for much of the progress we take for granted in our lives. And, as we've been discussing, nonprofit leaders are often unsung American heroes, balancing a range of responsibilities that can make a corporate CEO's job feel like a walk in the park. But our guest speaker that day was dead set on promoting the idea that everything that came before her was ineffectual and that she had the new formula for success.

Nonsensical Analogies

There is no formula—no "plug and play" analogy to be adopted by the world of giving. There are many choices and many ways to be an effective giver, but none are simple.

Although there is, of course, much ineffective philanthropy, there are also inspiring examples all around us of giving done right. And when done right, giving can and does have tremendous positive impact.

Yet many continue to insist that the answer lies in ill-suited investing analogies. It's confusing. What does it even mean to do your giving "like a venture capitalist"? My professor and his coauthors said it means taking steps like focusing on performance measures, having close relationships (including taking board seats) with—and building the capacity of—nonprofits, making large and long-term gifts, and having an exit strategy. Many of my business school classmates ate it up.

"Yes, let's all act like venture capitalists!"

But none of the ideas put forward in that *HBR* article were new to philanthropy, nor were they particular to venture capital. Moreover, it's just not a good comparison. Givers don't own nonprofits, nor should an exit strategy for a high-performing organization necessarily even be the goal. Givers should continue to support those organizations that are delivering results against shared goals for the long haul. Oh, and the venture capitalists I know care about one thing: their ability to make outsized financial returns.

Why would that motivation be a good analogy for those who care about making a difference in the world?

Finally, while a company's success is defined by its profit and growth relative to its competitors, nonprofits usually don't solve anything by themselves; they're part of a complicated ecosystem of organizations addressing related issues. The for-profit world is all about *competitive* dynamics—what's Lyft's market share relative to Uber's? The giving and nonprofit world is all about *collaborative* dynamics—how does a homeless shelter work in relation to a drug treatment center to achieve a shared goal of better outcomes for homeless people suffering from addiction?

Perhaps as a result of this recognition, many of the same people who promoted the notion that we should focus on an organization's growth in the way venture capitalists do—including the guest speaker in my business school class—are now embracing the idea of "systems change." The notion of systems change is based on the recognition that the challenges philanthropy addresses are complicated and interdependent. This is something those with experience in the nonprofit sector have been saying for decades.

Mario Morino, the tech entrepreneur and investor-turned-giver I mentioned in the Introduction, cofounded Venture Philanthropy Partners in 2000. At the time, he saw a venture capital model based on General Atlantic's approach, which had been so crucial to his company's ability to grow when he was an entrepreneur, as a great analogy for philanthropy.

Venture Philanthropy Partners has done much great work to help vulnerable youth in the Washington, DC, area. But Morino now concedes that his giving work has been more difficult than investing and that the analogy didn't work. While Morino feels the approach was valuable in helping nonprofits instill better discipline into how they function and think in the longer term, the model had to be adapted to consider the differences of the nonprofit world and its inherent complexity. "These decisions have a degree of social complexity that is far greater," he said.

Warren Buffett also knows a little about investing. After pledging some $30 billion in Berkshire Hathaway stock to the Bill & Melinda Gates Foundation in 2006, the investing guru explained that he did it because what he knew was business, not giving. In business, he explained, the goal is to look for easy ways to make money, but "in philanthropy, the most important problems are those which have already resisted both intellect and money."[2] Andrew Carnegie famously said he reached a point in life when he was going "to stop accumulating and begin the infinitely more serious and difficult task of wise distribution."[3] So, if you don't believe me, take it from those who have deeply immersed themselves in both worlds: Giving effectively is distinctly difficult—far more so than investing.

Giving Everywhere

Adding to the complexity is the range of choices donors face today about how to channel their giving. Should I just write a check? Should I give in coordination with others through one of the burgeoning numbers of new giving circles? Should I give to or through my local community foundation? Through a donor-advised fund at a national commercial gift fund? At the cash register? In response to the people approaching me on the sidewalk? At my doorstep? Or, if I have significant resources, should I establish my own foundation, a family office, a limited liability company (LLC), or all of the above?

Before we address these questions, let's take a moment to look at the giving landscape in this country, which is vast and diverse. About 70 percent of the more than $400 billion in total giving comes from living individuals, 8 percent comes from bequests, and 5 percent from corporations. Another 16 percent comes from foundations.[4]

The overall giving level in the United States is more than 2 percent of GDP. It's as high as it is for a host of reasons, including the American tradition of citizens coming together to form associations (about which de Tocqueville famously commented) and the introduction, in 1917, of the charitable deduction into the tax code. Add to that the relative lack of a government-provided social safety net of the kind Europe and Canada offer their citizens, and you have the American philanthropic and nonprofit sector. Whatever your views about the role of the American government, there can be no denying the role of giving as a vital engine of American compassion, association, affiliation, and creativity.

Like nonprofits, givers are diverse, coming in all political stripes and affiliations and spanning all distinctions of race, socioeconomic status, sexual orientation, and gender identity. So, too, are the ways to give varied and diverse.

Just Say No

One of the ways you can give is by doing so when you're asked, whether by people at your door, at the cash register, or by coworkers raising money for this or that. But you shouldn't just instinctively say "yes." There are few strict rules I'd suggest following in the world of giving (and we'll get to all of them in this book), but here is one: Just say no to people who ask you to make giving decisions in the moment or who push you to give primarily based on emotion or slick marketing messages. Or at the very least, ask for time to think about it. That's hard, of course, because those people are everywhere.

Dan Pallotta has been one of them. He rose to prominence as a for-hire fundraiser, organizing events to raise money for charities, before his company collapsed in 2002 amid charges that too little of what was raised went to the nonprofits and too much to Pallotta's company.[5] He reemerged years later, stepping back into the spotlight with two books about nonprofits and a widely viewed, and misleading, 2013 TED talk in which he insists that nonprofits don't invest nearly enough in fundraising.

While that's certainly true in specific instances—some smaller nonprofits struggle to dedicate needed capacity to fundraising—the facts tell a different story about the overall picture. We've already discussed that total giving in the United States leads the world and has grown steadily (although many nonprofit leaders worry that changes in the tax laws the Republican-controlled Congress passed in late 2017 may lead to some decline in giving)—keeping pace with GDP growth and beating it by a good margin in some recent years.

But if the impressive fundraising numbers don't convince you, think about your day-to-day experience. If yours is anything like mine, it feels as if every evening your phone rings with requests to fund cancer research, support police and firefighters, help the homeless, and so forth. Long infomercials on cable news channels promote organizations helping veterans, cancer patients, and abused animals. Every trip to a store to buy something now seems to be accompanied by a request at the cash register to give. And with uncanny timing, the doorbell seems to chime just as you settle down for dinner, rung by a college student working a summer fundraising job for a nonprofit who is ready to launch into her spiel.

I had that summer job once, when I was in college. "Hi, I'm Phil. I'm from Oregon Fair Share," I'd begin. "We're the organization fighting to make health care more affordable for everyone here in the state." I was pretty good at it, and I believed in the cause. But I'm sure those who were writing checks as I stood on their stoops or sat at their kitchen tables after they'd invited me in, didn't carefully think through their decision. And I know they didn't realize that I was basically paid on commission—with a big percentage of what they gave going straight to me.

I get why some nonprofits hire companies like the one Pallotta ran, or telemarketing companies, or college kids to press donors to give. They do it because it works, at least sometimes.

I know it's hard, and I've given in myself, but smart givers will just say "no" to these types of requests, saving their contributions for the organizations they choose thoughtfully based on their personal (or, in the case of foundations, institutional) goals and strategies. If you want to do the most good with your giving, you'll never give just because you were asked. You'll give because you consciously decided how to allocate your precious charitable resources. Take the literature. Jot down a website address. Be polite to those whose difficult job it is to have doors slammed in their faces. "Thanks so much for telling me about this work," you might say. "But I have different giving priorities, so I think it's a no for me." Or, if you're open to considering the pitch, say, "I like to take my time to carefully consider my charitable giving decisions, so could you leave me some information to review?"

If that doesn't work, then close the door or hang up the phone. Don't give until you've had the opportunity to carefully consider your decision.

What about requests from people you know—your coworker, for example, who is participating in a race to benefit research on a terrible disease, or your niece, who is raising money to benefit a local food pantry as part of a school project? Sometimes, for social or familial reasons or simply to support someone you care about, you will want to say "yes." That's fine, but I suggest you create a budget for these kinds of contributions and stick to it. You should try to keep it below 20 percent of your total gifts if you're an individual giver.

If you work for a foundation and are stewarding others' resources, then, of course, it's not your money. You should always be aligning giving either with stated goals and strategies or with the intent and directions of the donor or board you serve. Either way, the goal is the same: to make conscious giving choices on your or your organization's terms, rather than reflexively responding to terms someone else sets.

The Right Vehicle

To feel most confident about the effects of your giving, you'll want to feel good about how you do it—through what vehicle and with what support and counsel. Just as choosing the right car is personal—a tall person doesn't want a Mazda Miata and a Floridian doesn't need all-wheel drive—so, is choosing the right giving vehicle.

If you're giving a few thousand or hundreds of dollars a year and you already have a sense of where your giving will go, you can simply write a check or give online. This is the right approach for many, including those whose giving is primarily about affiliation and relationships rather than making a difference. (I hope not you, if you're reading this book.) Perhaps they're giving to their alma mater or to the hospital that looked after them or a loved one (known as "grateful patient" giving). They're not necessarily interested in maximizing the impact of their giving or exploring the range of possibilities for making a difference. These gifts are almost like dues for affiliation or membership or, in some cases, thank-you presents.

Most of us do some of this. When I've given to the university I attended, it's in great part from a sense of gratitude for all the financial aid the institution provided me, without which I couldn't have made it through. For most people, some portion of their giving falls into that category (and is part of the 20 percent not aligned with goals we discussed earlier), and that's fine. These institutions do much good, but they also have significant endowments, and in many cases, a high proportion of the students or patients they serve aren't particularly needy.

So, I hope you will consider carving out a significant portion of your giving to try to do the most good you can do. We'll discuss how to decide on what, exactly, your goals should be in the next chapter. But if you're giving more than hundreds or a few thousands, say $5,000 and above, or if you just want to get more serious about your giving (at whatever level), you'll be interested in what seems to be an ever-proliferating range of ways to give. The options feel endless.

One such option is a giving circle. Think of it as a book club with a philanthropic mission. Giving circles have become much more popular in recent years.[6] As of 2017, there are an estimated 1,600 in the United States—up threefold since 2007.[7] They've been particularly popular among women donors. They allow givers to pool their funding and make joint decisions about where and how to give.

Giving circles tend to be locally focused on a particular geographic community but often have a specific field focus, too.[8] For example, the African American Women's Giving Circle in Washington, DC, has a minimum contribution level of just $100 and pools its members' funds to "sustain African American women–led organizations and support promising or effective projects that address unmet needs of African American women and girls."[9] The Everychild Foundation in Los Angeles is comprised of some 200 women, each giving $5,000 annually. The group then awards one $1 million grant each year to a nonprofit working to help "children facing disease, abuse, neglect, poverty, or disability." The Everychild Foundation has inspired numerous other giving circles in other geographies that have emulated this model.[10]

Giving circles can be a great choice for those looking to connect with and learn from others with shared interests, and to pool their funds to have a greater impact together than they would alone. There seems to be a giving circle for just about everything. Just search online for your interest and your geographic region and you'll find giving circles near you. Whether you're a small giver or a big giver—and sometimes the bigger the giver, the more isolated you can feel—a giving circle is a great way to find community and connection.

Community Foundations

Some donors are looking not just for connections to other donors, but also for expert guidance, especially about giving options in their local community. For them, community foundations are a great option and, as one of my friends who runs one put it, community foundations, which are more than a century old, "are in some ways the original giving circles."

There are nearly 800 in the United States, covering almost every geographic region in the country. They're incorporated as public, tax-exempt charities, like the operating nonprofits they support. You can give to a community foundation and allow the professional staff there to use your resources to address what they see as the most pressing challenges. Or you can designate your support for a fund or area—say, education. Or you can establish a donor-advised fund (DAF) and recommend which organizations you would like to support. DAFs have grown dramatically in recent decades, with nearly $30 billion pouring into them from individual donors in 2017 alone.[11]

The first community foundation was the Cleveland Foundation, established in 1914 as a community chest of sorts. Today, the foundation has assets of more than $2 billion and makes grants of nearly $100 million every year in areas from housing to education to arts and culture. The best community foundations play a crucial leadership and convening role in the cities or regions they serve. They help define a change agenda for a community. That's what the Cleveland Foundation did in 1915 when it launched a study on the public school system that charted strategies for responding to the flood of immigrant children coming to the Ohio city.[12] That's what the Community Foundation of Greater Birmingham did when it helped create Railroad Park in the early 2000s and, more recently, a nearby light installation called LightRails, which has helped bridge the divide between the south and north sides of the city.[13] That's what the New Hampshire Charitable Foundation did in 2016 when it committed $100 million over ten years to close the opportunity gap among young people in the state, using grants, coalitions, and public policy to advance early childhood development; family and youth supports; substance use prevention, treatment, and recovery; and education and career pathways.[14]

The best community foundations also step up in moments of crisis. That's what the Community Foundation Boulder County did when it coordinated relief work in 2013 following severe flooding in that region of Colorado.[15] It's what the Community Foundation Sonoma County did in the wake of the 2017 fires in that area of California, establishing a resilience fund for long-term rebuilding in recognition of the fact that most postdisaster giving is focused on short-term response.[16] And it's what the Greater Houston Community Foundation did in the wake of 2017's Hurricane Harvey, establishing a relief fund that, by January 2018, had raised $110 million that the foundation then granted to nonprofits, "filling the gaps that are not met by other local and federal efforts."[17]

If you care about your local community and want to give back but aren't sure you want to spend the time to become an expert on the issues, give unrestricted money to your community foundation. If you want to retain more control over your giving but still want access to the local experts who work in a community foundation, establish a DAF. Many community foundations also offer a range of options in between. For example, a giver might set up a designated fund, which is designed to support specific organizations long after the giver's death but includes safeguards if one of the selected organizations goes under or has management issues. Nonprofits frequently establish "agency funds" at community foundations to take advantage of their investment expertise and ensure perpetual support for themselves. Many community foundations also run substantial scholarship programs, using funds donors establish for that purpose. There are also issue-based community foundations. The Pride Foundation, for example, seeks "to expand opportunities and advance full equality for LGBTQ people across the Northwest." Other options include religious-based giving vehicles, such as Jewish community foundations.

Community foundation staff are experts in helping givers think through giving options. Because they work for a mission-driven nonprofit, you don't have to worry that they're pushing you in any one direction to maximize fees or profits.

DAF Debates

DAFs have proliferated at community foundations, but their growth has been especially dramatic at the national gift funds, the biggest of which is Fidelity Charitable. In recent years, Fidelity Charitable has surpassed the United Way as the nonprofit organization that raises the most money in the United States—more than $4 billion annually.[18] It's now among the biggest grant-makers in the United States, not far behind the Bill & Melinda Gates Foundation in dollars out the door each year. Its nearly 200,000 donors value its convenience and ease of use, low fees, and range of investing options. But the biggest givers also get specialized attention from Fidelity Charitable staff, who provide advice and counsel on where and how to give.[19]

Fidelity Charitable and the other national gift funds affiliated with investment firms, such as Schwab and Vanguard, offer low fees and enormous convenience. A giver can establish a DAF with as little as $5,000 and can easily choose which nonprofits to support or change investment allocations while sipping coffee at her kitchen counter. This convenience factor is likely a leading reason that these funds have grown so dramatically in recent years.

DAFs aren't without their critics, who lament the fact that a donor receives a tax deduction for putting money into a DAF even if she doesn't grant out much for years (although, in fairness, the same is true of foundations). This deduction allows for huge short-term tax benefits, while operating charities see little benefit from the gift. Take the case of GoPro founder and CEO Nicholas Woodman, who gave $500 million worth of his company's stock to the Silicon Valley Community Foundation in 2014 to create an account to house the resources of the Jill and Nicholas Woodman Foundation, receiving much praise for his generosity. Four years later, according to the *New York Times*, "there is almost no trace of the Woodman Foundation, or that $500 million. The foundation has no website and has not listed its areas of focus, and it is not known what—if any—significant grants it has made to nonprofits."[20]

Some critics, such as Boston College Law School Professor Ray Madoff, have called for new regulations—for example, to require DAFs to spend out within a decade.[21] She and philanthropist Lewis Cullman critique DAFs in a coauthored 2016 article in the *New York Review of Books*:

> Donor-advised funds have been a bad deal for American society. They have produced too many private benefits for the financial services industry, at too great a cost to the taxpaying public, and they have provided too few benefits for society at large. When we consider their overall effect, we see that rather than supporting working charities and the beneficiaries they serve, they have undermined them. Congress should enact a rule requiring that donor-advised funds be distributed to operating charities within a reasonable period of time in order to assure a regular flow of money to working charities.[22]

Indiana University's Patrick Rooney argues that "there appears to be little substantive evidence" to support the claim that many donors simply park their money in DAFs.[23] Defenders of DAFs, including community foundations and national gift funds, maintain that DAFs have made giving easier. They say DAFs are a better, more efficient alternative for many who would have otherwise formed their own charitable foundation. They argue that the Woodman example is rare, that the vast majority of DAFs make distributions every year, and that payouts from DAFs average more than 20 percent annually, much higher than the typical payout at most foundations or, for that matter, most endowed nonprofits, like colleges and universities.[24] They note that while DAFs have grown dramatically, they remain a much smaller segment of total giving than private foundations. Hundreds of community foundations adhere to and are accredited through a set of National Standards for US Community Foundations that require, among other practices, that DAFs not remain idle. Fidelity Charitable and other national gift funds likewise have policies that don't allow for DAFs to sit idle indefinitely. Finally, defenders note that while DAFs have grown dramatically, they remain a much smaller segment of total giving than private foundations.

Missing from this debate, at least as I write this, are sufficient data and analysis to reveal the impact of DAFs on nonprofits. Is the increase in giving to DAFs resulting in a net increase in funds available in the near term to nonprofits, as proponents imply, because it's either spurring new giving or replacing the establishment of foundations (which pay out at a lower rate on average)? Or is the increased use of DAFs leading to a decrease in funds available to nonprofits, as critics suggest, because it's replacing checkbook giving, which would have gone straight to nonprofits but is now sitting in accounts that may be spent down slowly? Data about the answers to these questions should inform any policy debates about DAFs.

What does this all mean for you? You should discuss your choice of giving vehicle with your tax advisor or attorney, especially if you're giving thousands of dollars or more annually. I think DAFs are a convenient and useful way to manage your giving and can be an excellent choice. But whether you establish a DAF or a foundation, or do your giving from your checkbook, I hope you focus on doing as much good as you can as quickly as you can. Don't just let your dollars sit there, as the *New York Times* reports that Woodman has. While there's a strong case to be made for the role of perpetual foundations supported by endowments, individual givers should seek to get gifts out the door. There are so many pressing problems that charitable dollars can help address today.

Crucial Institutions

Historically, private foundations have been the vehicle the biggest donors—from Carnegie to Gates—choose for their giving. But in recent years, some prominent megadonors like Mark Zuckerberg of Facebook and Steve Ballmer of Microsoft have chosen to do their giving through other entities, such as an LLC or a family office—leading many to wonder whether foundations are yesterday's news. I don't think that's the case.

It's true that giving through an LLC or family office may give a donor more freedom to engage in political activity, and it's true that it frees donors from any obligations to be transparent about their giving. But the foundation form will endure, I believe, because of the advantages of having a single-mindedly focused and professionalized institution handle the giving of the largest donors. If you have more than $30 million in assets that you want to devote to charity, you should at least consider establishing a foundation.

Even if the rate of establishment of foundations were to decline, endowed foundations aren't going anywhere; they will remain a crucial part of the giving landscape. And foundations are unlike any other institutions in our society. Whether you're affiliated with one, considering establishing one, or doing your giving from your checkbook or through a DAF (and it's worth noting that many givers use multiple vehicles for their giving), it's crucial that you understand the role foundations play. Moreover, many of the lessons of foundations are broadly relevant to individual givers.

It's important to learn about foundations' contributions to progress in this country as well as about where they've come up short. As you evaluate nonprofits, one good sign is if they receive support from your local community foundation or a major private foundation you respect—because it's foundation staff's jobs to make smart decisions about who to fund. That doesn't mean they always get it right, of course, or that you shouldn't support organizations that haven't yet garnered foundation support. But it does suggest the nonprofit has made it through a process of demonstrating its merit.

There are roughly 100,000 foundations in the United States. Collectively, they control nearly $800 billion in assets and make $58 billion in grants each year.[25] Most are small and unstaffed. The largest several hundred staffed foundations control a majority of foundation assets and giving in the country. Endowed private foundations have tremendous freedom. As Joel Fleishman has argued, "foundations have long been for good and ill, the least accountable major institutions in America."[26]

For good and ill. For foundations, their greatest virtue is their greatest vice. On the positive side, freedom from accountability means an ability to take on issues other actors in our society cannot or will not. This freedom is what allowed the Robert Wood Johnson Foundation to take aim at smoking in the United States in the 1990s, often battling tobacco companies, which contributed to significant declines in smoking rates, especially among teenagers. It's what allowed the Ford Foundation and Rockefeller Foundation to support advances in agricultural production in developing countries in the 1950s and 1960s, known as the Green Revolution, reducing famine and malnutrition. It's what allowed foundations to support efforts that have led to greater human rights, stronger communities, and decreases in poverty and disease. From the creation of *Sesame Street* to the establishment of our country's 911 emergency response system to the discovery of vaccines and cures, foundation giving stands behind many of the good things we value (as well as many we too easily take for granted) in this country and around the globe.

Freedom and Responsibility

But this freedom that foundations enjoy to tackle the issues others can't or won't—this lack of what former W. K. Kellogg Foundation staff member Joel Orosz calls a "salutary external discipline"—has its flip side.[27] During my seventeen years working with foundations, I've seen it more than a few times. I've seen ineffective, isolated foundations that undermine rather than support grantees' effectiveness. Foundations whose leaders and board members believe they know best but get it wrong. Those that promote and fund strategies that don't work and that those they're intended to help don't support. Foundations that are secretive, sharing little information about their priorities or about what has worked and what hasn't. Those that say, "If our grantees don't like us, we must be doing something right," and that fail to recognize that strong relationships with nonprofits are essential to effectiveness.

The givers behind foundations, as well as their staffs and boards, reside in a bubble of positivity, surrounded by grantees and aspiring grantees. It's a dynamic that has informed many jokes about the changes that going from, say, a nonprofit job to being a foundation executive seem to cause. "Suddenly, I was better-looking, thinner, and funnier than I ever had been," many foundation leaders have kidded to me, in so many words. I've heard versions of this joke at least one hundred times, and I'll admit to laughing every time as though it was the first time I'd heard it. (I did so especially when the joke-teller had the potential to support the organization I lead. Don't judge me. I bet you'd do the same!)

At their worst, givers and foundation leaders come to believe all the praise that's heaped on them and become detached from reality. The larger the giver, in terms of dollars out the door each year, the greater the risk of this kind of self-inflation and detachment. The natural tendency of grantees and aspiring grantees to tell givers what they think they want to hear is only intensified when the stakes are higher.

Of course, leaders of any powerful institution can become isolated and insulated, but the giver is even more at risk. The isolated, insular giver or foundation CEO confuses media mentions, appointments to boards and commissions, and invitations to speak at major conferences with effectiveness. They make pronouncements with increasing authority and certainty. They issue premature declarations of success without sufficient evidence or in ways that claim credit for others' work, leaving everyone unsatisfied except for the giver. Failures go unacknowledged. And in the case of staffed foundations, the CEO and others on staff might even talk about their foundation and its resources as though they were their personal resources.

People often ask me what compels givers, whether individuals or foundation leaders, to do this work of giving well. My answer is always the same: the moral imperative to do the most possible good with the resources with which they're entrusted. American foundations are, after all, tax-advantaged institutions. Donors establishing them benefit from the charitable deduction, and foundations are subject only to a small annual excise tax of either 1 or 2 percent of investment earnings, depending on payout. More broadly, individual giving is advantaged, too, under the tax code. With these advantages should come some sense of real responsibility.

Thankfully, most givers act responsibly, in my experience. But, as we know, some don't.

Giving Under Scrutiny

Givers of all types are under more scrutiny today than they were even five years ago. As historian Benjamin Soskis noted, we have come out of a "brief, balmy" season—which he argues is a historical aberration—when big givers received only praise and little critical scrutiny.[28] Megan Tompkins-Stange, assistant professor of public policy at the University of Michigan's Ford School, describes the shift:

Ten years ago, critical discussion around philanthropy was limited. In one survey, nearly 60 percent of civic leaders could not name a single foundation, and another study found that 98 percent of press on foundations was neutral or positive in tone. In 2006, Warren Buffett's $30 billion gift to the Gates Foundation was described in the press using almost exclusively celebratory terms. In the perpetually crisis-oriented narrative surrounding education, foundations represented admirable sources of hope and levers into the logjam of K–12 policy. A former student of mine summarized the general ethos of the time: "I trust the billionaires." Starting around 2012, however, this trust began to erode—echoing a pattern that has repeated itself in three distinct waves over the last century in which foundations have faced scrutiny with regard to their political involvement: in the early 1910s, early 1950s, and late 1960s. This most recent wave was triggered as national foundations became more vocal and visible in federal education reform efforts, and several high-profile philanthropic experiments began to be challenged.[29]

More and more books and articles are questioning the motivations and the efficacy of big givers. Former Ford Foundation executive Michael Edwards has been among the most eloquent and consistent critics of those, such as Matthew Bishop, formerly of the *Economist*, who have written glowingly of "philanthrocapitalists." Edwards argued in a 2013 op-ed in the *Chronicle of Philanthropy* that "philanthropy is supposed to be private funding for the public good, but increasingly it's become a playground for private interests."[30] Journalist Anand Giridharadas, author of *Winners Take All: The Elite Charade of Changing the World*, has claimed that "even as they give back, American elites generally seek to maintain the system that causes many of the problems they try to fix—and their helpfulness is part of how they pull it off." As a result, he argued, "their do-gooding is an accomplice to greater, if more invisible, harm."[31] Education expert Diane Ravitch has slammed what she calls the "billionaire boys club" of the foundations of Bill and Melinda Gates, the Walton family, and Eli Broad for what she sees as an antidemocratic attempt to import market-based principles into public education.[32]

Liberals lament the influence of conservative philanthropy, like that of Charles Koch, on policy, while conservatives see George Soros and Open Society Foundations lurking behind the curtain of liberal policies. Both perspectives are partly accurate and frequently exaggerated. Philanthropy's influence on policy is nothing new and isn't likely to change. My aim is to help you, if you're a large-scale giver, use your influence responsibly and in a way that elevates, rather than crowds out, the voices of those with little power in our society. And if you're a small-scale giver, this information is also relevant, so you can be discerning about which funders to follow and which to be wary of.

New entrants to the world of philanthropy are issuing critiques, too. In a blistering *Wall Street Journal* op-ed, Napster cofounder and early Facebook investor Sean Parker wrote,

> The executive directors of most major private foundations, endowments and other nonprofit institutions are dedicated, first and foremost, to preserving the resources and reputations of the institutions they run. This is achieved by creating layers of bureaucracy to oversee the resources of the institution and prevent it from taking on too much risk.[33]

Parker's critique is typical of too many in Silicon Valley who have barely begun their own philanthropic work but are convinced that there's nothing to learn from those who came before them. Oddly, pronouncements about philanthropy and the nonprofit sector from those with practically no experience with or knowledge about either are routinely given visibility and credence. This concept is difficult to understand.

Parker's crude caricature may apply to the worst among foundations and nonprofits. But to suggest this is the norm is akin to using the Enron or Wells Fargo scandals to impugn the ethics of all in business. Still, it's important to be mindful of just how prevalent these critiques are becoming. They're increasing in frequency and coming from a variety of directions.

This is all happening in an environment in which anything deemed "establishment" is under fire. The word has become a political liability. The simmering disaffection that manifested itself in the Occupy and Tea Party movements has now gone mainstream, as we can see in the 2016 US presidential election or in the Brexit vote that same year in the United Kingdom.

Trust in the institutions we created to protect us has eroded as those institutions have failed to live up to our expectations. From the abuse scandal in the Roman Catholic Church to the practices of our biggest banks pre–Great Recession to the killing of unarmed African Americans by police, citizens are asking whether any institutions can truly be trusted. "We now operate in a world in which we can assume neither competence nor good faith from authorities, and the consequences of this simple, devastating realization is the defining feature of American life at the end of this low, dishonest decade," wrote MSNBC host Christopher Hayes in the 2012 *Twilight of the Elites*—which now appears to have been a rather prophetic book. "Elite failure and the distrust it has spawned is the most powerful and least understood aspect of current politics and society."[34]

In this new climate, givers of all types—but especially the big ones—will need to work extra hard to nurture and maintain trust. One way they can do this is by ensuring that they're connected to those they seek to help, and that their approaches to problem-solving are welcome.

That may seem obvious, but it's hard to do.

Staying Grounded

Listening to and engaging with those you seek to help has always been crucial if you want to be effective. It's even more crucial now because the distance between the haves and the have-nots has widened. However well-intentioned, givers can be seen as the embodiment of the "establishment"—outside powers imposing their will on communities. Givers who seek to design and implement "solutions" in a top-down way will meet increasing resistance as citizens rightly rail against a process that leaves them out of the conversation.

Big givers have work to do in this area. CEP's research suggests that grantees—who arguably are in a good position to judge—don't see foundations as adequately understanding the needs of their intended beneficiaries.[35] As a former foundation official told me recently, "We fund a lot of movements, but we can be mistaken for the oligarchs."

Indeed, sometimes foundations have acted too much like the oligarchs, behavior that will increasingly be ineffective in an era in which "new power" is challenging top-down, old-school power from the ground up.[36] Grant Oliphant, president of the Heinz Endowments, which has more than $1.6 billion in assets and makes grants of $80 million a year, put it this way: "The days of Richard King Mellon and Davey Lawrence deciding they would clean up Pittsburgh's air and water are done. That doesn't happen anymore, even for organizations like ours that presumably wield power because we give away money."[37]

Oliphant's point is not that givers aren't free to operate in a top-down way. They clearly are. Rather, he argues that they won't be effective this way, not in a society in which people distrust institutions intuitively and expect to have a voice. The most effective givers understand these dynamics.[38]

In a 2016 survey CEP conducted of foundation CEOs, listening to and learning from the experiences of intended beneficiaries came out on top of a list of twenty-four promising practices for increasing impact. Listening to and learning from the experiences of grantees was the runner-up.[39] These big givers understand that to do their best work, they need to stay connected to those on the front lines. But understanding is one thing and doing is another.

Staying Humble

The best givers stay humble. As the Rockefeller Brothers Fund's Stephen Heintz puts it, "audacious in ambitions, humble in approach."[40]

Knowing that it takes a long time to succeed, effective foundations have performance indicators and feedback loops that let them know how they're doing along the way and how they can do better. When possible, they're open about what they're learning, even when it's that their efforts fell short. But I've seen many inspiring examples of givers who, often quietly, just get it done.

Take Rose Letwin, whom we met earlier, and the Wilburforce Foundation. "I grew up in a small midwestern farm town and have always had a passion for animals," she explained. "I moved to Seattle in the 1970s and fell in love with the outdoors. These interests led me to volunteer at a wildlife rehabilitation center, where I faced the devastating truth that many of these animals, once healed, had no home to return to. Seattle and its surrounding communities were growing rapidly, and there were fewer spaces where wild animals could just be."[41]

Wilburforce's approach has relevance to givers at all levels, including individuals giving hundreds or thousands of dollars annually. It's about humility. And it's about respecting those closest to the ground—both their time and the knowledge they hold.

Wilburforce's mission statement reads, "We help conserve important lands, waters and wildlife in Western North America by supporting organizations and leaders advancing strategic solutions." Notice the first two words: "We help." The foundation is aware that it's just one player.

But it's also focused on results and understands that it achieves them with the organizations it funds, as well as with other funders. The foundation identifies geographic areas of focus based on the science related to ecological impact, the opportunities in—and threats to—those areas, the capacity within the area in question, and the need.

Through this process, Wilburforce zeroes in on the areas where it can make a difference. And because the work is local, the organizations Wilburforce supports are often small, as we discussed. "Every place is different, and the constellation of organizations to do the needed work is going to look different," said Paul Beaudet, the executive director.

Wilburforce's staff often wear shorts and sandals to work, and several bring their dogs in every day. But don't let their laid-back appearance fool you. They are an incredibly smart, analytical, and passionate bunch. "We take our work seriously, but ourselves lightly," said Beaudet.[42]

Wilburforce regularly collects feedback from its grantees—through CEP's Grantee Perception Report (GPR)—and makes changes based on what its leaders learn about how they can better support those organizations to meet their shared goals. The foundation is one of the highest-ranked funders among the hundreds whose grantees CEP has surveyed on dimensions such as impact on grantees' fields, understanding of grantees' fields, advancement of knowledge in grantees' fields, influence on public policy in grantees' fields, approachability when a problem arises, fairness of treatment, and responsiveness. (The foundation made its results public on its website, which is why I am free to share them.)

Wilburforce's model is focused on relationships. "At the very basic level, solid relationships with grantees are critically important because grantees are a very good source of information for us," explained Beaudet. The nonprofits Wilburforce supports "are the ones doing the on-the-ground work. They're likely to have a much more nuanced and deeper understanding of the context for the work that needs to be done in the particular places that we care about. If we have high-quality, long-term, trust-based relationships with grantees, we believe that we'll have better knowledge around which we can make smart investments in their organizational and programmatic capacity, helping them to more efficiently and effectively achieve their outcomes."[43]

The staff at Wilburforce have made specific changes in response to feedback they received from nonprofits the foundation supports, such as simplifying grant application processes, awarding more multiyear grants, creating a fast-track process for grants of $50,000 or less, scheduling one-hour-long conversations with every nonprofit before an application or renewal, and targeting comprehensive nonmonetary assistance more narrowly to those groups that the foundation has identified as being its highest priority for these services.

Wilburforce works to help the organizations it funds achieve their shared goals and realizes that to do that well, the foundation staff need to listen humbly and make changes based on what they learn. The changes may seem minor, but they lead to better relationships with grantees—relationships that generate results.

Relationships matter, not just with grantees but with those you seek to help. CEP interviewed leaders at foundations that do this especially well and saw three commonalities in how they approach their work:

- They see the nonprofits they fund as the experts.
- They recognize the importance of spending time in the communities and fields in which they work.
- They hire staff who come from those fields and communities.[44]

Getting close to those they seek to help matters for individual givers, too, and it often means opening yourself up to some tough and painful emotions.

Closing the Distance

Jason Hackmann comes from the small, rural town of Winfield, Missouri. He describes his childhood as ordinary, growing up in a lower-middle-class family. He graduated from his small high school—his graduating class had just sixty-eight students—in the spring of 1995.

That's also when his brother was killed by a drunk driver.

The crushing loss of his brother fueled Hackmann's ambition to be successful and to break free of the small-town life he'd grown up living. He built a successful career, eventually founding a life insurance agency in St. Louis that caters to wealthy clients. After his first child was born, in 2004, Hackmann began thinking about what really mattered to him. "It was at that time that I began my journey back to Christ," he told me. His past giving, he confessed, had been made with "ulterior motives" related to his business interests.

It was on a vacation in Turks and Caicos in 2008 that his perspective changed. One day on the beach, Hackmann said to his wife, Jennifer, that he felt uninspired by the books he had brought on the trip. Jennifer pulled out a just-released book and suggested Hackmann read that. The book was called *Jantsen's Gift: A True Story of Grief, Rescue, and Grace,* by Pam Cope. It chronicles the author's story and the link between her loss of her fifteen-year-old son to an undiagnosed heart ailment and her desire to help others, particularly to do something about child slavery in Ghana.

Hackmann connected with her story, reading the book in a day, and decided he, too, wanted to do something about the issue. "If my brother hadn't died, and I hadn't felt that pain, I wouldn't have opened myself up to this work," he told me. "I realized how God uses tragedies to help others and what the possible purpose of my brother's death was."

Four months later, Hackmann found himself taking a trip again. But this time he was in Ghana with Jennifer, leaving behind their three children, the oldest of whom was five. "Our friends thought we were crazy," he said. Getting involved in this way changed Hackmann. "For the first time in my life, I wanted to do something, and I wanted nothing in return. I just wanted to help another human being," he explained.

Hackmann would be in Ghana ten times over the next three years, seeking to understand how to do something about the fact that children as young as three were being sold as slaves to Ghanaian fishermen. He spent time with and gave money to small, local nonprofits working to help affected children and spoke with many of those children himself.

He couldn't get out of his head the six-year-old he had met on his first trip who was a slave to a fisherman. Hackmann described the boy's withdrawn, remote demeanor: "He had no smile." The organization Hackmann was working with sent him a photo a year later of the same boy, now freed, smiling broadly. "I realized, 'Holy shit. Giving is better than receiving.' My mom always told me that, but I never believed it."

Over time, Hackmann contributed more than $1 million to a large Christian nonprofit, the International Justice Mission, helping to persuade its leaders to seek to end childhood slavery in Ghana, which he believes is achievable by 2022 or 2023. Hackmann has devoted much of his energy to this and related efforts, even launching a charitable offering from his company and dedicating all the profits to the cause.

"The more you hurt, the more you help," Hackmann told me. Getting close to a problem as searing and unfathomable as childhood slavery is emotionally taxing. But it also inspired Hackmann to do work that has given a new level of meaning to his life.

Hackmann's giving has helped children become free. "This work is part of God's calling for my life," he said. "What some people might see as amazing coincidences, I see as part of God's plan for me."[45]

As with many Americans, Hackmann's giving has been motivated by his religious beliefs, which have inspired him to get close to suffering and to try to do something about it. Others' motivations come from different sources. But whatever impels givers to get close to those they seek to help and to open themselves up to the suffering of others, the result is better-informed and more-effective giving.

"We have too many people trying to problem-solve from a distance," said Bryan Stevenson, founder and executive director of the Equal Justice Initiative. "And when you try to problem-solve from a distance you miss the details and the nuances of the problems, and your solutions don't work very effectively."[46] Stevenson urges people who want to make a difference to "get proximate" to the people and problems they seek to address.[47]

That's what Jason Hackmann did.

Results

The effects of good giving are everywhere. Hackmann's giving has played a role in freeing formerly enslaved children. Wilburforce has contributed to preserving millions of acres of land in the Pacific Northwest, protecting wildlife from extinction and preserving natural ecosystems. When you drive through that breathtaking part of our continent, which I know well, having grown up there, and marvel at the untouched natural beauty, you may not ever stop to think that giving has played a crucial role in protecting it.

But it has.

Or take another example. Newspaperman Charles Edward Marsh founded the Public Welfare Foundation in Washington, DC, in 1947. Public Welfare, which was until recently run by Mary McClymont, has nearly $500 million in assets and makes more than $20 million in grants annually. McClymont spent her entire career in the nonprofit sector, having served as executive director of Global Rights, an international human rights capacity-building organization, and as president and CEO of InterAction, the largest alliance of US-based international development and humanitarian nongovernmental organizations. She's a quiet leader, but with daunting smarts and a total commitment to results, she gets it done.

Public Welfare has been a driving force behind criminal justice reform. The foundation's work has been especially impressive in juvenile justice, shining a light on the appalling rates of incarceration of children in the United States and supporting crusaders such as Stevenson (who is also the author of *Just Mercy: A Story of Justice and Redemption* and whose Equal Justice Initiative has helped free death row inmates and influenced policy with respect to imprisonment of children). Using research that demonstrates that incarceration of children for minor and nonviolent offenses leads to high levels of recidivism and a slew of other bad outcomes, the foundation has helped change state policies through support for state-based advocacy. As a result, the juvenile incarceration rate has dropped by more than half in the past twelve years.[48]

Sometimes effective philanthropy is about avoiding bad outcomes. The Rockefeller Brothers Fund, for example, spent years trying to foster more-productive interactions between US and Iranian officials in the interest of diffusing tensions between the countries and avoiding war, helping support and plan some fourteen meetings between 2001 and 2008. "For many of the participants, it was the first time they ever spoke to someone from the other side," Trita Parsi, founder and president of the National Iranian American Council, wrote. "Beyond providing the two sides with a deeper understanding of their respective political systems, limitations, and calculations, the meetings also connected key players on both sides who later came to have leading roles in the nuclear negotiations."[49] The foundation, in other words, laid the groundwork for the 2015 US-Iran nuclear deal. Although President Trump pulled out of the deal in 2018, it still resulted in a period of decreased tensions between the countries, and therefore increased safety for all of us.

Yes, it's true that some givers squander their opportunities for supporting positive change. But it's also true that many deliver, often in ways that remain invisible to the American public. Giving by individuals like Hackmann and by Letwin and her foundation, as well as foundations like Public Welfare, Rockefeller Brothers Fund, and scores of others, strengthens our country and the world.

No matter whether you're giving away thousands or millions of dollars during your lifetime, being effective as a giver is a choice. And it isn't easy. The elements of giving done right, which I'll discuss in the chapters to follow, sound like what it takes to be effective in anything: clear goals, coherent strategies, disciplined implementation, and good performance indicators. But in every case, doing it well is uniquely challenging in ways I'll explain. It takes commitment, humility, and a willingness to understand the nuance.

꧁꧂꧁꧂꧁꧂

Chapter 2 Review: Giving Guidance

1. **Giving isn't like investing.** In fact, investing in companies to make a profit is a terrible analogy for giving. In giving, performance measures are elusive, and success usually takes multiple organizations acting in coordination. Giving effectively is uniquely challenging, requiring its own unique discipline and set of skills. Furthermore, investment implies ownership, and givers don't own their grantees.

2. **Don't give just because you were asked to.** Take the time to make a careful decision—which is impossible to do with a college student at your doorstep or a telemarketer on the phone. Give in accordance with your goals and strategies—which we'll turn to in the next two chapters—not the slick marketing message, infomercial, or telephone call of the day. Balance the head and the heart and make decisions on your own terms.

3. **Find the vehicle that makes sense for you.** It may be a donor-advised fund, a scholarship fund, or a field-of-giving fund at your community foundation, a giving circle, or a private foundation. There are many ways to give, and the challenge is to find the right one based on your interests and goals, your level of giving, the time you want to spend on your giving, and the amount of support you feel you need.

4. **Learn from the big donors' and foundations' lessons.** Among those lessons is that effective giving that's rooted in an understanding of needs can contribute to tremendous progress, but that out-of-touch or complacent givers can easily squander the opportunity to do good. Giving done right requires understanding the organizations you fund and the people, fields, and communities you seek to affect. It requires humility and patience.

⚒ 3 ⚒

A TOUGH BALANCE

CHOOSING YOUR GOALS

L ESLIE AND MARK Sillcox had successful careers as information technol-ogy executives. They knew they wanted to make a difference with their philanthropy but weren't sure where to focus. They considered a range of options. Finally, thinking about what had mattered in their own lives, they settled on education.

Leslie had been a teacher before a career switch that led to serving as chief information officer at Goldman Sachs when the company went public in 1999. She told me she sees "education as the platform through which you change life outcomes." Even once she and Mark achieved clarity about the area in which they wanted to work, they tried not to rush in.

"We wanted to be hands-on, to be proximate," Mark explained over coffee near the couple's New York apartment. So they mentored students, volunteering their time and developing relationships with the people their philanthropy would ultimately seek to help.

"We knew the kids," Leslie explained. "We mentored them. We sup-ported them. We chose our goals through a combination of analysis plus understanding." As they describe it, the objectives of their foundation, which makes several million dollars in grants annually, is "to contribute to the steadily growing number of young people in New York City who over-come socioeconomic barriers to graduate from public high school—and then from college—prepared for meaningful employment and robust civic participation."

Their foundation supports organizations and schools that have strong evidence of success, and they seek as much as possible to stay focused on their clearly articulated goal.

"We've tried to be pretty strict about our mission and not stray," Leslie explained. Mark described the mix of passion and dispassion that this takes. "Do something you're passionate about," he advised. "But don't become emotional about it."[1]

Not So Simple

Giving done right starts with clear goals. The fewer the better, in general, because the more you try to do, the harder it is to do it all well.

Sounds simple, right? But it's not nearly as easy as it sounds. Which goals should you choose? How do you choose goals when there are so many pressing problems? How do you stay focused when challenges are so interrelated?

These are the questions the Sillcoxes started with, as every effective giver must. They are the basis for success, for making a difference, for having an impact. And, here, again, it's important to be skeptical of the conventional wisdom found in most general guides for donors. These guides advise givers to focus on the heart. The authors of these guides don't judge whether some goals are worthier than others. I think the heart is also key—you need to really care about your areas of focus. But I'd urge you to use your head, too, as the Sillcoxes have.

Even proponents of a data-driven, strategic approach to philanthropy have taken what some have referred to as a "goal agnostic" approach. One well-respected and thoughtful how-to book for givers advises that "the choice of philanthropic goals is essentially subjective," arguing that "the most fundamental determinants of a donor's goals are his or her interests or concerns."[2] Rockefeller Philanthropy Advisors (RPA), in a guide to "finding your focus," says that "many funding appeals seek support on the basis of urgency. But what's the most urgent issue? There's obviously no objective answer to that question."[3]

Or is there?

The Princeton philosopher Peter Singer, the originator of the "effective altruism" movement, harshly critiques the RPA guide, saying, "This is the wrong question to ask, but even if it were the right question, the answer would be wrong. 'What is the most urgent issue?' is not the right question to ask because a potential donor should be asking, 'Where can I do the most good?'"

Singer and other effective altruists believe that not all goals are created equal. They argue that there is, in fact, an "objectively best cause" and that it's your moral duty to support it—to focus on the goals that will allow you to do the most good.[4] The implications for Singer are to support causes abroad, where the costs to save a life are much lower than in the United States. He believes givers should support organizations that are, for example, providing bed nets to stave off malaria, which is a leading killer of children in developing countries, or preventing trachoma, the most common cause of preventable blindness.

What's Worthy?

While many have taken a data-driven approach to strategy in philanthropy, arguing—rightly, I believe—that some strategies are more effective than others to achieve particular goals, Singer takes a data-driven approach to goal selection, seeking to analyze how to do the most good per dollar spent.[5] Does this mean Singer thinks donors shouldn't give to support, say, the addition of a new wing to a local museum? Yes.

He says you shouldn't give to the museum—not when you can cure or prevent blindness for just $100 per person. Singer is relentlessly rational in making the case that it's difficult to justify goal agnosticism. He suggests that by choosing to support certain causes, you're forgoing the opportunity to save or dramatically improve lives.[6]

Among those I know who are givers or advisors to givers, most reject Singer's arguments—whether because they disagree with them or because his arguments make them uncomfortable (or both), it's hard to know. (For the record, his arguments made me uncomfortable and made me question choices I've made over the years, which of course is his aim.) But I think his case, which he outlines in his books, *The Life You Can Save* and *The Most Good You Can Do*, is powerful and worth consideration. It's probably right that not all philanthropic goals are equally worthy, morally.

The area where Singer's influence and that of the effective altruism movement appears strongest is among Silicon Valley donors. Most notably, Facebook cofounder Dustin Moskovitz and his wife, Cari Tuna, a former *Wall Street Journal* journalist, have been open about the influence effective altruism has had on them as they launched their foundation, Good Ventures. When I asked Tuna whether she was a follower of Singer's during a session at CEP's conference in 2015, she demurred somewhat, saying, "not everyone thinks the same way" in the effective altruism movement.

"The thing that I am really excited about is working to improve the lives of other people as much as we can, and that at the core is what to me effective altruism is all about," she told me and the conference audience.[7] Moskovitz has a reported net worth of nearly $10 billion—so his and Tuna's philanthropy, which is still in its early stages, will be the largest-scale and highest-profile effort to put effective altruism into practice.[8]

There is, indeed, a strong case to be made for rejecting goal agnosticism and grappling with the moral questions Singer raises. But the heart matters, too. Unlike Singer, I think giving locally is important, as it responds to a deep-seated human need to help those in your community. And, unlike Singer, I believe there's an important role for giving that supports arts and culture—and the humanities. Givers must weigh a host of considerations, including their values and (if relevant) religious beliefs, and decide on the goals that best suit them.

Giving effectively is tough work, so you need to be committed to it for the long haul. Mario Morino, whom we met earlier, said, "I ask new donors, 'What do you care about most?'" Then he advises them to "get in there and learn" by "talking to the end clients"—those they seek to help—and "bearing witness." He said that, based on his own experience as a giver, "I tend to try to slow them down. They want to do something, but they don't know enough yet."[9] It's important to take your time to choose your goals.

In the end, as I believe Singer would agree, you're free to make any choice you like. But you should at least engage the question of where you can do the most good as well as what incites your passions and stirs your heart. As you do, keep in mind that if you live in the United States and you itemize in your tax returns, you benefit from tax advantages as a giver. Institutional givers are also tax advantaged, as we've discussed. Recognizing that tax revenue has been forgone should compel you to seriously reflect on your obligations and push yourself to go beyond just what is appealing to your heart.

Head and heart both matter in goal selection.

Roots and Branches

Another frequent argument about the choice of goals is that givers should focus on the "root causes" of problems. In this school of thought, philanthropy that salves—rather than solves—problems such as hunger is inferior. The CEO of a large, relatively new multibillion-dollar foundation—one of the fifty largest in the country, thanks to its young, living donor—contrasted his approach with that of other foundations. He told me, "We're focused on root causes, unlike others." I was puzzled. What he meant was that they don't want to deal just with the effects of a problem, such as homelessness. They want to get at what led to the issue in the first place, which involves understanding root causes such as unemployment, substance abuse, and mental health issues.

I was puzzled by this man's comment because givers have long tried to do this. The focus on root causes is often described as though it were superior and recently conceived; a 2015 *Forbes* article points to it as a "trend."[10] But that's not the case. Examples of a root-cause approach go back centuries. Writing in *Outlook* magazine in 1907, Daniel Gilman noted the power of major philanthropic gifts as a "new force in civilization," praising the "far-sighted" perspective of the new donors of his day, such as Andrew Carnegie and Margaret Olivia Slocum Sage.[11] Gilman didn't use the phrase "root cause," but what he described is the same concept. Indeed, this was the perspective that informed John D. Rockefeller to support the Rockefeller Sanitary Commission for the Eradication of Hookworm Disease in 1910, virtually eradicating the disease in southern states, where it had been prevalent, in just four years.[12]

William Schambra, the conservative critic of foundations, has noted that big, institutional philanthropy in the United States has been focused on root causes since its earliest days. He points out that the earliest major American foundations, and the givers behind them, took a "scientific" approach to their philanthropy, sometimes to terrible effect. Schambra notes that some of the efforts to address root causes have been among the most shameful episodes in the history of philanthropy, citing the eugenics movement in the 1930s, which the Rockefeller Foundation supported.[13]

Schambra is right about the history. He's also right in pointing out the dangers of a focus on root causes if it's done in a way that assumes donors know best and attempts to impose "solutions" on society. But the horror of the eugenics example, or the caution it offers about the imposition of solutions by those who think they have the answers, is hardly reason to give up on the idea that when we can get to the underlying causes of serious issues, we should.

There are many great examples of philanthropy that have addressed root causes of issues for the good, as in the case of hookworm, often improving lives dramatically and even saving them. Some are mundane and simple, but powerful. Consider the efforts of successful industrial chemist John V. N. Dorr and his wife, Nell, in the 1950s. In the book *Give Smart: Philanthropy That Gets Results,* Thomas Tierney and Joel Fleishman tell the story of how Nell Dorr recognized that "after dark, especially in bad weather, headlight glare from oncoming traffic made drivers either hug the center line of the highway or swerve away from that line onto the soft shoulder of the road—sometimes with tragic consequences."

The Dorr Foundation lobbied the state of Connecticut to test Nell's theory that painting a white line on the far-right side of the road would increase safety for drivers and pedestrians. Based on the positive results, the practice began to spread, with a lot of work by the Dorr Foundation to make the case. "As a result of the foundation's money" and efforts on Dorr's part, "an increasingly mobile population became a lot safer, and thousands upon thousands of lives were saved," Tierney and Fleishman wrote.[14]

Focusing on root causes can be powerfully effective, as it was in this case. When your teenager walks into the house at 11:30 p.m. after driving home, you probably don't think, "Thank God for the Dorr Foundation, without which my daughter might have veered off the road, crashed, and died tonight." But it would be reasonable if you did. Dealing with the root cause of something is powerful because it prevents bad things from happening.

That said, a focus on root causes isn't somehow superior to other forms of philanthropy. Nor is it the only type of philanthropy that can be considered strategic or results-driven. Reducing car accidents and the injuries and deaths they cause is a great achievement, but so is improving the emergency room outcomes at hospitals where the victims of car crashes are rushed—even if that effort doesn't get to the root causes of the injuries. Givers and nonprofits can be more or less strategic and effective, yielding better or worse results, when dealing with issues such as disaster relief, feeding the hungry, or helping ex-inmates get back on their feet to lead productive lives.

Yes, of course, we'd all like to permanently solve a problem. That is possible, in some cases. Polio has been nearly eradicated, thanks to the efforts of the World Health Organization, United Nations Children's Fund (UNICEF), the Rotary Foundation, and, more recently, the Bill & Melinda Gates Foundation. That is a huge achievement. Wherever we can permanently eliminate a problem, we should. But givers can also make a huge difference by reducing harm from something that cannot be permanently eliminated—or hasn't been yet.

You shouldn't assume that a focus on roots is necessarily superior. Trimming branches is also important.

Realism

Whatever you decide to do, I encourage you to approach the articulation of philanthropic goals with clarity about where you're choosing to intervene in a problem or context. Regardless of what you decide, and whether you focus on root causes or not, you'll need to articulate your goals as clearly as you can—and with an awareness of what others are doing.

As you do this, you need to be realistic. I've seen givers with hugely ambitious goals that seem detached from the reality of how difficult it would be to achieve them. "We're going to reinvent public education," one foundation staffer told me. But as much as foundations have spent in education—it's commonly the largest program area at large foundations—their grant dollars (even if all of them were devoted to education) are a drop in the bucket compared to total government education spending. So, is that a realistic goal? A related question is whether that's even an appropriate objective for a giver operating in a democracy.

Givers sometimes get intoxicated by the dollar signs. I've heard talk of "disrupting poverty," as if doing so would be as quick to accomplish as Uber's "disruption" of the taxi industry. But the philanthropic road is littered with the carcasses of wildly successful business people who thought they'd be able to *single-handedly* address some stubborn social problem in the same time frame and with the same approach with which they made their millions or billions.

It never happens.

Given how challenging it is to make progress on stubborn problems, it's crucial to remember that givers operate in a larger context of other givers, each with their own goals. You shouldn't assume you have to start from scratch or come up with something different than what others have done. Remember that you're not competing with other givers; choosing to have the same goals as others should be seen as a smart choice, not a failing. Sometimes what's most useful is for a donor to follow the lead of others to increase the resources being directed at a problem. After all, no giver can accomplish much alone.

I don't want to suggest that philanthropy shouldn't take on the biggest, thorniest problems. I think it should, precisely because it's the societal actor with the most freedom to do so. But it's no coincidence that when a number of the largest foundations decided to try to do something about climate change, they did so together—as when the David and Lucile Packard, William and Flora Hewlett, and McKnight Foundations founded the ClimateWorks Foundation in 2008. The effort has since expanded to include other funders, such as the Oak Foundation, John D. and Catherine T. MacArthur Foundation, and many others. With nearly $1.4 billion committed directly to the ClimateWorks Foundation since its establishment—and numerous additional foundations partnering, collaborating, and aligning billions of dollars more in funding—it is likely one of the biggest "giving circles" in the world.[15]

The leaders of these foundations knew it was foolish and naïve for any of them to believe they could make a difference on climate change acting alone, even though they lead some of the largest giving institutions. So, they wisely aligned efforts. Even acting together, the odds are long, and they've certainly had their challenges. But they have determined that the potential benefit is so great that it's worth a shot, even if it's a long shot. I'm glad they did.

Realism involves looking at the giver's resources relative to the scale of the problem. This sober look at dollars relative to the challenge should lead to two realizations:

- It's crucial to work in alignment with other actors, including other givers.
- The more resources that can be devoted to a goal the better, which should lead to fewer goals rather than more—though it's tough to guard against "goal drift."

Competitive Frameworks, Misapplied

On the first point, here again we see the damage of analogies to business, where the focus is on a single institution in a competitive, zero-sum environment. This was the framing of one of the more damaging articles for the effective practice of major philanthropy of recent decades, published in *HBR* in 1999. The article urged foundations to focus on what they could uniquely do, select "the best" grantees in the manner of "investment advisers in the business world" (there's that investment analogy again), and focus on "unique positioning" and "unique activities."[16]

The article imports notions that make sense in a competitive context but are counterproductive in a noncompetitive one in which the ultimate goal is impact, not profit. Unfortunately, countless givers—including many of the largest foundations in the country—brought in the authors' firm, FSG, to help them find their "unique position" and define strategies that were too often top-down, isolated, and therefore inevitably ineffective. To its credit, FSG has since changed its tune and has shown more understanding of the very different dynamics that exist in the world of giving than in the world of business. But it took too long, with too many missed opportunities along the way. Too often, big givers fall in love with the ideas of big business, especially when they're being promoted by someone with a high profile and a big marketing budget. But the contexts, as we've seen, are dramatically different—and so must be the approaches.

The stubborn historical fact, which should have been a revelation to absolutely no one, is this: Nothing of real consequence has been accomplished when our toughest societal problems are tackled by a single entity acting alone. Sadly, those who believe that what they gleaned in business school, in the business world, or from business "gurus" can just transfer over to giving seem to have to learn this lesson the hard way.

Goal selection shouldn't focus on uniqueness. Quite the opposite—it should happen with an eye toward overlap and opportunities for collaboration.

Narrowing

On the second realization that flows from realism—devoting as much to a goal as possible—givers need to make tough decisions about what they will *not* do so that they avoid undertaking many disparate initiatives and doing none well. Few of the largest foundations focus on just a single goal. In a survey of CEOs of large foundations CEP conducted, 6 percent said they had one programmatic goal; 68 percent had between two and five; 16 percent had six to nine; and 10 percent had ten or more. It's hard to imagine being able to maximize your impact as a giver while pursuing more than ten goals.[17] I've seen foundations I think could make a strong case that they're doing this effectively, but it's certainly rare in my experience.

Avoiding goal drift isn't as easy as it sounds, though. In business, the overriding objective is clear: drive profits. Focus is easier to maintain because if something isn't increasing profits or showing the potential to do so, you stop doing it. When McDonald's introduces a new product, say Mighty Wings or the McHot Dog (real menu items from recent years), it becomes clear quickly whether they will sell. If they don't, McDonald's takes them off the menu—as it did in these cases. The data are clear on what works and what doesn't.

In giving, it's much more complicated. If what you're doing isn't working, you won't necessarily get the kind of rapid and powerful feedback that McDonald's gets. So you keep going, adding goals, thinking "maybe we'll be more effective in addressing Goal One if we also get at the related issue we're addressing through Goal Two."

After all, you can do so many things when you're a giver—as many as you like, really—and the temptation is powerful because there are so many worthy causes. Even once you've settled on goals, it's hard to stay focused when it often seems logical or even necessary to do something adjacent to what you were doing—say, for example, to move from early childhood education into adult literacy when you realize parents aren't reading to their kids because they can't read. But where does it stop? What about poverty—how can kids learn if they're hungry? And can we do anything about poverty without changing government policy? And so maybe we need to do advocacy in addition to giving?

Pretty soon, focus is lost.

Philanthropic Drift

About a decade ago, I met with a widely respected retired foundation executive I'll call Mike. He had worked at two of the largest foundations in the country in senior roles. Over lunch, Mike told me a story.

At one of the foundations where Mike worked, a new CEO had been named. As often happens with appointments of CEOs of large foundations, the foundation's board had selected someone with little experience in philanthropy and little familiarity with the nonprofit sector. The staff was concerned. What did *this* guy know?

The new CEO, who I will call Bob, was now to lead what was one of the oldest, largest, and most respected foundations in the country. This foundation gave hundreds of millions of dollars in grants each year. Staff members wondered how to best bring their new leader up to speed. Noting that Mike had the most experience in philanthropy of anyone on the staff, it was decided that he would offer to orient Bob to the world of philanthropy. "You talk to him, Mike," staff members said. "You can help him understand foundations."

Bob was eager to learn and asked Mike many questions over tea in Bob's large, ornate office. Finally, as their time ended, Bob looked at Mike and said, "I have one more question for you, Mike. What is the greatest mistake you fear I will make?"

"That's a good question," Mike said. "I think the greatest mistake you will make is that you'll decide on goals and strategies for the foundation and then you will be reading the newspaper and you will read about a terrible problem, and you'll say, 'We need to do something about that!' And you'll walk into the foundation and set in motion a process that leads to the creation of a new program area."

"Six months later," Mike continued, "you'll be shaving and listening to NPR, and you'll hear about something else. Something that moves you and that feels connected to other issues you're working on at the foundation. And you'll walk into the foundation and set in motion a process that leads to the creation of a new program area."

"And this will keep happening. And then," Mike went on, "after five or ten years, you'll walk into the offices of the foundation and you'll see office after office and cube after cube, and you'll look out across the place, and all the busy people, and you won't really have any sense of what it all adds up to."

Mike told me this story and paused for dramatic effect. He said that, despite the warning he had given, that's exactly what Bob proceeded to do over the decade that followed. He made exactly the mistake Mike predicted he would make. So much so that Bob's successor massively reorganized the foundation, shuttering programs and letting go dozens of staff in the name of greater focus and clarity.

So often, well-meaning givers, both individuals and institutions, try to stay focused, but over time they end up spreading their limited resources across more and more goals and strategies. Philanthropic drift is hard to combat.

The Downside of Hyperfocus

So, the lesson is clear then, right? Stay focused! Every management guru says the same thing, more or less. Jim Collins, speaking at CEP's conference in 2009, put it this way: "Disciplined action begins with piercing clarity about what you choose to not do. In a world awash with opportunity for contribution, it's what we choose not to do," that matters, said Collins, "because there is so much to do."[18]

I cite that Collins quotation all the time. I agree with it. I think too many givers fall into the trap of adding goal after goal. Unlike in the case of McDonald's, there aren't naturally occurring feedback loops to let them know they've lost focus. But I also think it's more complicated than it seems. Too narrow a focus can generate its own issues.

Look at the Bill & Melinda Gates Foundation, the largest foundation in the world, with some $45 billion in assets. Many observers, including me, praised Bill and Melinda Gates for the degree of focus they maintained at their foundation as it got up and running. Quite unlike the foundation where Bob had been brought in as CEO, there weren't going to be ten different program areas at the Gates Foundation, with dozens and dozens of priorities and initiatives within each. There would be focus. Early on, the primary areas were global health and US education.

In those first years of the foundation's work, Bill Gates emphasized that he would focus on global health but not global development.[19] But over time, he and his staff realized that they couldn't achieve the goals they set for themselves in global health without paying attention to global development. They recognized that they couldn't do one without the other. Look at the foundation's website today and you'll see a global development program that includes emergency response; family planning; global libraries; integrated delivery; maternal, newborn, and child health; nutrition; polio; and vaccine delivery—and that's a narrowing from what the website listed in 2016. In addition, there's a global policy and advocacy division, which includes tobacco control, development policy and finance, and global education learning.[20]

Were Bill and Melinda Gates wrong to add programmatic areas and goals to their foundation? Is their giving now too diffuse? Or were they right to do this because their global health goals would never have been achievable without also focusing on global development? What use, for example, is a vaccine if it can't be delivered to those who need it because of a lack of infrastructure, such as roads and bridges?

These are difficult questions, and I certainly don't have all the answers. But the Gateses' experience illustrates the degree to which the bromides about "focus, focus, focus" can fall short in philanthropy. Scale is obviously relevant here. Bigger givers can more easily have more focus areas and still be effective.

Yet smaller, individual givers face similar challenges. The Sillcoxes realized that some of the students who were achieving great success academically because of the programs they supported were having all they worked for threatened because they were undocumented. They had arrived in the New York area from Latin America, often fleeing violence, and were finding that, despite their academic success, they couldn't get financial aid for college. In some cases, they faced the risk of deportation. So, the Sillcoxes began supporting the Safe Passage Project, which provides pro bono legal counsel to undocumented minors.

"They are really willing to listen and learn," Safe Passage Project executive director Rich Leimsider said of the Sillcoxes.[21] They recognized that issues are interrelated.

Focus is hard to maintain. The challenge is to strike the right balance between the natural drift that tends to pull givers into too many areas with too many goals and a telescopic focus that misses the larger context in which a problem resides. You'll never be certain what that right balance is or whether you've found it, but that's why you need to continually assess and challenge yourself.

Here, again, a key consideration is what others are doing—including other givers, nonprofits, and, when relevant, government and corporate actors. Sometimes, givers can coordinate to ensure that they each support different, and complementary, aspects of an approach to reaching a goal. For individual givers, I think part of the reason for the rapidly growing popularity of giving circles, which I described in Chapter 2, is the realization that givers can be more effective together than they can operating alone.

Understanding Your Role

To be effective, givers need to be simultaneously ambitious—willing to take on tough challenges—and humble about the role they play. Givers can articulate goals at the level of outcomes, such as "to reduce poverty in the greater Los Angeles area." They can also articulate goals that are more modest and focus on supporting others to achieve their goals, such as "to strengthen organizations that are working to reduce poverty in Los Angeles." Most larger givers and foundations choose the former type of goal, but it's perfectly respectable, in my view, to take a more modest approach—and to focus your giving on supporting organizations that are working to achieve outcomes. Regardless of how you frame your goal, though, you'll need to productively engage the organizations and other actors you need to work with to achieve your goal.

You don't have to look far for examples of givers who, although well-intentioned, didn't engage the people they needed to engage to ensure alignment toward a common goal. In Newark, New Jersey, for example, Facebook founder Mark Zuckerberg made a $100 million challenge grant—announced to much fanfare on *The Oprah Winfrey Show* in 2009—to turn around the city's failing school system. Other donors and foundations matched Zuckerberg's grant. As the journalist Dale Russakoff has documented, everyone agreed that the Newark schools were broken, but the effort fell apart amid distrust from teachers and families who weren't consulted about the best ways to fix them.[22]

Between Zuckerberg's gift and the others who met his challenge, $200 million was spent to improve the schools, but the gains were modest, at best. The failure to live up to the hype in Newark was partly about strategy, a topic we'll explore in the next chapter, but it was also about goal articulation. To many of the givers outside Newark who were involved in the effort, the goal was as much about proving a point about how to combat teachers' unions as it was about improving Newark's schools for its students and families. The fundraising presentation consultants from McKinsey prepared for then–Newark Mayor (now US Senator) Cory Booker touted Newark as a "blueprint for national replication." Leaders of key local organizations, including major local foundations with crucial knowledge, weren't even consulted, according to one who told me this directly. Russakoff observed that the "language of national models left little room for attention to the unique problems of Newark, its schools, or its children."[23]

Although there are some more recent signs of progress in Newark, which some connect to this effort, the results fell far short of expectations. Of course, failure will happen when givers are ambitiously seeking to take on issues other actors can't or won't. But failure will be almost inevitable if you seek to go it alone, imposing change from the top down. A similar fate befell those who supported the infamously autocratic Washington, DC, public school chancellor, Michelle Rhee. In the words of Kaya Henderson, who Russakoff described as Rhee's "far more collaborative" successor, "Movements that don't include beneficiaries are doomed to fail." Russakoff noted that "voter backlashes" against "school reform" in other cities "revealed the tenuous nature of disruptive changes made without buy-in from those who have to live them."[24]

Henderson's and Russakoff's cautions apply to goal selection and, as we will see in the next chapter, to strategy choices as well. Givers are doing work to help others—that's what philanthropy is, after all. So, it's crucial to engage and consult with those you seek to help. They know what will help better than you do!

From Categories to Goals

Too many givers aren't clear on their goals. They can tell you the category of their giving: "We fund education," or "We support the environment." But they can't tell you what they hope to achieve. Without goal clarity—"I am seeking to improve the quality of high schools in Omaha, as judged by the number of students who go on to two- or four-year colleges"—it's tough to make decisions about what to support, much less how to gauge progress. Push yourself and those with whom you're doing your giving, whether family members or staff colleagues, to get clear about your goals.

It's not easy, and you might not get there right away. And it's especially challenging for big givers and for big families, in which many people are often involved in giving decisions.

Hotel tycoon Conrad Hilton Sr. founded the Conrad N. Hilton Foundation in 1944. The Hilton Foundation has grown considerably and today has assets of $2.8 billion, which will double upon the death of Barron Hilton, the founder's son. My CEP colleagues and I started working with the foundation in 2007, when it commissioned a GPR, which, as I've described, allows foundations to understand how their nonprofit grantees rate them on a range of dimensions and puts those results in a comparative context.

At the time, Barron's son Steven Hilton was the CEO. He had joined the foundation as a program associate in the early 1980s, when it was, in his words, "almost on autopilot" and "generally very reactive." Hilton's predecessor began professionalizing the foundation, a process Steven Hilton contributed to and continued as he assumed more leadership. By 2006, Hilton, who was now the CEO, was moving the foundation from its early focus on just a handful of nonprofits to a set of programmatic goals and strategies, in consultation with a board comprised mostly of Hilton family members. He hired Edmund Cain, who had served as head of the Carter Center's Global Development Initiative, as his vice president for programs. When we surveyed the foundation's grantees in 2007, the foundation was rated among the lowest in our comparative data set for its clarity of communication of goals and strategy.

Fast-forward a decade and it was among the highest-rated large foundations on this same dimension.[25] How did they do it? The foundation's website now clearly articulates goals in areas from improving life outcomes for young people transitioning out of foster care to ending chronic homelessness in Los Angeles County to preventing avoidable blindness to disaster preparedness, relief, and long-term recovery. The foundation—which is now led by seasoned philanthropy and nonprofit executive Peter Laugharn with Steven Hilton in the role of board chair—performs unusually well among large foundations on more than just clarity of goals and strategies. It leads most of its peers on a range of dimensions measured in the GPR, including perceptions of its impact.

The Real Experts

One of the reasons for the high ratings is that the Hilton Foundation is seen by the nonprofits it funds as "collaborative" and "open" to a "free-flowing" exchange of ideas about goals and strategies. The board and staff recognize that the foundation achieves nothing alone. "We did not see ourselves as above our grantees—that we had the answers, that we are smarter than them," explained Hilton. "It was the opposite. We listen."

The Hilton Foundation's goals connect to the vision of its founding donor and include some that focus on root causes and others that deal with alleviating near-term suffering. The foundation's efforts to address homelessness in Los Angeles County, for example, with its emphasis on long-term and holistic solutions to this challenge, has become a model emulated throughout the country. Among the programs of one of its primary grantees, the Corporation for Supportive Housing, is an effort that empowers formerly homeless people to become advocates.

The Hilton Foundation's effectiveness is rooted both in its clarity about its goals and in the way in which it has engaged those closest to the issues in shaping those goals. The staff there are quick to point out that the real experts are those closer to the issues, including nonprofits and those they seek to help. For his part, Steven Hilton credits his involvement with giving—through his work at the Hilton Foundation—with profoundly affecting his life, "giving me a sense of purpose and meaning."[26]

So, it's important to get clear on your goals. As you do, you should consider Peter Singer's plea to think about where your dollars can do the most good. But also consider your passions and what touches and inspires you. You will need that passion to sustain you when the work gets hard, and it will. Consider whether you want to focus on root causes or to address short-term needs. Obviously, both are needed, but neither is necessarily superior. Amazon's Jeff Bezos, in an attention-generating 2017 tweet requesting advice about his philanthropy (which is likely to be rather significant given his estimated $80 billion net worth), noted, "I'm thinking I want much of my philanthropic activity to be helping people in the here and now—short term—at the intersection of urgent need and lasting impact."[27]

But don't just ask your Twitter followers for advice. Try to understand what nonprofits working on the ground on the issues you care about think the goals should be. Most important, assuming your philanthropy seeks to better people's lives, try to understand what the people you seek to help think the most important goals are. Engage, as the Hilton Foundation has, those working to address the problem as well as those whose lives you seek to improve. They have the most informed point of view of all on what would be most helpful to them.

I suggest considering these questions as you think through your goals. Where can I do the most good? What can I realistically accomplish given my resources? Who shares my goals among other givers, nonprofits, and other actors? How do my goals connect to other goals and priorities? And, can I achieve one without working on the other? Do those I seek to help have the same goals for themselves that I have for them? Can I clearly explain each goal in a sentence or less?

Think through each carefully because your giving goals matter. Everything that follows—the choice of strategies, how you work with nonprofits, how you assess results, what to do beyond giving to complement those efforts—depends on having clear goals. Your pride in your progress will depend on goals that you feel good about and that you feel are worthy and wisely chosen. It's not easy to choose, nor is it easy to determine the right number of goals. But it's crucial.

From your goals, everything else follows.

⋞⋞⋞⋞⋞

Chapter 3 Review: Giving Guidance

1. **Not all goals are equally worthy, so don't just "follow your heart."** Yes, you need to be passionate about your giving. But you should also consider where you think your dollars can do the most good. Take into account your feelings of responsibility to your local geographic community but weigh also the potential to inexpensively and significantly affect lives for the better—or even to save lives—in developing countries.

2. **It's not true that the only worthy goals are ones that focus on so-called root causes.** You can do a tremendous amount of good, and be either effective or ineffective, whether you're focused on addressing pressing needs or getting to root causes. Neither approach is necessarily superior, and our world needs both. Be aware of where you're

intervening to address a problem and how your giving relates to the giving of others.

3. **Don't be afraid to simply do what others do and align your goals with those of others you respect and admire.** Unique positioning isn't relevant for givers in the same way it is in a competitive context, and it can be harmful. The fact is, you'll need to share goals with many other actors if you want to achieve them.

4. **Get specific and clear on your goals, not just categories of giving, and seek to find the balance between focus and recognition of the relatedness of issues.** Staying focused is difficult, in part because issues are so interrelated. Both hyperfocus and philanthropic drift can be problematic, so finding the right balance is key. If you add a goal, think about whether you also need to subtract one.

$\approx 4 \approx$

STRATEGY DONE RIGHT

ACHIEVING YOUR GOALS

P at Reynolds-Hubbard grew up in Topeka, Kansas, and San Francisco, where her family moved when she was eight. Her father was a lawyer and her mother a teacher, and she admired her parents' commitment to service and their involvement in the civil rights movement. She knew, as she put it, that she wanted to serve.

She had worked with foster youth in one way or another for much of her professional life, serving as child welfare director for San Francisco County during the mid-1990s. "It just drew me in," she said.[1] She was struck by the dismal life outcomes for former foster kids in California. Within eighteen months of "aging out" of foster care, a quarter of boys were incarcerated. Many others were homeless.

When Reynolds-Hubbard took a job in philanthropy, she knew she wanted to do something to change that statistic. The goal was clear, and it was a good and worthy one.

But how to do it? By strengthening the foster care system? Promoting adoption? Helping former foster kids get through college? All of the above? When dealing with complicated problems, it's often hard to know what strategy is most likely to achieve the desired result.

This was the challenge facing Reynolds-Hubbard and her employer, the San Francisco–based Stuart Foundation, two decades ago. The Stuart

Foundation was founded in 1941 by E. A. Stuart, the entrepreneur behind the Carnation Company, and now has $500 million in assets and makes about $20 million in grants annually across several areas. Struck by the grim statistics about the lives of foster youth, who leave the system at age eighteen, the staff and board of the foundation wondered what they could do. Reynolds-Hubbard was responsible for grantmaking in the child welfare area. "We spent time with these young people and built relationships. We heard their stories, and we did our best to understand them," she recalled.[2]

The conventional wisdom at the time was that adoption, or any kind of long-term relationship with a caring adult (referred to as "permanency") outside the foster system, was impossible for older children. Those working with foster youth believed it. But Reynolds-Hubbard wondered whether it was true.

"I heard them say how much they missed certain relationships and that they felt alone," she said. "For example, they would be very upset if their social worker was changed and they weren't notified. . . . It just kept needling me that they don't have parents, don't have support. That's a big deal, and we had just assumed that permanency can't work after children get older."[3]

Testing a New Approach

In 2000, Reynolds-Hubbard set out to test the conventional wisdom.

First, the Stuart Foundation's Child Welfare Program funded research by outside consultants to learn what others had been able to accomplish when seeking permanency for teenagers. "We did find people around the country; not a lot, but a few who were doing some innovative and successful work, and it was very, very inspiring," Reynolds-Hubbard told my colleague when we interviewed her for a CEP case study.

The next step was bringing the people succeeding in this work together with child welfare colleagues in California and Washington. There were skeptics. "Some people couldn't understand why I was having this meeting on youth permanency," said Reynolds-Hubbard.[4] But, eventually, the approach the foundation tested was shown to work and expanded across the state and then nationally.

That didn't happen easily. Reynolds-Hubbard told me that it was hard to get people working with foster youth to change their approaches. "Information alone didn't do it," so the foundation invested in coaching to help county workers, for example, adapt to the new insights about what was effective. Similarly, the expansion beyond California took investment. "We held national convenings several years in a row," Reynolds-Hubbard recalled.[5]

But, over time, the approach to foster youth changed across the country. Indeed, there is evidence of a change in attitudes nationally about adoption of older foster children. In California, the number of children in the foster care system dropped dramatically between 2001 and 2015.[6]

Aware that there are few cure-alls, Stuart and other funders backed complementary strategies, including supports for former foster youth attending college. They did so in the same manner—working collaboratively, seeking feedback, starting small, and expanding based on evidence of success. Crucially, Stuart also did something too few funders do—it invested in a data system that allowed all the relevant players to track a group of agreed-upon indicators. That way, everyone could accurately gauge the efficacy of different approaches.

The Stuart foster youth story has lessons for both institutional and individual givers. It's about the courage to challenge conventional wisdom and a refusal to accept that better outcomes aren't possible. It's about the patience to do research, learn, iterate, and be data-driven while also recognizing data sets alone don't change behavior. It's about a willingness to change based on what works and what doesn't. It's about listening to those you seek to help. Finally, it's about humility—the foundation's staff didn't assume they had all the answers.

The Stuart Foundation was, of course, just one of many actors. Tellingly, when we approached then-president Christy Pichel in 2008 about profiling Stuart's efforts as an example of good foundation strategy, she was hesitant. She and her colleagues saw the strategy as shared, not "theirs," and she didn't want to take all the credit.

Indeed, that humility is perhaps the biggest part of what made them effective at strategy.

Four Types of Givers

If goals are the *what*—specifying what, exactly, you want to achieve as a giver—then strategy is the *how*. Strategy is about the logic of how you will allocate your resources to achieve your goals. It's about supporting what works: what will help you make progress toward your important aims.

Those at the Stuart Foundation involved in the child welfare effort in the late 1990s and early 2000s were what we at CEP would call "total strategists." "We've seen in our Child Welfare Program that having a really clear strategy, using clear data that allow us to adjust our strategy as we go along, and staying focused on that strategy has helped us be successful," said Pichel.[7]

My colleagues and I have carefully analyzed the use of strategy at foundations. In several studies between 2006 and 2011, the first of which was led by CEP's Ellie Buteau and Kevin Bolduc, we examined foundation CEOs' and program officers' approaches to making decisions, looking at private and community foundations and conducting interviews, surveys, and case studies. When we examined these givers' approaches to making decisions about resource allocation, we found that most said they had a strategy, but fewer were describing decision-making that met our definition of strategy. This is how we define it:

> Strategy is a framework for decision-making that is focused on the external context in which the foundation or donor works and includes a hypothesized causal connection between use of philanthropic resources and goal achievement.

In other words, it's about logic. It's about having reason to believe that giving to certain organizations will help you achieve your goal. It's really that simple—but it's hard to have the discipline to do it, day in and day out, as a giver. That's where the passion and emotion come in. The emotional desire to have a real impact is what compels givers to get strategic. It is the heart that compels effective givers to use their head. We see givers get more strategic as their frustration grows because they don't have the impact they seek.

Based on our research, we developed a typology of four kinds of givers. My experience with individual givers suggests this typology applies equally to them. I have seen both individual donors with means large and small and staff at foundations large and small fall into these categories. As I will explain, my view is that these are in order of least to most effective:

◊ **Charitable bankers** are decidedly nonstrategic. Like bankers reviewing loan applications, they describe making decisions in terms of processes for reviewing, making, or denying individual requests. They rarely mention the external context. Most charitable bankers develop goals and decision-making frameworks based on historical practice and priorities—what they or others before them have done. Most givers start as charitable bankers—responding to requests without a lot of clarity about what they're trying to achieve. For foundations, it means seeing what proposals come over the transom and then figuring out which ones to approve. For individuals, it means responding to requests from those with whom they interact—at the cash register, over the phone, at work, when they see friends. For both types of givers, what's missing is clarity of goals and logic to guide decisions to achieve those goals.

◊ **Perpetual adjusters** describe themselves as in the midst of change—revising giving priorities or deciding whether to change how much they allocate to particular areas. They try to appease a broad range of stakeholders. Noted one, "I think our job as allocators of resources is to be there not only to listen to the communities but also to be open to new communities that are here, new issues, new and different things that are coming up." Individuals and institutions that are perpetual adjustors are always shifting, always adding something, and they can't tell you much about how it all coheres.

◊ **Partial strategists** differ from charitable bankers and perpetual adjusters in that they often link their goals to external factors and generally use external data to develop their approach. Partial strategists can cite at least one example of a strategy, yet for much of what they do they cannot articulate a logic connecting the use of resources and goal achievement.

Ꝺ **Total strategists** work diligently to ensure continued fidelity to their goals and their strategies. Their goals are well-defined. Nearly all total strategists take a proactive approach to their giving—they're not just responding to requests. Given their outward focus, strategy development for total strategists is primarily analytical and relies heavily on data about the external context. Foundation staff can be total strategists, but so can individuals. It's about a relentless focus on what will allow you to achieve your goals—and about ensuring that all decisions are guided by that focus.[8]

Which are you?

FOUR TYPES OF GIVERS

Being a Total Strategist

If you really care about maximizing the chances of making a difference with your giving, you'll want to work to be as close to a total strategist as possible. Total strategists are focused on supporting what works. When they don't know what works, they participate in disciplined tests to find out, the way the Stuart Foundation did. They go bigger when—and only when—they have confirming evidence.

Sometimes, reliable information about the best strategies to allow you to achieve your goals is readily available. You can simply fund what works. For years, for example, there's been a consensus among scientists and the world health community that insecticide-treated malaria bed nets are the best way to prevent deaths from malaria. So, if your goal is to reduce deaths related to malaria, a good giving strategy is to support organizations providing malaria bed nets.

But even when we know a lot about what works, it's usually more complicated than it looks. It turns out that some efforts to encourage use of bed nets are more successful than others. It's one thing to provide a mother with malaria bed nets for her children. It's another to know she'll use them. Different approaches, from sending text message reminders to providing stories depicting the benefits of using bed nets, might yield different results in terms of actual use.[9] Moreover, mosquitoes have developed resistance to the insecticide used in malaria bed nets, potentially weakening their effectiveness.[10] So, yes, supporting organizations making bed nets available is a good strategy for reducing malaria deaths, but there's still much work to be done to figure out what specific approaches are working best—and then to identify which organizations are using them.

Strategy in philanthropy isn't easy even in the best circumstances in terms of available evidence because even when something *seems* like it would make sense, even when there's evidence that it might work or does work, that doesn't always mean it will work in practice or in every context.

Bill Gates—the biggest giver of them all—found this out the hard way.

Chickens Come Home to Roost

In 2016, Bill Gates decided to donate 100,000 hens in developing countries, in partnership with the nonprofit Heifer International, to combat extreme poverty. He had written a blog post about the wisdom of raising chickens as a way out of poverty. "It's pretty clear to me that just about anyone who's living in extreme poverty is better off if they have chickens. In fact, if I were in their shoes, that's what I would do—I would raise chickens," he wrote.[11]

While the wisdom of this effort may have been clear to Gates, it wasn't necessarily clear to everyone else. In fact, the Bolivian government rejected the help, calling it "offensive."

"Cluck You: Bolivia Rejects Bill Gates' Donation of Hens," blared a headline in the UK newspaper the *Guardian*.[12] "He does not know Bolivia's reality to think we are living 500 years ago, in the middle of the jungle not knowing how to produce," said César Cocarico, the country's minister of land and rural development. "Respectfully, he should stop talking about Bolivia, and once he knows more, apologize to us."[13]

Givers sometimes feel like they know what's best for those they intend to help. It's perfectly clear to them: They've got *just the thing* to address the problem. Sometimes they're right; sometimes they're wrong. Let's assume that, in Bill Gates's case, raising chickens is indeed the best thing someone living in extreme poverty can do. The problem is this: It doesn't really matter whether Gates is right if the people he intends to help—or those who stand between the donation and the people—don't think so. Or if they're insulted by the suggestion.

In this case, the Bolivian government spoke up and rejected the help. But, often, nonprofits and other key actors bite their tongues, for fear of alienating those with the purse strings. The result can be a kind of charade, in which the giver never hears what people really think about the strategy du jour, and in which nonprofits play along, or pretend to, to secure funding. Some people, inside and outside the Bill & Melinda Gates Foundation, have suggested to me that this is what happened with the foundation's work in education. They point to the foundation's effort to break large high schools into smaller schools, for example, although others within the foundation say that work was more effective than many believe. When the foundation moved away from small schools, it focused on revamping and toughening teacher evaluation efforts only to see that initiative, like its predecessor, fall short of expectations. Similarly, efforts to push a common core curriculum have met resistance from those who felt it was being imposed from the top down.

To its credit, the foundation and Bill Gates himself have been open about the missteps, but only after a lot of upheaval—for schools, staff, families, and teachers. It's likely that this disruption could have been avoided with more listening, more research, and perhaps a more limited effort to test the hypotheses before betting big.

"We haven't seen the large impact we had hoped for [in education]," Bill Gates conceded in his and Melinda Gates's 2018 annual letter. Perhaps the right lessons weren't fully internalized—by the donors or the foundation's staff—from earlier failures. In that same letter, Melinda Gates seems tacitly to acknowledge as much, saying that now, "Everything we do in education begins as an idea that educators bring to us. They're the ones who live and breathe this work."[14] Time will tell whether this more ground-up approach to strategy really takes hold at the Gates Foundation.

I'm not trying to pick on the Gates Foundation, which has done much good and important work—some of which we'll discuss a little later. My point, rather, is to show how easy it is to get caught up in what seems like it just makes sense without checking to make sure it does make sense to those closer to the ground, including those you're trying to help.

It's the same hurdle that tripped up Mark Zuckerberg in Newark. And it's the same one that befell givers big and small that gave to PlayPumps International, which raised tens of millions of dollars to install water pumps across Africa that would be powered by children playing on a merry-go-round. As William MacAskill and others have documented, the pumps largely went unused. Turns out, the merry-go-rounds, which needed continual pushing rather than being able to glide around after a few good running pushes, weren't fun to play on—and were both more expensive and less efficient than traditional hand pumps. People in the communities that were intended to benefit from the PlayPumps didn't like them. Once again, the givers got infatuated with an idea or innovation—it sounds great, after all, to think clean water could result simply from kids playing on a merry-go-round—and imposed it on others.

And, once again, it didn't work.[15]

"Strategic Philanthropy"

Given stories like this—and they're legion among nonprofit leaders—perhaps it's not surprising that there has lately been a kind of backlash against so-called strategic philanthropy. More and more, people are questioning whether givers should be so focused on strategy.

I got a call from a board member of a significant foundation, which was undertaking a search for a new president. She was on the search committee and wanted my thoughts on the search. I asked her to fill me in on the context. "Well, I'll tell you this," she said, a tone of exasperation in her voice. "We're done with 'strategic philanthropy!' We have had enough of that approach."

She told me that, after a president who had been a big advocate of strategy, the foundation was ready to move in a different direction. "He just didn't know what he didn't know. And so we didn't have the impact we wanted," the board member said of the CEO. "It's time for us to listen. And to really respect the nonprofits we support with our funding, who are the ones on the ground doing the work, after all."

I realized that her issue was not with the concept of strategy—of pursuing the set of activities that would be most likely to help the foundation achieve its goals. It was with what the term "strategic philanthropy" had come to mean, which was something very different. Strategic philanthropy implied to her a way of working that lacks heart and is isolated and top-down, focused on the "uniqueness" of individual actors as though they were competitors in an industry. To her and many others in the nonprofit sector, strategic philanthropy looks something like this:

A plan is cooked up in a fancy conference room by high-priced consultants with MBAs in business casual garb with great PowerPoint skills; adopted by donors, foundation leaders, and program officers; then unceremoniously rammed down the throats of those doing the hard work on the ground. Nonprofits receiving funding are told to execute the plan but have no voice in its development. Years go by under the "new strategy" before there's a growing realization—within the donor's mind or among the foundation staff and board—of what has been long known but unspoken by nonprofits getting funding and others: It isn't working! Too many assumptions had been made, too many inappropriate analogies to a business context offered up. And too much underestimation of complexity, leading to unintended consequences and no—or, even worse, negative—results.[16]

Thoughtful givers recognize that strategy in philanthropy is different from strategy in business, but the CEO who was being replaced simply didn't get that. He saw himself as a business-savvy savior who was turning the foundation around by employing strategic philanthropy, which to him seemed also to mean his way or the highway. His attitude, and I've spoken to people who come from the business world who see themselves in this light, seemed to be that we should all be grateful that he was willing to take his talents to the nonprofit sector, fancying himself the LeBron James of philanthropy.

This belief that business experience offers exactly the right tools to be a great giver is quite common. One community foundation president, whose board includes significant individual givers who made their money in business, confided in me one evening at a conference dinner, whispering so his board chair across the table wouldn't hear: "Every single one of my board members thinks they can do my job better than I can. Look, I came out of business, too, but what I know now that they don't is how hard it is to do this work well. They don't get it."

Over time, those who promote a conception of strategy that's pulled straight out of the business world will find it just doesn't work. But let's not throw out the baby with the bathwater. To me, the issue isn't strategy, per se, which is essential to having impact in philanthropy. The problem is bad strategy or, often, well-designed strategy implemented badly. And yes, bad strategy does, indeed, happen too often. But it's no more reason to reject strategy than my being a (very) bad singer is a reason to reject music.[17]

Not a Business Concept

So, what happened when it came to strategy in philanthropy? What went wrong?

Here, again, it's the business school professors and philanthropy consultants invoking business metaphors who led philanthropy astray. It all started with the 1999 *Harvard Business Review* article I discussed in Chapter 3, with its unrelenting emphasis on the need for "uniqueness" and "distinct positioning." The problem is that the authors failed to acknowledge—or perhaps didn't understand—crucial differences between business and philanthropy, arguing instead that the underlying logic of strategy in philanthropy is the same as in business.

Strategy isn't a business concept; it has meaning in any number of domains from sports to chess to war (the word itself derives from "army" in Greek). Crucially, strategy in philanthropy, unlike in business, isn't about uniqueness or distinct positioning. It's about a shared approach across institutions and people that recognizes and appreciates the challenge of understanding cause and effect when working on the toughest challenges. In business, your strategy should be yours alone, given the competitive dynamics. In philanthropy, if your strategy is yours alone, it will almost surely fail. The *HBR* article was influential because it offered simplicity, boiling down "strategy" to a simplistic checklist. But, as Warren Buffet famously said in another context, "beware geeks bearing formulas."[18]

In too many conceptions of so-called strategic philanthropy, the giver is the locus of strategy—and of control. Philanthropy evaluation consultants Patricia Patrizi and Elizabeth Heid Thompson described the situation well in 2011. "Not only are plans often separated from implementation, they're often developed in isolation from those doing the work—the grantees supported to execute the strategy. It is difficult to think of a setting where this would be good practice."[19]

I've seen it up close. Years ago, I shared results of a grantee survey we had conducted, through our GPR process, with the staff of a foundation as well as with the living donor who established it. I let them know that grantees didn't feel the foundation was approachable when problems arose. I also told them that grantees said the foundation put much more pressure on them to modify their priorities to get funding than was typical. In both cases, our comparative data showed the individual giver and his foundation to be at the extreme, and not in a good way.

But, to my surprise, they were pleased with this result, seeing it as a vindication that what they were doing was working. "The nonprofits we are supporting don't yet understand what we know about what needs to happen," one staff member said. "And we're pushing them to follow our strategies and to ramp up their performance. So, we see a strained relationship as a sign that we're doing something right." This is a common view: People describe poor relationships to my CEP colleagues and me as the inevitable collateral damage of a focus on impact.

Unfortunately, though, this kind of heavy-handed approach almost invariably fails. "Grantees need to be treated as the central partners that they ultimately are in the strategy process. They are not only the main executors of strategy but have the on-the-ground knowledge and experience essential to sort the wheat from chaff in strategic thinking," wrote Patrizi and Thompson.[20]

Second Thoughts

Far too many people in the philanthropy world have adopted a mindset in recent years that's a little too "command and control." This mindset also affects those who didn't come from business. Take Paul Brest, former president of the William and Flora Hewlett Foundation (and former dean of Stanford Law School) and someone I admire as thoughtful and committed to effectiveness.[21] Brest, who has been among the most ardent proponents of strategic philanthropy, often points to the analogy of a pilot charting a flight path when discussing the concept.[22] He argues that donors and nonprofits need a "causal model"—a strategy—just as much as a pilot needs a flight plan.

But this analogy has never quite worked for me. First, it makes the work all sound too simple. Feedback to a pilot flying a plane is clear and essentially real-time, such as, "you're on course" or "you're off course." Not so in philanthropy.

Second—although, in fairness to Brest, he makes clear that strategy is needed for both philanthropists and nonprofits—it often feels to many grantees as though foundations and donors see themselves as the pilots and nonprofits and the people affected as passengers who don't have any relevant input into the best route to take to get to the destination. Indeed, sometimes the feeling of being a grantee or intended beneficiary can be as frustrating as being a passenger on a long-delayed flight, with little or only incomplete or inaccurate information available and a sense of utter powerlessness.

Nonprofit grantees and intended beneficiaries aren't just along for the ride that the givers chart. They're crucial navigators.

Increasingly, even those who have advocated for a more donor-centric version of strategy are recognizing that it's tougher than it looks. Brest wrote in 2012, "We have also learned through painful experiences about the challenges of implementing even well-thought-out strategies."[23] Another of the chief proponents of strategic philanthropy, Hal Harvey, coauthor with Brest of the 2008 book *Money Well Spent: A Strategic Plan for Smart Philanthropy*, went further, penning a regretful op-ed in the *Chronicle of Philanthropy* in the spring of 2016.

Harvey, who served as a program director at the William and Flora Hewlett Foundation and as a leader of both the Energy Foundation and the ClimateWorks Foundation, wrote about his evolving views of strategy: "I sometimes feel I owe the world an apology. The book's ideas and arguments are important and legitimate, but I did not properly anticipate the potential side effects of this concept, and some of them are nasty indeed." He went on to describe the "delusions of omniscience" among givers who "begin to see themselves as the origin of intelligence as well as the arbiters of money." Harvey said an effective giver—his op-ed spoke to foundation staff, but the lessons apply more broadly—should act "as a humble synthesizer rather than an omniscient leader." He said givers need to "listen, gather, synthesize, test. Do these for real, not as a fake front. Build the strategy around what you learn."[24]

Harvey wasn't saying strategy isn't important, although some misread his piece that way. Rather, he was suggesting that there needs to be a humbler approach. Indeed, a second edition of Brest and Harvey's book, released in 2018, reflects an admirable evolution in their thinking. I respect Harvey's candor in admitting that he did get some things wrong. I wish more would follow his lead.

When to Go Big, When to Go Home

Even as there's some growing recognition of the unique challenges of philanthropy, the tendency—which seems especially prevalent among new givers in Silicon Valley—remains to assume there's a breakthrough answer, a technical fix or innovation that the philanthropist can create and then impose. Recently, many have called for more "big bets" in philanthropy.[25] In certain situations, in which there may be a single solution to a problem, big bets make sense: when searching, for example, for a vaccine or a cure to a disease (though even then, there's the question of how to deliver it).

So, then, "why not encourage philanthropists and foundations to seek out and make" big bets more generally? asked William and Flora Hewlett Foundation president Larry Kramer, Paul Brest's successor first as Stanford Law School dean and then again as the president of the Hewlett Foundation. "Because social problems—at least the big ones that really need and can benefit from philanthropy—are difficult, complex things."

"Physical diseases can be cured by inventing a drug or vaccine, but social problems are seldom susceptible to one-shot solutions," he continued. "There are no silver bullets, no shortcuts, when dealing with poverty, racism, climate change, education, women's rights, or income inequality, to name only a few of the significant problems that philanthropy addresses; working seriously on these requires a different mindset altogether."[26]

The area of education funding offers perhaps the most sobering reminder of the challenges of "strategic" and also "big bet" philanthropy. Over the past decade and a half, individual givers and institutional ones have focused on specific interventions that were seen as key to "transforming" education. As Hewlett's Kramer explained, "Massive amounts of philanthropic resources have been wasted on efforts to improve the American education system by 'disrupting' this or that aspect of it. Just ask the people of Newark. Or the District of Columbia. Or New York. Or Los Angeles.

Small classrooms are the answer! Choice is the answer! Charter schools will solve our problems! We need only get rid of the teachers' union! So much money is spent in a futile search for silver bullets."[27]

To find strategies that work takes diligence, patience, and humility. Givers need to avail themselves of existing research, talk and listen to non-profits and intended beneficiaries, and be willing to adopt others' successful strategies as their own rather than insisting on uniqueness. In areas where it's unclear what works, givers can help support disciplined experimentation. Sometimes big bets make sense. But, at other times, what's needed are little bets to test approaches—with expansion to bigger bets coming only when something has been shown to work.[28]

Some of the education initiatives of the Gates Foundation, such as its effective teaching initiative, were likely too big a bet to make based on the available evidence, and the foundation would have been wiser to test them more on a smaller scale first. Thomas Kane, who worked as a deputy director within the K–12 program at the Gates Foundation and is now at the Harvard School of Education, said as much in October 2018, writing, "Instead of providing large, multi-year grants for districtwide scale-up, the foundation should have invited applications to conduct pilot programs on a smaller scale first."[29]

But when we know something works, then—and only then—is it time to go big. That's what the Gates Foundation has done with immunization, providing more than $2.5 billion to Gavi, the Vaccine Alliance (the global alliance for vaccines and immunization) and contributing to a reduction—by half—of the number of children under the age of five dying worldwide.[30] A 2018 article in *Wired* describes the scale of the achievement: "Launched with $750 million of Gates' money in November 1999, Gavi has averted some 10 million deaths in seventy-three of the poorest countries in the world. In 2000, just 1 percent of the population of those countries received the pentavalent vaccine (covering diphtheria, tetanus, pertussis, hepatitis B, and Hib); by 2016, that number was 76 percent."[31] If we're to critique the Gates Foundation for getting it wrong on education, we should give it credit for its contributions to progress in global health. And the progress has been simply stunning—an inspiring example of giving done right.

The key is to understand which approach is needed when. Context is everything. Again, big bets on proven strategies make sense when we know with confidence that something is effective. But when something is untested, it's irresponsible to go big. What's needed first is disciplined testing of approaches to identify what works—limiting the potential negative impact of the learning process. What's needed is the kind of approach that staff at the Stuart Foundation took, funding something with the explicit idea that they were testing it to see whether it worked and would only support it further if it did.

Individual Givers Need Strategies, Too

Strategy isn't just for big foundations. Individual givers can also identify the strategies—and specific nonprofits implementing those strategies—that make sense for achieving a goal. An individual who wants to support efforts to reduce deaths from malaria, to go back to that example, can consult sources such as GiveWell, which carefully analyzes the efficacy of different nonprofits. Among its recommended charities is the Against Malaria Foundation, which provides funding for long-lasting, insecticide-treated bed net distributions in developing countries.[32]

Indeed, GiveWell is a great resource for those who want to find and put money behind the strategies that will help them have the maximum impact for their dollars. Unlike widely used nonprofit rating websites like Charity Navigator, which still rely primarily on measures like overhead ratios that tell you nothing about strategy and impact, GiveWell is interested in identifying which organizations are delivering results. The organization analyzes the impact of a nonprofit's efforts, not the line items in their budget. GiveWell's work is labor-intensive and primarily focused on organizations in developing countries, so it's not comprehensive. But it's a great place to start for those interested in saving or dramatically improving lives abroad. For those more focused on making a difference in their local communities, whether by supporting a vibrant arts and culture sector or addressing inequality of opportunity for children, the local community foundation is an invaluable resource for identifying the strategies and organizations with the best evidence of effectiveness.

Whichever strategies you pursue, don't assume they're fixed. Instead, find ways to get feedback about how it's going. When we looked at total strategists in our research, we saw that they were in fact more likely than their less-strategic colleagues to solicit external feedback to iterate and improve their strategies. We also noted that the presence of a strategic plan is overvalued relative to the day-to-day use of logic as a guide to make decisions and iterate strategy.[33] It's not about the plan on your shelf; it's about the way you make decisions each day.

Every giver, individual and institutional, should be able to answer these questions in the affirmative:

- Can I describe the goal(s) and strategy(ies) for my work in a way that's understandable without others needing to ask for much clarification?
- Do my colleagues, spouse, or family members describe our philanthropy in the same way that I do?
- Can I point to data-based analysis of the external environment that contributed to the development of my strategy?
- Do I regularly review or assess progress toward goals of the giving I do?
- Do I gather input from others to help me refine my strategy?
- Have I recently turned down a request because the request didn't fit my strategy—even though it did address my goals?[34]

Disaster Philanthropy

Sometimes, disaster strikes. Something happens that compels you to give, but you don't have a strategy yet and you don't know anything about what strategies will be most effective. Moreover, there's no time to do research. What do you do in the face of a hurricane, tsunami, or earthquake that is causing enormous suffering? Too many make the same mistake we discussed in Chapter 2: They respond to whomever is asking or whomever has the big, recognizable brand name, like the American Red Cross.

That's what Ben Smilowitz did when Hurricane Katrina hit in 2005. Smilowitz was a recent college graduate, in between jobs, with a background in campaign organizing and youth civic engagement. He didn't have money to contribute, but he figured he could put his organizing skills to work as a volunteer helping with response to the hurricane.

The Red Cross deployed him to Mississippi and, within hours, he was appalled by what he saw. Efforts to help were disorganized, and people were being turned away based on what Smilowitz believed were nothing more than prejudices. He has since learned that what he saw is all too typical in disaster response.

"Groups that actually have the capacity on the ground to respond" aren't the ones getting donations, Smilowitz explained to me. Instead, it's the brand-name organizations that may have a high profile that get the support, but don't have the community knowledge and contacts to be effective. "Most of the money that pours in after these events does not reach the local organizations on the ground," he said. But it's often these organizations that understand the needs best and are best positioned to help.

Smilowitz has set out to change that, founding the Disaster Accountability Project. It's a watchdog organization and has, for example, taken the Red Cross to the carpet for shortcomings in its 2013 response to Hurricane Sandy. But it's also a resource, through its SmartResponse website, to help givers find organizations that are well-positioned to help in the wake of a disaster.

Effective giving strategy in the wake of a natural disaster—just like effective giving strategy pursuing other aims—should be driven by those closest to the challenges and those with roots in the affected communities. SmartReponse actively seeks out information from organizations in the US and around the world and curates "how to help" lists so that, when disaster strikes, givers can quickly find local organizations to support. Smilowitz is just getting started, and needs more support to realize his vision, but his effort has the potential to transform post-disaster giving—connecting those who want to give with those best positioned to make good use of those resources.[35]

I'd argue that the Red Cross frequently does crucial work responding to disasters—it's not always wrong to give to them. But it shouldn't necessarily be the default, either. It's crucial that givers also listen to local organizations in affected communities and find out what's needed. Days after Hurricane Harvey hit in 2017, a colleague I will call Nancy, an executive at a foundation in Houston, found herself on the phone with a wealthy individual donor in New York. She told the donor what was needed, but the donor had her own ideas. "We don't want to do that," she told Nancy.

"It was ridiculous," Nancy vented. "There was an outpouring of generosity from all around the city and around the world. Much of that giving did tremendous good. But much of it went to waste. People donated box after box of clothes, but that's not what was needed! My daughter was volunteering at a nonprofit that literally threw out donations that weren't needed, including a pair of donated stiletto heels. Stiletto heels? Seriously?"

We all want to help. But we need to make sure we're doing so in a way that's responsive to the real needs of those affected.

Prioritizing short-term relief over either preparedness or long-term rebuilding is another mistake that's frequently made in responding to disasters. Bob Ottenhoff runs the Center for Disaster Philanthropy, which seeks to change this in part by establishing funds to which individuals and institutions can contribute. These funds take the long view, granting dollars out for rebuilding over time, as needs become clearer.

"Seventy-five percent of all disaster giving is for immediate relief," Ottenhoff explained, noting that it mostly happens in the thirty days after an event. "When the media coverage ends, so does the giving." Frequently, too much is raised for immediate relief, he noted, and too little for the intermediate and long term. Wise donors will look to support these efforts, and the Center for Disaster Philanthropy can be a resource to them.[36]

Whether giving in response to an ongoing challenge or a disaster that strikes, givers need to be smart about what they hope to achieve and, therefore, what approach makes sense. They also need to be aware of what others are doing. Every giver operates in a larger ecosystem of other givers.

A Strategic Push for Civil Rights

This awareness of what others are doing is a key quality that effective givers share. It is, for example, what helped make the work of big givers effective over the past two decades in the area of civil rights for LGBT people. Early on in our efforts to study strategy, my colleagues Kevin Bolduc and Ellie Buteau interviewed the late Rodger McFarlane, then executive director of the Gill Foundation in Denver, Colorado. Created by Tim Gill, the software entrepreneur who founded Quark, the Gill Foundation today has about $230 million in assets and makes about $10 million in grants annually.

We were struck by the degree to which McFarlane and the Gill Foundation exemplified a total strategist approach, so we highlighted the foundation in our research reports and a video we produced, which we shared at the 2007 CEP conference. The foundation was focused on civil rights for LGBT people and took just the kind of data-driven, iterative approach that was consistent with what we saw in total strategists.

Initially, Gill worked with other funders and grantees to get hate crime legislation passed in a number of states. But it monitored results, and when the foundation realized that the hate crime laws weren't driving down crimes targeting LGBT people, they moved on to support efforts to educate prosecutors and law enforcement. Eventually, they saw results. They were clear on their goals and relentlessly strategic in their approach, recognizing the need to constantly test their assumptions—hate crime legislation will lead to fewer hate crimes—and then learn and iterate and improve their strategies.

We chose to highlight Gill in part because the foundation illustrated that being strategic and being focused on civil rights were not in tension, as some had insisted. Quite the opposite. I remember several foundation executives thanking us for highlighting a foundation focused on gay rights. I also remember a foundation leader taking me aside at that 2007 conference to tell me we shouldn't have chosen something "so controversial." None of these leaders would have predicted the scope of change that would come over the next decade. Much of that success is owed to the strategic and coordinated approach of Gill, the Evelyn and Walter Haas, Jr. Fund (a San Francisco foundation with about $500 million in assets from the Levi Strauss fortune), and other foundations that came together in what was called the Civil Marriage Collaborative—a jointly funded $153 million collaborative effort. These funders pooled resources, recognizing that they'd be more effective together than they could be separately.

The approach these foundations took was an iterative one, as they constantly took in new data on what was and wasn't working and adapted their efforts on that basis. Speaking at CEP's conference in May 2015, Sylvia Yee, former vice president at the Haas, Jr. Fund, said that she hadn't "dared dream" that marriage equality would come so quickly. "We started our work simply and small," she said, noting that their approach "evolved over time." She said that "we gave ourselves and our grantees the time to muck around, to learn and to make mistakes" but then, based on that learning, the collaborative got behind a common strategy.[37]

Yee described the way the funders shifted their emphasis away from a focus on "equal rights" when research showed this message wasn't resonating with the public. "Messaging tended to highlight the many rights and benefits—including rights as basic as hospital visitation—that restrictions on marriage had denied to gay couples. The losses of 2004 and afterward [when many states explicitly banned gay marriage through constitutional amendments and ballot initiatives] showed that this argument was falling flat with the public."[38] So, the funders paid for psychographic research to figure out what people were thinking about marriage equality. "On the basis of that research, my colleagues and I arrived at a crucial insight," Yee explained. "When we straight people think about marriage, we don't think about hospital visits or taxes or dental plans. We think about love, family, and commitment."[39]

This insight led to a change in the language and images used in the effort to change "hearts and minds," with an increased focus on the perspectives, for example, of parents who wanted their gay children to be happy. This approach contributed to shifts in public opinion and policy that culminated in the 2015 US Supreme Court decision guaranteeing the right to marry for gays and lesbians.[40]

Gill, Haas, Jr., and the other foundations didn't double down on something that wasn't working, insisting that their strategy was the right one despite evidence to the contrary. They learned and adapted. Their goals were clear, and they stuck with their work for the long haul, even when things looked tough. But their strategic plan evolved; it was more like a wiki or a Google doc than something static, constantly evolving and with many contributing to its editing and improvement.

While there's much more to be done, of course, progress in LGBT rights is a shining example of philanthropic strategy at its best. It isn't fixed. It evolves based on what it learned about what works. It's shared across many actors and is much, much more difficult than strategy in business.

Givers should embrace the unique challenge of strategy in philanthropy, doing the hard work of seeking to understand what are more and less effective approaches, listening to those in the best position to know, and constantly learning and iterating to get better. It isn't easy. It requires a humility and a learning mindset that characterizes effective givers from the Sillcoxes to the Hilton Foundation to Pat Reynolds-Hubbard to Sylvia Yee. It requires a collaborative approach that recognizes strategy must be shared across many people and organizations working to solve a problem, because very little in philanthropy can be accomplished alone. It's not easy, but it is worth it.

Because when it's done right, it can pay off in ways that transform society.

⋟⋌⋋⋌⋟

Chapter 4 Review: Giving Guidance

1. **You need a strategy to guide your efforts to achieve your goals.** Strategy is about the logic of your decision-making—for example, supporting a focus on "permanency" among foster youth because it will lead to better life outcomes or supporting the use of bed nets because they've been shown to reduce deaths from malaria. It's about funding approaches that have evidence to support their efficacy. Or, when you're supporting something new, for which no evidence is available, it's about making sure to ask how progress is being judged and revising as appropriate.

2. **Good strategy is different in giving than in business.** Absent a competitive context, strategy plays out differently. It's not about the giver having all the control. It's about a collection of different actors working together and responding to continual feedback. Strategy is crucial in philanthropy, but it needs to be applied in a way that is mindful of the unique challenges of working on the most vexing, complicated,

and interdependent issues. Support existing, effective strategies when you can, rather than charting your own path.

3. **Strategy needs to be iterative to be effective.** Typically, the challenges philanthropy seeks to address are complicated and interdependent, with cause and effect difficult to predict. As a result, strategy should not be fixed but dynamic. Effective givers revise their strategies as they learn.

4. **It's not enough to be sure yourself that something works.** Others—from the nonprofits you fund to the people you seek to help—must agree. This means it's crucial to listen carefully to nonprofits as well as those you seek to help. Good strategy is informed by those closest to the ground and is shared across organizations. Sometimes, such as in response to disasters, the best approach is to give to good organizations in the affected communities—and then to let them figure out the best strategies for achieving the shared goal of alleviating suffering.

ESSENTIAL PARTNERS

SELECTING AND WORKING WITH NONPROFITS

M Y FAMILY'S SATURDAY night had started out well. My wife, Lara, and I had decided to splurge on a nicer dinner than was typical for us. We, along with our daughters Ava (11 at the time) and Margo (7), were celebrating something—I forget what—and we decided to make a reservation at a restaurant in Harvard Square in Cambridge.

The girls were excited about going "somewhere fancy," and Lara and I were looking forward to a menu with more-interesting choices than our standard go-to family joints. We all got dressed up, at least relative to our usual weekend garb, and headed out. "Will the waiters wear white gloves?" Margo asked, bouncing up and down in the back seat of the car. "Don't think so," Lara answered.

We were seated quickly in the dimly lit restaurant, a favorite of Harvard faculty and Boston-area movers and shakers. About five minutes after our salads were served, Lara and Ava began whispering to each other and looking at something. I followed the direction of their stares and saw three mice scurry under the table where a sophisticated-looking older couple were obliviously enjoying their dinner. Then, I saw another mouse under the table of a young couple who looked like they might be on a first date, also blissfully unaware. And another by the door to the kitchen.

"Mom, there are mice everywhere," Ava whispered.

All three of us knew that Margo, our youngest, happily eating her salad, wouldn't be at all pleased if she saw the mice. She's not a big fan of rodents. So, Lara got up, telling Margo she needed to use the ladies' room, to calmly and discreetly inform the restaurant's staff of their rodent infestation while I made conversation with Margo to distract her. Their response was wholly unsatisfactory. They said that a door had been open during an event at the restaurant that afternoon and that it was really not that big a deal. We weren't buying the explanation and thought it was, in fact, a big deal. We left the restaurant before our entrees arrived.

What did I do when we got home? I trashed the place online, of course, on every site I could find, from Yelp to TripAdvisor. I also swore never to go there again. After all, there are a lot of other great restaurants in Cambridge.

Why am I telling you this story? Because it stands in stark contrast to another story I want to tell you, this one about giving.

The very next week after our fateful restaurant visit, I had a terrible interaction with a program officer at a foundation that was funding CEP. I was treated as though I didn't know what I was doing—not someone who had been working with some success in the field for a number of years—by someone who seemed unprepared for our meeting or, for that matter, for the demands of his job. He told me what he thought I was doing wrong in my job, citing "facts" that weren't even accurate. When I pushed back gently, he doubled down. I decided to just go along with it, pretending to agree.

By the time our meeting was over, I was silently fuming. But had there been some analog to Yelp for foundations at that time, I wouldn't have written anything about the interaction.

Not one word.

Why? Because he would have known it was me, even if I didn't name him (he had only a dozen or so grantees he was responsible for, and I couldn't assume any others were as mad as I was), and I would have jeopardized CEP's chances of receiving funding. And the stakes were high because his was one of a handful of foundations that could provide CEP the level of support I was talking with him about.

So I swallowed my pride and stayed quiet.

Choosing

Givers often gravitate to the analogy of customers when discussing those they fund: their grantees. For example, Dave Peery, managing director of the Palo Alto–based Peery Foundation, wrote, "we think of grantees as our customers and act accordingly."[1]

I get what he's trying to say and appreciate the sentiment behind it. But this thinking doesn't quite make sense. It's a bad analogy. Givers don't have customers. After all, the money is flowing in the opposite direction: Customers pay for something; grantees are recipients of funding. As a result, as my two stories illustrate, the power dynamics are totally different: In most industries, customers have choices, meaning businesses will, at least in theory, pay a price for ignoring their preferences.

While I can choose which restaurant to go to, most of us who lead a nonprofit don't necessarily feel that we have a choice of who we raise money from. We look to raise money from almost anyone we think will give.

The choice about whether to establish a relationship lies with the givers. So, being great at giving begins with choosing wisely the organizations that are best positioned to help you achieve your shared goals—through implementation of what are hopefully also shared strategies. You'll want to ensure this alignment from the beginning and not force a fit where there isn't one. Funders and nonprofits need to work collaboratively in a relationship that, by virtue of the challenges they face, is unique. Each party brings distinct strengths to the effort: the nonprofits as the doers and the funders as the ones who have the resources and also a unique perch that allows them to see across fields and communities, convene, and bring valuable non-financial resources to the table, too.

A variety of sources of information exist to help you begin to develop a list of prospective grantees. In certain areas of giving, there are highly vetted nonprofits that you can give to with confidence. If, for example, you're convinced by the arguments of philosopher Peter Singer that you should focus on alleviating poverty in developing countries, you can go to GiveWell or to thelifeyoucansave.org, which Singer founded, to learn about nonprofits doing highly effective work. You might support Living Goods, which trains community health promoters who go door-to-door providing health products and education and treating common causes of child deaths. Or you might give to the Schistosomiasis Control Initiative, which facilitates school-based distribution of deworming tablets, protecting children from debilitating diseases and improving school attendance for less than seventy-five cents per child.[2] Another option is to give through givedirectly.org, which allows you to send money directly to people living in extreme poverty internationally—a particularly powerful, if simple, intervention. If, however, you wish to give locally, or to issue areas not covered by these sites, you'll have more work to do.

Once again, your community foundation can be a crucial resource; community foundations exist to help you navigate these choices. You'll also likely turn to friends and family for ideas. Perhaps you've heard from other givers about organizations you respect. Once you have a list of organizations that you think align with your goals and strategies, you'll want to dig in and better understand each organization. As you do, it's important to know that every nonprofit should be able to clearly answer three basic questions:

◊ What are we trying to achieve (aims)?
◊ How are we seeking to achieve it (strategies or programs)?
◊ What information do we have to assess progress (results)?

GuideStar, which has for almost two decades made available on its website the required filings that nonprofits must submit to the IRS (called Form 990s), now offers nonprofits the opportunity to put the answers to these questions on its site—and tens of thousands do. It also provides seals of "transparency" for the degree to which they share this information. Even small nonprofits should be able to answer these questions. Judging organizations by their answers is a much more effective way to select nonprofits than gauging the percentage of their budget spent on overhead, which, as we discussed earlier, can be a misleading and sometimes even counterproductive way to assess nonprofits. To be sure, it's not as easy as comparing financial ratios. But it tells you about what matters—what organizations actually achieve, in terms of results.

Seven Pillars

When the work nonprofits describe matches up with your goals and strategies as a giver, they're a viable potential recipient of your giving. But if you're making a large gift, you'll want to go deeper. In 2014 and 2015, philanthropist Mario Morino (mentioned in earlier chapters) convened a group of nonprofit leaders (myself included, although my contributions were minimal) to discuss what differentiates high-performing nonprofits. The group defined achieving high performance for nonprofits as: "To deliver— over a prolonged period of time—meaningful, measurable, and financially sustainable results for the people or causes the organization is in existence to serve."

It then identified seven pillars of excellence in a document, which can serve as a resource to givers and nonprofits alike, called the Performance Imperative. The seven pillars are:

1. **Courageous, adaptive executive and board leadership.** Included here are principles such as, "Executives and boards embrace their responsibility to deliver meaningful, measurable, and financially sustainable results" and "Boards are strong, assertive governors and stewards, not just supporters and fundraisers."

2. **Disciplined, people-focused management.** Among the tenets of this pillar are leaders who "recruit, develop, engage, and retain the talent necessary to deliver on the mission" and "provide continuous, candid, constructive feedback to team members."

3. **Well-designed and well-implemented programs and strategies.** Key elements here include "leaders and managers select or design their programs and strategies based on a sound analysis of the issues and evidence informed assumptions about how the organization's activities can lead to the desired change (often referred to as a 'theory of change')."

4. **Financial health and sustainability.** Included here are that "the board and senior management establish strong systems for financial stewardship and accountability throughout their organization," and "the board, management, and staff build and participate in budget

processes that are oriented toward achieving results and not just conducting activities."

5. **A culture that values learning.** Among the elements here are "the board, management, and staff recognize they can't fully understand the needs of those they serve unless they listen to and learn from constituents in formal and informal ways."

6. **Internal monitoring for continuous improvement.** Chief among the principles of this pillar is that "the board, management, and staff work together to establish quantitative and qualitative indicators tightly aligned with the results they want to achieve, for each program and for the organization as a whole."

7. **External evaluation for mission effectiveness.** It's crucial that "leaders complement internal monitoring with external evaluations conducted by highly skilled, independent experts."[3]

This is a good list of qualities to seek in the organizations to which you contribute. The Performance Imperative goes into more detail about each of these pillars—I have quoted selected elements above—and an accompanying self-assessment allows nonprofits to gauge themselves on each one. Few organizations will be strong on every dimension, but the seven pillars are a good reference for assessing capacity. If you're making a significant gift to an organization and you believe its leaders are struggling in one or more areas described in the Performance Imperative, you can ask them how you can help them improve.

If this all sounds like a lot of work, that's because it is. "You've got to spend the time with an organization" if you're going to really make a significant gift, advised Morino. "You've got to bear witness. You've got to spend time with the end clients."[4]

It isn't easy to figure out whom to support. As we'll discuss, assessing nonprofit performance isn't straightforward because the approach needs to vary dramatically depending on what the organization is trying to achieve. That's why efforts to create something like a Morningstar for nonprofits—a central resource to compare effectiveness of diverse organizations with a set of common metrics—are misguided and inevitably fail.

Small and Effective

If you're focused on particular issues within specific geographic communities, it's important not to overlook the small, unsung organizations that may be doing amazing work but lack a high profile, or even any dedicated fundraising staff. I'm talking about organizations like Epiphany Community Health Outreach Services (ECHOS) in Houston, which was formed in 1999 and caters to what executive director Cathy Moore described as "poverty-stricken, vulnerable families." ECHOS connects "people in need with the health, social, and educational resources that can improve their lives."

This means providing services from children's immunizations, to blood pressure and glucose screenings, to child checkups, to vision and dental care. ECHOS staff members help clients with the paperwork to be eligible for a county health care program for the poor or for food assistance and other benefits. ECHOS also helps with basic needs, providing food from its food pantry, English classes, computer literacy training, and a domestic violence support group. With nine staff members and a budget of $500,000, ECHOS struggles to meet the needs of all its prospective clients, many of whom are undocumented and essentially all of whom are desperate for help.

But to see the staff at ECHOS at work is to see effectiveness in action. It's an organization totally focused on executing its mission with excellence. I visited on a hot June day in 2018, the temperature already in the mid-eighties when I walked into the modest, cramped space on the campus of the Episcopal Church of the Epiphany. It was 7:15 a.m., and the staff was already assembled and discussing their plans for the day as a growing group of clients waited outside for ECHOS to open at 8:00 a.m.

Moore has a laid-back leadership style, allowing her staff to run the meeting and chiming in with many questions. When a debate broke out about how best to ensure a fair system for clients waiting for multiple services, she was quick to change her mind when staff challenged her proposed solution. "You're right, you're right," she said. "Let's go with your approach." She trusts her staff. They each carry a sense of passion and caring to their jobs.

At 8:00 a.m., though, Moore took charge as she strode into the waiting room. She had told me that, judging by the numbers there, it was likely to be a slow day compared to most. If this was slow, with more than twenty-five people already waiting, I wondered what busy was. The mood was tense and quiet. A Latina grandmother with her young grandson sat, head bowed, next to a tall, white man in his twenties sporting at least a dozen tattoos and a ripped T-shirt. A middle-aged man in a wheelchair sat in the doorway, moving out of the way for a Vietnam veteran in full biker gear who walked in just as the five-foot-two Moore broke the silence with her booming voice.

"Welcome! We are glad you are here! Welcome to ECHOS. Thanks for choosing to come here," she said in English, her colleague translating to Spanish. I imagine Moore likely knew well that most didn't view it as their choice to be there, but she wanted to treat each person with a sense of dignity and to convey respect for them in her words. She was trying to shift the power dynamic between those who needed help and those who could offer it.

"We know you sometimes have to wait a long time here, and we apologize for that," Moore continued, noting that a staff member would check everyone's paperwork right there in the waiting room to ensure no one waited needlessly. "Has that ever happened to anyone who has been here before, that you waited only to find out you didn't have the paperwork you needed?" she asked.

"It happened to me," the man in the T-shirt said. "But it was my fault. I should have known."

"No, it was *our* fault," Moore said. "It was our fault and we changed that based on feedback from our clients. We want to make sure no one waits when they don't have to. So now, the first thing we do is check everyone's paperwork so we can send them back to get what they need before they wait."

"No, really, it was my fault," the man said.

"No, it was our fault," Moore said, as people began to laugh.

The mood had changed now, the waiting room filled with smiles and nods. Another staff member passed around candy. Moore knew exactly what she was doing: building the trust and goodwill that would allow her staff to be as helpful as possible to each client. Over the hours that followed, each client met privately with an ECHOS staff member, and many more arrived.

I asked one man in his thirties who was coming to get help renewing his eligibility for the county health care program what he would do otherwise. "Just go into debt for my medical expenses, I guess," he told me. Two of the ECHOS staff are former clients. "I just want to pay it forward after what ECHOS did for me," explained Yuri Valenzuela, who first walked through the organization's doors at age fifteen, as a client. She started as a volunteer in her thirties and then joined as a full-time, paid employee.

Janice Guirola works twelve hours a week as the intake coordinator. She told me she had met Moore just six months after she'd lost her job in sales and found herself desperate enough to come to the ECHOS food pantry. When Moore realized how personable she was, and that she was completely fluent in Spanish and English, she hired her.

ECHOS and organizations like it are well-known by those they serve. Every one of the many clients I spoke with answered the question of how they heard about ECHOS the same way: "friend" or "amigo."

But ECHOS isn't as easily found or widely known by donors. "It's really hard when you're a very small organization and wearing every hat," Moore told me. "It makes it hard to be good at fundraising. We have had no problem finding clients," she said, noting that lines sometimes form as early as 5:00 a.m. outside the ECHOS doors. "Donors? Not so much." Thankfully, the Episcopal Health Foundation in Houston has provided ECHOS with invaluable grant support, but there's still a need for much more. Moore hopes to be able to bring on a full-time fundraiser so she doesn't have to do it all herself while running the place.

A giver needs to try to find nonprofits that fit with their goals and strategies, are well-run and making a difference but might not be well-known— the organizations that are quietly getting it done. You should get to know your community and spend time visiting organizations if you can, then look closely at who the foundations in your community are supporting—both your local community foundation and any significant private foundations that are focused in your region. Once they've identified potential recipients, one way for individual givers who have the time and inclination to get to know them better is to volunteer.

Volunteering is what retired attorney Bob Bennett was doing at ECHOS the day I was there, and he told me with great pride of the role ECHOS played in the wake of Hurricane Harvey, and of the way staff and volunteers rose to the occasion to help those in need. Bennett coordinates the logistics for the vision screenings ECHOs provides.

"You're making such a difference," I remarked.

Bennett, who is also a donor to ECHOS, looked at me intently, a little perplexed, and paused. "No. They're making a difference for me," he said.[5]

Volunteering can indeed be a powerful experience. Greg Baldwin, the CEO of the website VolunteerMatch, which links volunteers to volunteering opportunities, noted that volunteering is a "hugely significant social phenomenon in America." About one in four Americans volunteer each year.

It's important to be sure first, of course, that the organization for which you're volunteering genuinely wants your help. A 2015 *Boston Globe* article noted that nonprofit staff often dread the legions of corporate volunteers that arrive to help them because they can't help in the ways that are needed. But the nonprofits go along anyway—a powerful and depressing example of the power dynamic between funders and the funded—because they want the corporation's philanthropic support. "It's the dirty truth of corporate volunteer projects: They may make good photo ops and sound virtuous in a company's annual report, but nonprofits often dread them and suffer in silence," wrote *Globe* reporter Sacha Pfeiffer.[6]

But it doesn't have to be that way, of course, if you're careful to ensure that your interests and the nonprofits' needs and expectations are aligned. When they are, volunteering can be a great way to make a difference. It's helpful to the organization and it's good for you, too. It's been shown to correlate with happiness and health. And it can also make you a better giver.

"It's like doing field research," Baldwin said. "It makes you more effective. It anchors the importance of giving and gives it meaning, emotional connection, and grounding."[7] It also gives you a front-row view of how an organization is led, what kind of staff it employs, and the results it achieves. If you have the time, it's worth the effort.

After all, selecting the right nonprofits to fund and building strong relationships with them is essential to effectiveness. It may not be glamorous or trendy, but you won't make progress in pursuit of your philanthropic goals if you don't get this right.

A Unique Relationship

Once you've made a gift or grant to an organization, especially if it's a large gift, there's a strong power dynamic in place, which brings us back to the inapt comparison between customers and grantees. A nonprofit leader we surveyed described a foundation as "elitist" and "out of touch" and said the foundation's staff seemed "to have their own priorities and operate with an arrogance that they can fix the world's problems, when they are not actually engaged in collaboration with the constituents they claim to serve." Given sentiments like this, I've heard over the years from many who hoped to start some kind of anonymous feedback tool for nonprofits to provide feedback to big givers, especially foundations. The first person who pitched me this idea compared it to the restaurant guide Zagat; now the analogy is most commonly Yelp. Recently, a website called GrantAdvisor has tried to make this idea a reality. But even though the site has been up and running for a year as I write this, and has received a fair amount of attention, only a few foundations have more than twenty reviews, and most of the reviews are positive. That's because nonprofit leaders perceive being critical as a great risk.

Seventeen years ago, when CEP was just getting off the ground, my colleagues and I met with many big givers who were keenly aware that they didn't know what the nonprofits they supported thought about what it was like to work with them. They understood that they resided in a bubble of positivity, surrounded by those who had every incentive to tell them what they wanted to hear. To many of these givers, this recognition was deeply unsettling. They wanted to understand whether they were helping the nonprofits they supported to be effective in the ways they hoped; whether the nonprofits felt their communications were clear; and whether their application processes, in the case of grantmaking institutions, were seen as useful or as mindless wastes of time. They felt uneasy about not knowing. They

badly wanted to know, so that they could improve and become more effective in their work with the nonprofits they were funding.

In response, we developed a comparative, confidential grantee survey.
The idea behind what eventually became the GPR was that only a credible
third party could ensure that grantees could be candid, confident that their
individual identities would be protected. Moreover, only a comparative process could allow givers to learn from the results. That's because, on many
dimensions, grantees—no matter how cynical they might be about donors
in general—rate those that funded them highly on an absolute scale. It's a
little like the difference in how voters often view Congress and their con-
gresspeople: they're down on Congress in general but tend to be positive on
their specific representative. So, the key question is, how do grantees rate
the grantmaker relative to how other grantees rate similar grantmakers?

It's only through these kinds of comparative data that a foundation
or a United Way or a family office's philanthropy arm can understand its
strengths and weaknesses in the eyes of its grantees and then set out to
do something about them. My colleagues Kevin Bolduc, Judy Huang, and
I—with encouragement and guidance from CEP board member Phil Giudice—developed and iterated the GPR survey with a lot of input from grantmakers. It was adopted much more rapidly than any of us expected. There
was strong demand for candid feedback and for information to contribute to
improvement in the giver–grantee relationship. The GPR allowed funders to
finally understand how they were seen—the good, the bad, and the ugly—
relative to other funders. It also allowed us to develop a comparative data
set on nonprofit perceptions that can yield insights for givers big and small.

Supporting Organizations, Not Just Programs

We've established that grantees are neither customers nor investees. A
third, frequently invoked analogy is to compare grantees to contractors like
the guy who fixes your roof. Of the three analogies, this at least is sometimes
appropriate.

There are indeed occasions when givers will want a particular thing
done and won't have much long-term interest in the health of the organization they're funding. An example might be a research project focused on

a particular topic related to the strategy a foundation or individual is pursuing; for example, when the Stuart Foundation wanted to explore whether there were any places in the country that were successfully promoting adoption of older foster youth. In cases like this, perhaps those best positioned to do that research are at a university or a firm in which the giver has no particular long-term interest. In these instances, nonprofit grantees are indeed like contractors, doing a specific piece of work for the funder.

"Purchasing services" is the way Paul Brest and Hal Harvey describe this form of funding.[8] Givers, especially foundations, will want to do this sometimes, and when they do, the best tool is a restricted grant or gift with clear parameters on how the money is to be used. The problem is that, today, this is the default approach for big givers. The overwhelming majority of foundation support is provided through these kinds of grants.

Fully 65 percent of grants in CEP's data set of tens of thousands of grantee surveys fall into this category of program-restricted funding. Only about 20 percent are general support or unrestricted. (The remaining grants are for specific types of funding, such as capacity building or capital projects.) Foundation Center data show a similar pattern. Furthermore, both CEP and Foundation Center data show little change year over year, as we discussed in Chapter 1.

This doesn't make sense. If nonprofits share goals and strategies with their donors, then the nonprofits should be able to allocate their resources in the ways they see fit. Our research at CEP has shown that there are three specific aspects of the way gifts and grants are made that tend to correlate with grantees' views that their donors have a positive impact on their organizations:

◊ The gift or grant is unrestricted.
◊ It spans multiple years.
◊ It's large.

You don't have to do all three; each one is good and helpful. All three at once is even better, of course. Yet this kind of funding remains hard to get. Fewer than 8 percent of the grants represented in CEP's data are unrestricted, multiyear, and six figures or more annually. For 30 percent of the hundreds of foundations in our data set, fewer than 2 percent of grants have these characteristics.

Why does this matter? I asked Gregg Croteau of UTEC, the organization working with young people involved in gang activity that I described in Chapter 1, what his biggest challenge is, and he didn't blink. "We don't pay enough," he told me. The street workers he employs to engage with gang members have brutal, demanding jobs. They show up in hospital rooms and at funerals after shootings; they visit young people in jails; they break up fights. And they make just over $40,000 a year. "Being able to elevate the salaries of our core group of youth workers would be huge," Croteau told me. Then, he could more easily attract and retain the best people. To do that, he needs more unrestricted as well as long-term support.[9]

A grantee responding to one of our surveys put it this way: "We have had continual funding from the foundation. However, every grant is for one year. This makes it difficult to recruit expert staff who need a reliable job. . . . Talented young leaders with families are difficult to recruit in such an insecure environment." Wrote another, "I would be remiss if I didn't plug for multiyear general operating grants, as this is really what we need to be sustainable and stable. . . . We have two other multiyear grants, and it makes employee retention and planning *so much* easier when I can hire someone and guarantee a job (if they perform) beyond a year at a time."

To be fair, there are a number of foundations that provide 30 percent or more of their grantees this kind of support, such as the Weingart Foundation, Hewlett Foundation, Oak Foundation, Omidyar Network, and Marguerite Casey Foundation. In addition, several big foundations have recently announced that they will significantly increase the proportion of unrestricted support they provide to grantees.

Yet many other foundations remain deaf to the pleas of nonprofits. "Our advice would be to listen to what nonprofits and other community stakeholders outside of the foundation/grantmaker community are saying about what types of support equip, rather than hinder, their collective efforts to address our community's social issues," wrote another of our grantee survey respondents. "This is particularly critical when making hard and fast funding rules, such as no funding for indirect/overhead costs, or no multiyear/on-going funding, or withholding 50 percent of payout until the grant term has closed." Another grantee pled with givers to "provide a more steady flow of income to nonprofits that have a proven track record. Many [donors] only provide [support] to new initiatives, which is fine. But nonprofits with a track record of success need long-term funding to sustain a proven operation."

To their credit, individual givers tend to give more unrestricted dollars, in part because they're not as well positioned as staffed foundations to track how their funding is used after a gift is made. Still, too many focus on "overhead rates" when deciding where to give, rather than on the organization's accomplishments. Individual givers should consistently support organizations that they believe in and that have evidence of results. It's in your interest because, whatever the area is in which you're doing your giving, you need strong organizations to do the work. So, you should give in a way that makes organizations strong.

Rather than building strong, trusting relationships, too many givers still seem to think that the opposite approach yields results. Take the example of one individual giver who responded to a survey CEP conducted about the community foundation through which he gives. He wrote that a nonprofit leader to whom he directs gifts through his donor-advised fund at the community foundation "confessed to me over breakfast that their meeting with [the foundation] is *the* most intense that they have all year and the meeting they spend the most time and effort prepping for. As a donor, that is very good news."

But it may not be. Too confrontational a dynamic between givers and nonprofits can undermine effectiveness.

What Nonprofits Value

When we created the GPR, we developed a survey instrument that covers a range of interactions and perceptions. Questions in the survey address topics such as:

◊ grantees' perceptions of foundations' impact on fields, communities, and organizations;

◌ selection, reporting, and evaluation processes;

◌ communications and interactions; and

◌ assistance beyond the grant.

The GPR has now been used by some 320 institutional givers, many of which regularly repeat the process to gauge their own progress. CEP administers the grantee survey online, confidentially, to grantees, and reports their responses in aggregate with other survey responses. We strip open-ended comments of any identifying information and relay the quantitative ratings and qualitative data to foundations through an interactive portal that allows them to compare their ratings to those of peer foundations—selecting peer groups and exploring segmentations (such as differences in ratings by program area or geography) in real time.

Our data set includes tens of thousands of surveys of grantees and allows us to examine what matters to nonprofit grantees. One key measure is grantees' views of their relationships with their funders, based on a composite of five related survey questions that our analyses have shown to be especially important and highly related: fairness of treatment, comfort approaching the funder if a problem arises, responsiveness, clarity of communication of goals and strategy, and consistency of information provided. There are many other questions in the survey, but these five form our "relationships measure."

Understanding what best predicts good performance on our relationships measure tells us what nonprofits value. This perception is broadly applicable to individual givers, too. We see that the two most important dimensions are understanding and transparency.

◌ **Understanding** encompasses a range of dimensions captured in our survey, including understanding of a grantee organization's goals, strategies, and challenges; of the fields and communities in which the grantee works; of the social, cultural, and socioeconomic factors that affect the grantee's work as well as the intended beneficiaries' needs; and the extent to which the giver's funding priorities reflect a deep understanding of the intended beneficiaries' needs.

◊ **Transparency** is about clarity, openness, and honesty about goals and strategies, as well as the nitty-gritty of what the giver is learning about what works and what doesn't. Nonprofits understand that many givers are in the position to see across fields, communities, and organizations in ways that nonprofits can't—and the best givers share what they're learning openly with other funders and those they fund.

It's hard to be understanding and transparent. Understanding the organizations you fund and their context takes time and concerted effort—and a lot of listening. Sharing important information, including information about what is and isn't working, requires collecting it in the first place and then making it available in clear and helpful ways. This approach can mean distilling complicated evaluation reports or translating them into layperson's terms. But nonprofits value funders' unique ability to see across complex systems and communities. Funders, by virtue of their distinct perches, can help nonprofits see and make connections.

As if all that's not enough, three other factors emerge as important in our analyses:

◊ How helpful nonprofits find a funder's selection process to be
◊ How open they experience the giver to be to new ideas about strategy
◊ How much pressure they feel to modify their proposal to receive funding (less is better)[10]

These factors also contribute to strong relationships with those you fund.

If it sounds as if there's a lot you have to do well to form strong relationships, that's because there is. But it is possible for givers of all sizes and types to do this well. The Whitman Institute (TWI), a small foundation in San Francisco that makes $1 million in grants annually, was rated in the ninety-ninth percentile in our comparative database on the relationships measure by its grantees. TWI's coexecutive director, John Esterle, is coauthor of an important article suggesting that it's time to move relationships "from the kids' table to the adults' table" in conversations about impact.[11]

TWI's grantees describe a foundation that interacts with them in ways that set it apart. Said one, "Our relationship with TWI is perhaps the best of all the funders who support our work. They understand what we are trying to do. . . . The staff and the executive director are among the most approachable and personable in the foundation world." Another said, "TWI is a very atypical funder. They care about the work in a different way and are in partnership with their grantees in ways that most larger foundations couldn't imagine."

For TWI, it's all about building trust, and the foundation's staff members have worked to identify exactly what it takes to do this. Among the principles of their "trust-based philanthropy" approach are to provide unrestricted, multiyear funding; to "do the homework" to determine potential alignment with nonprofits to shift the burden of work; and "solicit and act on feedback."[12]

There are other exemplars, too, and some of them come in surprising packages that defy stereotypes. Take the Einhorn Family Charitable Trust (EFCT). David Einhorn is the founder and president of Greenlight Capital, a New York–based hedge fund. Not surprisingly, then, the foundation is data- and evidence-driven and focused on results and impact. Also not surprisingly, the foundation's staff take a high-engagement approach with their grantees, with a demanding selection process and significant assistance in addition to financial support. EFCT wasn't kidding around when it came to effectiveness and results.

But, unlike some of their peers in the hard-charging investing world, EFCT has adopted a respectful approach in its philanthropy, focusing on building understanding and being responsive to nonprofits' needs. The foundation has a deeply humble stance that sets it apart. EFCT describes it this way on its website:

> We take a relationship-based approach to grantmaking, working in close collaboration with each partner grantee to identify and maximize opportunities for success and ways to mitigate and address challenges. . . . Our grantees are the experts; therefore, we seek to develop partnerships that

provide maximum flexibility for grantees to apply funding in ways they identify will lead to the greatest impact.[13]

Einhorn's executive director, Jennifer Hoos Rothberg, also emphasized the importance of building trust. "We don't just call it partnership because we think it's nice," Rothberg told my colleague Ethan McCoy in an interview.[14] "It's the essence of every single thing we do." Grantees feel the same way, according to their feedback in the GPR: "Partnership" was the most frequently mentioned word grantees used to describe EFCT.

"It's Our Job to Learn"

"We say to potential partners, 'Let's start from a place in which you have the resources—what do you want to accomplish in the world?'" Rothberg said. "We want to give potential partners the opportunity to speak about what they want to see in the world in their own terms, not just fitting it into the foundation's terms."

It works. The organizations it funds are effusive about the impact of EFCT's support. The foundation is rated highly across many measures in the GPR.

The foundation asks a lot, but its grants are large and long in term: The GPR showed that the average grant size was north of a million dollars. Perhaps you're thinking, "Of course they get high ratings from grantees. They make huge grants!" But, in fact, size of grant is not a meaningful predictor of grantee ratings in our data set; indeed, CEP has worked with many foundations that get low marks from grantees despite large grants.

One EFCT grantee said, "Our application process involved the development of a strategic plan, which was very time-consuming but was also an important exercise for us to go through as an organization. As a result, we spent much more time on it than we would have on a typical 'grant application,' but it was also significantly more helpful to us as an organization." Another grantee said, "I have found the effort EFCT staff makes to get to know our organization, our goals, our challenges, and the nuances of our work to be so incredibly helpful. They have gained our trust and offered theirs, and have created such a positive partnership that I'm happy when they ask hard questions designed to help us improve."

EFCT's staff understand that strong relationships are crucial to impact. "Our partners know way more than we do about what it's going to take to accomplish the change we're both after. They're the experts," Rothberg said. "We're generalists. It's our job to learn as much as we can so that we can be knowledgeable and supportive."[15] EFCT uses the Performance Imperative's seven pillars I described at the beginning of the chapter and supports organizations' work to get stronger on those dimensions. Rothberg emphasized the importance of making grants to support "things that are often seen as unsexy" because they "are ultimately the things that lead to the sexy impact we are all after."

Crucially, EFCT is constantly seeking to learn and improve. Rothberg described the trust as a "total work in progress."[16]

"Capacity Building"

In recent years, there's been an increased emphasis on the idea that nonprofits don't just need financial support or volunteer hours to do relatively unskilled work, but that they can also benefit from technical assistance or capacity-building to strengthen them as organizations. Financial support is what nonprofits most need, of course, and CEP's research and analysis shows it is more highly valued than assistance beyond the grant.[17] Furthermore, as I mentioned before in the context of volunteering, we need to be sure that nonprofits really need and want whatever assistance givers come bearing.

When there's a genuine match between a nonprofit's needs and a giver's unique skills and experience, however, the results can be significant. A Silicon Valley foundation called RippleWorks, for example, matches business and technology experts with mission-driven organizations (nonprofit and for-profit) that need them. This allows a nonprofit like VisionSpring, which provides affordable glasses to poor people who need to see in order to work, to benefit from the expertise of Vijay Raghavendra, the senior vice president of engineering at Walmart.com. Raghavendra is helping VisionSpring select its first business-to-business e-commerce platform.[18]

That's important because there are an estimated one billion people in the world who need glasses but don't have them, and VisionSpring is working to change that.[19]

Just as individuals give time and expertise as well as financial contributions, foundations also provide more than just grant dollars. They will often directly assist with strategic planning or the development of fundraising capabilities. When done right, this assistance can be extremely valuable to nonprofits.

Additionally, some givers provide targeted grant support for specific organizational capacity needs, such as investment in technology or leadership development. These "organizational effectiveness" grants or gifts can be powerful because nonprofit leaders can spend money on strengthening their organizations' capacity guilt-free. Frequently, leaders feel they shouldn't allocate unrestricted support to something that doesn't feel like a short-term need. These kinds of targeted gifts and grants can help grantees set themselves up for long-term success.

In these efforts to help in ways that go beyond typical gifts or grants, givers must understand nonprofits' needs. We see in our research a disconnect between how well foundation leaders believe they understand the needs of nonprofits and how well nonprofits think their funders understand them. This disconnect underscores, yet again, the importance of listening well so that whatever assistance you provide is tailored to what specific nonprofits need.[20]

What It Takes: Ten Rules

Building effective relationships with grantees begins with the understanding that there's no analog to the dynamic between givers and the nonprofits they support. The relationship is unique, and in some ways fraught. As we've discussed, it requires a commitment to building understanding and to openness.

Here, then, are ten rules for working well with grantees, which I have gleaned through CEP's surveys of tens of thousands of grantees about hundreds of grantmakers—and from working with both exemplars and those struggling to improve their relationships with the nonprofits they support.

1. Don't force a fit.

Look for alignment between your goals and strategies and the goals and strategies of nonprofits. It's a mistake to think you can use the leverage you have over grantees to get them to adapt to what you think is right. Pressure to modify priorities contributes to less positive relationships. For example, grantees pressured in this way are less forthcoming with information about problems. So, it's crucial to prioritize alignment and fit and not try to force a match.

If you can't identify potential recipients of your giving that have goals and strategies aligned with your own, that should tell you something. After all, if those doing the work on the ground don't see your goals and strategies as the right ones, maybe they're not the right ones. Listen closely to learn from those who are, after all, closer to the action than you. If you're sure you have it right even though others don't see it, you have work to do to persuade those you will support—before you fund them.

2. Recognize that if you're a big giver, you live in a bubble of positivity—and take steps to burst the bubble and learn.

I've heard too many big givers insist that they know exactly what grantees think—that they are so down-to-earth and accessible as people that they have negated the power dynamic and created open, two-way communication.

They're wrong. The power dynamic *always* exists between the funder and the funded, and the only way to know grantees' views is to find creative ways to get feedback. For institutional givers, the GPR is a tool to allow you to hear from those you support. For individual givers, it's about making sure to ask questions like, "Is this helpful?" "What could I do differently to support you?" and, "What do you most need?"

3. Don't assume you have what it takes to strengthen nonprofits or build their capabilities. Ask what they need and then offer it only if you're positioned to do it well.

Being good at strengthening organizations takes focus and resources. If you're going to seek to strengthen the organizations you fund, find out what they need and what others are offering, and then ensure you have access to the skills and experience needed to do it well.

In addition, if you're a foundation leader asking your program staff to do this work, you'll need to ensure that they have the time and skills to do it effectively. Foundations that provide valuable assistance in addition to financial support typically have staff who manage fewer relationships with grantees than foundations that don't. For individuals, time is key. Make sure you can commit to regular, predictable hours. Volunteering can be a rewarding and effective way to contribute, but be sure to approach volunteering with modesty and a focus on what the nonprofit needs.

4. Don't restrict your gifts, and make them last.

For those organizations with goals and strategies that significantly overlap with yours, provide the unrestricted, long-term, significant funding that's most helpful to grantees. To make progress against shared goals requires strong organizations, but givers too often restrict funding—creating challenges and limiting nonprofits' ability to allocate resources in ways that make the most sense. Nonprofits need flexible support, and they should build up financial reserves of at least three to six months' operating expenses. Help them get what they need to be effective.

There's no reason a majority of your grants or gifts shouldn't be for general support. There are, of course, some examples where restricted funding makes sense—research, a capital project, perhaps an "organizational effectiveness" grant—but nonprofits desperately need significant unrestricted, multiyear support. Make sure your key grantees are receiving it.

5. Calibrate what you ask of nonprofits to the size of your gifts.

I've seen grantmaking institutions with hugely cumbersome selection and evaluation processes that are making small, one-year grants. I've seen individual givers with unrealistic expectations for the time and attention they'll receive given the amounts of their gifts. Givers should be conscious of transaction costs on both the giver and grantee sides, which take time away from more-important and valuable work.

Right-size your process requirements to the size of the grants or gifts you're making. If you require significant data collection and reporting, then provide the funding to support it. Don't issue "unfunded mandates" to the organizations you support.

6. If you have to make a restricted gift, allow for a decent "overhead" rate and offer as much flexibility as possible.

Givers often impose arbitrarily low overhead rates on program grants—saying, for example, that only 10 percent of a grant can support overhead or indirect costs such as rent. This means that the grantee is being paid less than the full cost of delivering the program, which creates all kinds of headaches and transaction costs on both sides. In the worst cases, it creates incentives for dishonest "creative accounting" as nonprofits scramble to figure out how to pay the rent when none of their grants will allow for those basic expenses to be covered—or at least not at the level required.

Pay for the full costs of programs you support. Several large foundations have recently revised their "overhead" caps on program-restricted grants, moving in some cases from 10 to about 20 percent. But even that may be much too low, according to research conducted by the Bridgespan Group.[21] Finally, allow for flexibility, recognizing that circumstances change. Focus on outcomes—what was achieved—not specific budget line items.

7. Prioritize relationships and make your expectations clear.

If you're a big giver, you'll be hiring staff or retaining consultants or advisors to help you with your giving. Too often, givers prioritize subject-area expertise above all else when looking for staff or advisors. But givers should also prioritize the ability to work well with a coalition of others because, as we've discussed, that's what it takes to make a difference when seeking to address our most stubborn societal problems.

Look for staff or advisors who will be open and transparent and who will also seek to understand the organizations you support and the contexts in which they work. Staffed foundations should make clear their expectations for how program staff will interact with grantees. The David and

Lucile Packard Foundation, for example, developed a set of four "grantee experience standards"—promises they make to grantees and that they communicate publicly.[22]

8. Use your unique vantage point and influence to help grantees do their work better.

Givers, especially big givers, have a bird's-eye view that no one else has—with the ability to look across communities and fields and observe what's working and what's not. These givers also have a caché that allows them to bring organizations together to learn from one another. That's what the Stuart Foundation did in its child welfare work. It's also what the Gill Foundation, the Evelyn and Walter Haas, Jr. Fund, and the other funders involved in the work on marriage equality did.

Nonprofits can benefit enormously when givers use their distinctive strengths to help everyone do their work better.

9. If you have to end a relationship with a grantee, do it well—transparently and with a lot of notice.

If you've been consistently supporting a high-performing nonprofit but, for whatever reason, won't be able to in the future, exit the relationship well. Nonprofits understand that givers' goals and strategies will sometimes change, but they need both time and support to weather these transitions. Be as clear and direct as possible about the end date and your reasons for parting ways, and do so as far in advance as possible. If you have relationships with other givers that might support the nonprofit, use them to try to help prepare organizations you will no longer fund for the future.

If you're ending a relationship because you believe the grantee is no longer effective, again, both notice and openness are essential. Give nonprofits time to turn things around before you pull funding, and provide them with opportunities to tell you their story about what's getting in the way of success. Sometimes, the only choice will be to end a relationship between a giver and a grantee, of course. But other times, you may be able to provide support that helps the nonprofit achieve the requisite higher levels of effectiveness.

10. Decline applicants in a way that's honest and respectful of their time.

This approach starts with clarity about goals and strategy and good communication. It will allow nonprofits to gauge their likelihood of funding. If your selection process requires significant time, consider a two-step approach, starting with a quick letter of inquiry that allows for an initial screening and ensures that applicants with little chance of success don't waste their time on the full process. When you have to decline a nonprofit, do so respectfully and with candor about why.

Remember that declined applicants will apply again. Today's declined applicants are often tomorrow's grantees. Moreover, those you decline will interact with others, including your current grantees. It's in your interest to treat them well, and it's also the right thing to do.

It's Mutual

These ten rules will help you build effective relationships with the nonprofits that you depend on to achieve your shared goals. Working well with those you support is difficult but crucial to effectiveness. As Paul Beaudet of the Wilburforce Foundation wrote, "Wilburforce can only succeed if our grantees succeed. And our grantees can succeed only if they are given the funding, tools, and resources they need to do their work."[23]

It's about mutuality.

A giver's past can help develop empathy for those on the other side of the table who are seeking funds. In response to one of our surveys, one grantee, frustrated with her foundation funder, put it this way: "They would benefit from hiring program staff that have significant on-the-ground experience working in the nonprofit sector. Most of their program staff come from the business world, where the management approaches and metrics for understanding successful outcomes do not necessarily transfer well to the work of nonprofit organizations."

The best givers are both analytical and empathic. Anthony Richardson, associate director at the Nord Family Foundation in Amherst, Ohio, which has $160 million in assets and makes $8 million in grants annually, primarily in Lorain County, exemplifies this: "We approach the work with a sense that we don't have all the answers, and until you engage the people that are in the space doing the work, responding on the ground, you truly can't have a sense of what is actually going on. It's about trust. It's about transparency, obviously learning, and just appreciating and understanding the ecosystem in which our grantmaking functions."[24] Perhaps it's not surprising, then, that the foundation's grantees see it positively, relative to other funders. The attitude Richardson describes is the right one for both individual and institutional givers.

Some givers seem to balk at the notion that, fundamentally, their role is to give money wisely and in a way that supports mutual goal achievement. But, indeed, this is the giver's crucial task. In the Introduction, I noted that the fundamentals of effectiveness are timeless and that, just as the aspiring soccer player can only develop her ball skills through hard work, the effective philanthropist has to work hard to get good. But, too often, I see philanthropists who want to do the fancy stuff before they have the basics down. They want to attempt a diving header or bicycle kick before they can even deliver a simple inside-of-the-foot pass. Master the fundamentals first, which in philanthropy means good selection of—and strong relationships with—grantees.

⪦⪦⪦⪦⪦

Chapter 5 Review: Giving Guidance

1. **Selecting the right nonprofits to fund takes time and effort.** Focus on the nonprofit's aims, approach, and results—not simplistic metrics like overhead or the percentage of budget spent on program. In certain areas of giving, great resources exist for identifying vetted nonprofits that match up with your goals and strategies. But in others, finding the right organizations will take time and effort. When you find the right nonprofits, support them with funding that they can depend on and that isn't restricted. Organizations need this kind of funding to pay salaries, invest in their infrastructure, and maximize their effectiveness.

2. **Be mindful of the unique power dynamics between givers and nonprofit recipients of your support.** Candid feedback is tough to

come by for givers, so you'll need to make extra efforts to build trust. Strong relationships between givers and those you support require both understanding and transparency. Remember that the nonprofits working on the ground are the experts. You can and should learn from them!

3. **Support beyond the money, or traditional gifts and grants, can help strengthen the organizations you support.** If you think you're well positioned to help beyond money, that's great. Just make sure it's what the nonprofits really need—and that you have the skills required to provide it. Then, and only then, make the commitment to helping in ways beyond your grant or gift.

⚛ 6 ⚛

NO EASY ANSWERS

ASSESSING PERFORMANCE

Y FRIEND—I'LL call him Steven—was not happy. He was a founder and board chair of a nonprofit working with the homeless. He was also very successful in his day job as a marketing consultant. He and his family made significant gifts to the nonprofit each year, in addition to the countless hours Steven put in, because they so believed in its mission, effectiveness, and staff leadership.

The source of his frustration? After a grueling, lengthy, and labor-intensive application process that a funder—a self-styled "venture philan-thropy fund" whose staff fancied themselves as operating like venture capitalists—had encouraged the organization to participate in, the request for funding had been denied. The reason? The organization's "cost-per-life-touched" ratio was too high relative to other organizations.

Cost-per-life-touched ratio? *What did that really measure?* he wondered, noting to himself that none of the comparison organizations served the homeless, an especially difficult (and expensive) population to reach. What did it mean to "touch" a life anyway? And how could you compare nonprofits that were working with people in widely varied ways with a simple ratio? His organization, which runs intensive programs, was being compared to organizations offering much more limited services. These other organizations might touch a life, but did they really have the impact that Steven's organization did?

He was so frustrated that he told the program officer at the fund, "I can give every poor child a lollipop if you want a low cost-per-lives-touched number! But that won't create impact." He also found it maddening that his organization had spent so much time answering so many questions as part of the proposal process—and then was denied support because of a ratio that could have been easily calculated before any other work was done.

The venture philanthropy outfit that denied Steven's organization was a much-celebrated poster child of the Harvard Business School (HBS) social enterprise program. It raised money from a number of ultrawealthy individuals, promising that it would "invest" wisely in high-performing organizations. It had been highlighted in HBS case studies.

The cost-per-life-touched ratio was, presumably, an attempt to create a standardized metric—an analog to profit or return on investment—that could be applied across a diverse "portfolio" of "investees." But it's really no better or more meaningful than that other overused and misapplied metric: the administrative cost or "overhead" ratio. It's another mistaken effort to dumb down measurement so that diverse nonprofits can be compared in the way companies are.

To be sure, when organizations have the same goals and are working in the same contexts, they should analyze comparative data on outcomes to understand their relative performance. But there is no universal measure to allow for impact comparisons of nonprofit organizations working in different fields or with different populations, and there never will be. That's why assessment in philanthropy and the nonprofit sector is infinitely more complicated than it is in business. It requires skill sets very different from—and, honestly, much more sophisticated and advanced than—those of the typical MBA.

As management guru Peter Drucker said, "Performance and results are far more important—and far more difficult to measure and control—in the nonprofit institution than in a business."[1]

Uniquely Challenging

If performance measurement for an operating nonprofit is tough, assessing the performance of givers, individual or institutional, is tougher. It's uniquely difficult due to four specific challenges: causality, aggregation, subjectivity, and timeliness.[2] I'll briefly describe each.

First, when it comes to causality, the key is to understand that it will never be possible to establish definitively the causal connection between what a giver has funded and the impact created through that funding alone. That's because it's impossible to know the counterfactual. Might tobacco use have declined even without the Robert Wood Johnson Foundation's efforts? Might there have been civil rights gains for LGBTQ people even without the work of the givers who focused on this issue? Might criminal justice reform have gained traction without the early support of major foundations?

We can never know with absolute, provable certainty. Nor can we easily attribute outcomes to particular givers. The goal should not be to find proof of impact. Rather, the focus should be on whether the available evidence suggests the giver is contributing to progress. Jim Collins has used the analogy of our courts, suggesting a standard of evidence in philanthropy that is less akin to the "proof beyond a reasonable doubt" standard of US criminal trials and more like the "preponderance of the evidence" bar set in civil cases.[3]

The second challenge, aggregation, relates to the lack of a universal measure. While a venture capital firm can look at a single, overall return on investment across its portfolio, a giver cannot. Imagine you run a foundation with a program focused on improving graduation rates for kids in your city and a program with an equivalent budget focused on reducing pollution in the same city. Imagine that, somehow—just go with me—you could understand that your giving contributed to a 10 percent increase in graduation rates through the first program and a 10 percent decrease in pollution through the second. How would you compare the two? Which is the better result?

This relates to the third challenge: subjectivity. You might believe that the increase in graduation rates is the more important accomplishment because more young people will have the opportunity to go on to college and good jobs. I might believe the decrease in pollution is the greater achievement because of the damage done to air quality, including the contribution to high asthma rates in the city. But your friend Sally, who leads the local chamber of commerce, might think that the new regulations that led to the decrease in pollution was too high a price to pay because it had a negative effect on business that she fears will curb future hiring, contributing to unemployment.

Who's right? It's a subjective judgment. In areas like reproductive health care, for example, one donor's positive outcome—access to safe, legal abortion—might be another donor's negative outcome. Here, again, we see how measurement in philanthropy differs from business. Democrats, Republicans, and independents all judge their 401(k)s by the same measure: returns. The higher, the better. But when it comes to their philanthropy, their personal values and beliefs affect what's considered a good result.

The fourth and final challenge is timeliness. The ultimate outcomes a giver is seeking to affect may take years—if not decades—to achieve. Sometimes, what looks like a failure initially can be a success ultimately or vice versa. The time horizons involved with making progress on vexing social problems pose many measurement challenges. It requires the creation of shorter-term, interim, inevitably imperfect measures that are either known to be or hypothesized to be related to the longer-term outcome.

So, performance assessment for givers is anything but easy, and it's only by facing that fact squarely that you can hope to do it well. Even then, it won't be simple. But don't let the perfect be the enemy of the good.

Nonprofit Assessment

In understanding the difficulty of assessing giving performance, it's crucial first to deeply understand the related challenge of nonprofit performance assessment. In this area, too, stereotypes and caricatures often get in the way of good practice. I can't tell you how many times I've heard it said that nonprofits aren't interested in assessing their performance. This was definitely the prevailing view at HBS.

It's the prevailing view in the business media as well. In the 2008 book *Philanthrocapitalism*, Matthew Bishop, who was then at the *Economist*, and his coauthor, Michael Green, wrote that "Whilst some people are skeptical about the invasion of MBA-enabled executives in suits into the Birkenstock world of charity, many philanthrocapitalists believe that the world of giving could benefit at least as much as business has done from a bigger role for professional intermediaries and advisers, and from the sort of transparency and accountability that exists in financial markets."[4]

The timing of the book's release, in the midst of the collapse of Lehman Brothers and the beginning of the Great Recession, almost made me feel sorry for the authors. But not quite. Because Bishop and Green were peddling a simplistic and erroneous narrative in which those in business have all the acumen and passion for results, and those working in the nonprofit sector are the problem—and don't care about assessing their work.

However, performance measurement is more challenging for nonprofits than businesses—and, as I've noted, they don't generally teach the measurement techniques and approaches that are needed in the nonprofit sector in MBA programs. Nonprofit leaders get this, and they care deeply about understanding their performance and impact. My CEP colleagues and I surveyed nonprofits about their practices, and this is what we found:

- Almost all nonprofits we surveyed report collecting information to assess their performance; still, many nonprofit leaders want to collect additional—or better—data.
- The nonprofits surveyed are mainly using their performance information to improve their programs and services, inform their strategic direction, and communicate about their progress; to a lesser extent, they are using it to share what they're learning with other organizations or to manage staff.
- A minority of nonprofits report receiving support from foundations for their performance assessment efforts.[5]

The group we surveyed consisted of nonprofits receiving some foundation support, so admittedly they may have somewhat better-developed practices in this area, but half in our sample have budgets of less than $1.4 million. Nonetheless, they're focused on assessment. The data, in other words, belie the stereotypes. These organizations do their level best to get the data they need, including collecting regular feedback from their intended beneficiaries. (Nearly 90 percent regularly survey those they seek to help, for example, and there are promising efforts I'll describe later to increase the quality and frequency of these feedback efforts.)[6] It's not that nonprofits aren't committed to assessing and improving performance. It's that they need much more support and resources to do this work to the extent they seek to—because performance assessment for nonprofits is a wholly different and much more complicated undertaking than performance assessment in business.

"Critics sometimes describe nonprofits as uninterested in—and incapable of—using data to improve their work," CEP's Ellie Buteau and her colleagues wrote. "But our findings paint a picture of organizations trying to understand their performance and using the information they are collecting to make improvements."[7]

Although there are foundations that do a great job supporting nonprofits in their work to assess performance, their numbers remain too few. Even those working at foundations in assessment roles agree. In a CEP survey of staff leading evaluation at larger foundations, 69 percent said that their foundations don't do enough to improve grantee capacity for data collection or evaluation.[8]

The place to start, as always, is by listening—seeking to understand what data the nonprofit believes it needs to learn and improve—because there is no one-size-fits-all set of measures. Let's take two examples to illustrate the vastly different approaches to assessment that make sense in different contexts: a children's museum and a youth development organization working with at-risk kids.

Different Strokes

The first organization, the children's museum, has the more straightforward assessment challenge. Its mission is "to bring to life the joy of discovery for children and their families through fun, creative, hands-on exploration of the world around them."[9] What data, then, would be important for the board and staff of the museum to gather to gauge performance? Obvious possibilities include number of visitors and surveys of parents and children—to see, for example, if they really are experiencing the museum as fun, creative, and hands-on. Ideally, the museum would collect both over time and compare them to other children's museums in similarly sized cities.

But that alone isn't enough. The staff and board would probably also care about the mix of visitors. Is it only affluent families who visit the museum, or is there socioeconomic diversity among patrons? This kind of focus on access might be in some tension with another important objective, which is that the museum be economically viable, perhaps generating enough revenue to cover costs, build an operating reserve, and allow for investment in new exhibits to ensure that the museum remains fresh and relevant.

So, presumably, the museum's leaders would need to monitor the mix of earned and contributed revenue relative to some agreed-upon goals, and, inevitably, there would be fairly complicated choices to be made about pricing. They would need to discuss the use of the facility for revenue-generating special events as well as the degree to which they should offer discounts or scholarships to museum programs for those unable to pay. The museum would need to balance the economic realities with the desire to serve all children, and it would need fundraising to close the gap between earned revenue and costs.

The museum might also be wise to monitor a range of information about its employees, including qualifications, turnover, diversity, and employee engagement and satisfaction—the kind of measures any high-functioning organization, for-profit or nonprofit, would want to monitor.

But the museum likely wouldn't seek to monitor any long-term changes in the life trajectory or educational outcomes of the children who visit it—even those who enroll in its summer day camps or other recurring programs. Given the relatively small role a museum would play in any person's life, it wouldn't make sense for the museum to hold itself accountable for that level of influence on a person, nor would it be practically viable to try to gather those data.

Measuring Impact on Lives

Assessment isn't simple for the children's museum, especially as it seeks to balance its need for financial sustainability with its desire to be open and accessible to all. But it's more straightforward for the museum than it is for many nonprofits.

Take, for example, a youth development organization that aims to *alter the life trajectories* of those it serves. Roca, based in Boston, has a mission "to disrupt the cycle of incarceration and poverty by helping young people transform their lives." That's a big goal to hold itself accountable for, and Roca takes it seriously. Operating in twenty-one communities, the organization runs a "four-year intervention model . . . based upon the theory that when young people are reengaged through positive and intensive relationships they can gain competencies in life skills, education, and employment that keep them out of prison and move them toward living out of harm's way and toward economic independence."[10]

An organization like Roca monitors a range of short- and longer-term indicators. In the short term, indicators include retention in its programs. But, unlike the children's museum, an organization working with at-risk youth to change life outcomes *must* monitor those it no longer serves—to track employment and incarceration rates, for example. Given its mission, it only knows if it's successful based on how its past clients' lives turn out.

While investing energy and resources in that monitoring, the youth development organization must also pay attention to its day-to-day operations: ensuring financial stability, retaining and engaging its staff, and so on. On these more operational dimensions, the children's museum and youth development organization may monitor some of the same metrics. But on the dimensions that are more closely connected to mission, the performance assessment approaches will be very different.

These are just two examples. Policy-oriented nonprofits face a different set of assessment challenges, as do multiservice human services organizations offering a wide range of programs serving a variety of populations. The point is that the right approach to nonprofit performance assessment varies widely. So, too, then, will the levels and types of support nonprofits need from their funders to do this work.

The Highest Bar

When possible, an organization that seeks to alter long-term life outcomes should compare the results for its participants to a population that is as similar as possible to the one it serves but that *did not* receive its services. Only then can it really know it's making a difference. This can best be done through RCTs (randomized control trials) like the ones BELL undertook to compare the academic gains of students with whom they'd worked against others who didn't go through their programs. RCTs are expensive, and many givers can't afford them, but that doesn't mean you can't learn from those that others have supported.

RCTs are also controversial. For example, critics argue that they don't sufficiently consider context—something shown to work in Denver might not work in Boise. Moreover, they argue that particular interventions cannot ever truly be "isolated," and that it usually takes a number of different interventions to address a complex social problem.[11]

Another criticism is that denying access to a potentially effective intervention to someone in need is unethical. This is the rationale Gregg Croteau of UTEC cites. In cases like UTEC's, where it's possible for an organization to offer a particular program to everyone who needs it, that's a good reason not to do an RCT. The BELL experience, in which the organization couldn't possibly reach every child in need, is more typical, which makes it possible to compare results without having to deny anyone anything.

Proponents of RCTs argue that it's the very complexity critics point to which makes it critical to ensure that specific interventions are contributing to progress—and that nothing is quite as effective as an RCT in doing so. "In fact, one of the advantages of RCT-based designs, which utilize both comparison groups and randomization, is that they isolate program impacts and protect against other complex and often hidden influences on their results (such as participant motivation) that commonly undermine competing study designs and lead to misleading conclusions," argued Patrick Lester of the Social Innovation Research Center.[12]

Lester is right, in my view. Admittedly, RCTs don't make sense in the many situations in which the goal is something other than changing the life trajectory for specific people. So it doesn't have a lot of applicability, say, for most environmental philanthropists or for those supporting arts and culture. But if you're seeking to dramatically scale a particular approach to solving some pressing problem, and your claim is that it will change the life outcomes of those you're seeking to help, you need to be pretty darn sure it works.

It's imperative in these cases to test an approach before potentially wasting millions of dollars scaling something ineffective. If efforts had been made earlier to rigorously assess programs like D.A.R.E. or Scared Straight—high-profile, heavily funded, and ineffectual efforts to keep children away from drugs and to steer them clear of crime, respectively—millions of dollars would not have been wasted. Take Scared Straight, which brings young people at risk of delinquency in contact with convicted criminals. It has repeatedly been shown not only to be ineffective, but to have the opposite of the intended effect: one meta-evaluation concluded that the program increased delinquency relative to doing nothing at all. The authors wrote that "evidence indicates that there is a greater probability than not that it will be harmful. Would you permit a doctor to use a medical treatment on your child with a similar track record of results?"[13] There is no excuse for continuing programs like this. We need to act on what we learn. If something doesn't work, or, worse, does harm, we need to either modify or scrap the program.

On the flip side, we should be giving more resources to what does work, especially to those programs that have been shown to be effective through repeated studies in multiple contexts, like those highlighted on evidencebasedprograms.org. Not all programs are equal. Some really are more demonstrably effective than others, and, given the choice, givers should support the effective ones. An RCT, while not right or relevant for all organizations, represents the highest bar for establishing results.

RCTs are expensive and almost invariably require significant philanthropic support. Givers in a position to provide the level of support needed for an RCT should be thoughtful and wise about which organizations are at a stage when they might benefit from one. Some questions to consider include:

✑ Is the organization doing something that, if effective, could benefit many more people than are currently being served?

ᗡ Are there early indicators of success based on other evaluations that give reason for optimism that the intervention is effective?

ᗡ Is the organization being considered for funding of an RCT staffed appropriately to execute at the level required for the trial?

Today, too few funders support RCTs. In a benchmarking survey of 127 mostly large foundations that CEP conducted in partnership with the Center for Evaluation Innovation in 2016, just 19 percent said they funded RCTs for their grantees.[14] Given the potential of RCTs, especially when replicated, to help reveal what really works, that number should be higher. A great value of RCTs is the knowledge they provide for other givers and for other organizations, not just the one whose program or work is studied. In a variety of areas of work—such as mentoring, for instance—there is now considerable evidence about which are the more effective practices. This means any mentoring program should be able to adopt the practices that have been shown to work, rather than starting from scratch.[15]

That's a big deal.

Building on Existing Knowledge

When givers know what works, they can fund it in a big way. That's what New York State Health Foundation did to improve the care of diabetes patients. Understanding that research had shown a link between certain protocols and better outcomes, but knowing that many doctors weren't familiar with those protocols, the foundation's staff supported the training of doctors. The foundation, which was created with funds resulting from the conversion of Empire Blue Cross Blue Shield from a nonprofit organization to a for-profit corporation, is one of many so-called health conversion foundations created in recent decades. Today, the foundation has about $300 million in assets.

Staff noted what was most effective and made grants to organizations working to ensure this knowledge was broadly understood and put into practice. The foundation didn't then track the outcomes of the patients because the protocol had already been linked to better outcomes. The foundation's leaders held themselves accountable simply for the increased number of doctors with the right training. That makes sense.

Givers of all levels, and in all issue areas, should tap into available resources to learn what has been shown to work. I've mentioned websites like GiveWell.org, thelifeyoucansave.org, and evidencebasedprograms.org, run by the Laura and John Arnold Foundation. There are many other resources, too. Education funders can look to the Institute of Education Sciences' What Works Clearinghouse. Health care funders can access the Cochrane Library. Criminal justice funders can go to CrimeSolutions.gov. Substance abuse and mental health funders can look to the National Registry of Evidence-based Programs and Practices. We know more about what works in a variety of fields than is often appreciated.[16]

Too often, givers and nonprofits—and perhaps especially new givers—fail to do what New York State Health Foundation did: take advantage of that significant existing knowledge. Also too often, givers and nonprofits alike don't share insights with others about what works and what doesn't. More than 70 percent of those leading evaluation at larger foundations believe their foundations don't do enough to disseminate evaluation findings externally.[17] That needs to change.

Much of the discussion in philanthropy over the past decade or so about "scaling what works" has focused on the growth of specific organizations with evidence of effectiveness. This, for example, is the approach the Edna McConnell Clark Foundation has taken, providing support to help nonprofits such as BELL, Nurse-Family Partnership, and Youth Villages to dramatically expand. This is a sound strategy that can be highly effective if those organizations are able to maintain excellence while scaling.

But scaling isn't limited to expanding specific organizations. Here, again, the analog to business has led us astray, with its focus on the growth of a specific organization, when what really matters most is the spread of effective interventions. Although those with a business orientation tend to assume there's greater efficacy and efficiency when a single entity does something rather than when a network of organizations does it, that isn't always the case in the nonprofit sector.

What matters, quite simply, is that efforts to achieve particular goals are effective. We can encourage more sharing of what works across organizations. What's most efficient and effective for spreading an effective practice will vary depending on the goal and context.

Support for Real Assessment

Good assessment is crucial for nonprofits. They need knowledge about what works, and they also need continual feedback to inform their work. But putting in place the data collection and analysis systems and processes needed to maximize effectiveness takes resources.

Not only do most nonprofits not receive any philanthropic support for assessment, they also often see givers' requests for data as prioritizing the givers' needs over their own.[18] It shouldn't be this way. Supporting nonprofits' efforts to collect and learn from the data they believe will help them become more effective is arguably one of the best investments a giver can make.

There are certainly givers that do this well, like the Mary Reynolds Babcock Foundation—a $200 million foundation located in Winston-Salem, North Carolina, making $10 million in grants annually—which was rated especially highly by its grantees in its GPR on dimensions related to support for performance assessment. Gladys Washington, deputy director at the foundation, said, "Grantees have the opportunity to tell us that the outcome they articulated six months prior has gone out the window because circumstances changed. We say, 'What happened? What's the learning from that? . . . We don't use [grantees' assessment processes] as 'gotcha' opportunities. We use them as learning opportunities."[19]

Washington's description is a useful reminder of the link between strong funder–grantee relationships and the ability to make sense of data together to learn and improve. Without strong, open, and trusting relationships, assessment becomes a dance of deceit. Evaluation reports are cherry-picked or distorted, and organizations that can market themselves as evidence-based and highly effective are seen that way even if the real evidence is scant. As a result, some nonprofits are seen as effective even though the data aren't there. It's difficult for anyone to speak out—grantees don't want to offend their colleagues or, worse, the givers that have made the success of their grantees their claim to fame. The individuals and foundations that have supported the organization have bought into the idea of its success and don't want to open themselves up to the possibility that they may have been misguided. And, because assessment is so difficult, it can be hard to know what's really going on, so growth becomes the metric. Givers assume that the support from other funders is a signal of efficacy and get on board. At its worst, a kind of herd mentality sets in.

Givers should do everything they can not to fall into this trap. They should constantly bring the discussion back to the data and evidence and be open about what works and what doesn't. It's important to reward nonprofits for openness about failure, rather than punishing them. Givers should be open, too, about their own missteps. That kind of openness, especially when the data are not what they hoped for, actually increases credibility and enhances givers' reputations. More importantly, it leads to greater impact.

Assessment Complexities

Foundations and individual givers alike are prioritizing assessment. We know that foundations have, over the past decade or so, increased their efforts to collect data to help them learn and improve. They recognize that if they are to insist that grantees assess themselves, the givers should do the same. That point is clear from our research and from CEP's growth, as well as from their increased interest in and attention to assessment and evaluation. While even the earliest philanthropists cared about assessing results, the difficulties associated with doing it well have made it rarer than it should be. Foundation CEOs believe there's considerable room for improvement.[20]

What, then, to measure? Tracking progress against the big goals that givers pursue—reduction in juvenile incarceration, increased college attendance by former foster kids, improvements in college readiness among high school students, and decreases in carbon emissions—is essential. But that's not nearly enough because the giver is just one of many actors and because, often, the time horizon on progress is long. If individual or institutional givers only monitor those *end outcomes*, they will have little data to gauge progress and make well-informed course corrections.

Givers need to establish additional indicators connected to strategy and to assumptions about how their giving is contributing to progress. According to a 2011 CEP research report focused on foundations, "While evaluation remains an essential component of how foundations approach assessment, our latest survey results suggest that the adoption of more indirect—or proxy—measures that speak to foundation performance has intensified. Almost half of CEOs are combining these indicators in an effort to assess overall foundation performance."[21]

Some do this especially thoughtfully, developing overall assessments that can inform board and staff discussion about how the foundation is doing and how it can do better. James Knickman led evaluation at the Robert Wood Johnson Foundation for many years and then became the first CEO of the New York State Health Foundation, which I mentioned in the context of its work on diabetes.

Knickman was one of the few foundation CEOs to come to his role with an evaluation background, and he was committed to ensuring that the foundation was continually learning, improving, and getting results. So, New York State Health Foundation posted a chart of performance goals publicly to its website, along with results. Some of its metrics directly connected to the programmatic goals it sought to achieve, such as the number of "evidence-based diabetes prevention programs" operating in the state. But other indicators were based on the foundation's hypotheses about what facilitates ultimate effectiveness, such as grantees' ratings of staff responsiveness, as recorded by the GPR, or data on the diversity of the leadership of organizations it supports. The foundation's leaders are open with this information and with results of all the external evaluations it commissions. They know that part of the way they contribute to the common good is through helping others learn about what is and isn't working.

External evaluators are crucial resources for big givers. Trained professionals who can help givers learn about their progress in an area of giving can be key partners to inform learning and improvement. Ideally, givers should engage the question of how they will evaluate progress early in the strategy development process, rather than waiting until later to involve those who will help evaluate results. As one of my mentors, former Edna McConnell Clark Foundation president and former CEP board member Michael Bailin, has observed, too often evaluation in philanthropy resembles an autopsy rather than a checkup on a living patient. The best approach to assessment focuses on learning.

The Rockefeller Brothers Fund, Commonwealth Fund, and others have developed approaches to performance assessment that combine indicators from a variety of sources into an overall appraisal that board and staff discuss. Foundation boards and CEOs should insist on this. None of the indicators will be perfect, and all need to be interpreted in context. But it's crucial to be disciplined and diligent about performance assessment.

Even at larger foundations we analyzed in the benchmarking study we conducted in collaboration with the Center for Evaluation Innovation, we saw that the ratio of program staff to evaluation staff is ten to one. While half of respondents said the foundation's spending on evaluation had increased relative to the program budget, it remained insufficient at many foundations. Just 35 percent of foundation staff with evaluation responsibility believed their foundation understands quite or very accurately what it has accomplished through its work when it comes to the fields their foundations seek to affect, and just 22 percent felt that way relative to the communities their foundations seek to affect.[22]

If even the biggest givers struggle with assessment, how can individual givers approach this challenge? It's important for individual givers to be realistic about what you can assess. You don't have a team of people to help you. You can't know everything about your giving or about the performance of the organizations to which you give. But there are some key questions you can ask. I suggest a simple, annual review of these three in particular:

❧ **Does your giving match your stated goals and strategies?** Review all gifts and calculate the percentage of total dollars given that align completely, the percentage that's partially aligned, and the percentage that fall outside your goals and priorities. Individual givers who want results should aim to have at least 80 percent of their dollars in the first category. If you aren't doing your giving through a

DAF, Giving Compass offers a useful tool for tracking your giving on its website—along with a slew of other helpful resources.

◊ **Do the organizations you support have evidence of progress you find compelling?** Review each organization's website or, if you're a giver at a significant enough level that you're interacting directly with staff, ask the question directly. Don't expect precision, but the evidence, both qualitative and quantitative, should suggest progress. If it doesn't, the organization should be able to describe what it will do differently based on what it has learned. If it can't do that, it may not be a worthy recipient going forward.

◊ **Who are the big givers supporting the goals and strategies you support, and what can you learn about their efforts and their assessment of progress?** Often, these givers will devote significant resources to assessment. If you're focusing your giving on the same goals they are—and if they're open about what they're learning—you can benefit from their evaluation work. Because the result is more giving toward what's effective, everyone wins.

Bursting the Bubble

One basic first step givers can take is to get candid and comparative feedback. This may be less relevant for smaller-scale individual givers, but bigger givers, whether individuals or institutions, will need to take stock of their relationships.

That's what Mary Vallier-Kaplan did in 2004. She still felt new to her job at what was a relatively young foundation, Endowment for Health, when she commissioned a GPR. She didn't expect the three-year-old Endowment, a grantmaker focused in New Hampshire with $75 million in assets at the time, to receive high marks across the board. But the results were so disappointing to Vallier-Kaplan, who was vice president and chief operating officer at the time, that when she received the findings, she didn't share them with the other foundation staff for three or four days.

On a number of important dimensions in the grantee survey, from perceived understanding of grantee organizations to quality of interactions, the Endowment received lower ratings from its grantees than almost all other foundations whose grantees CEP had surveyed at the time. One grantee wrote, "The foundation must place some trust in the ability of its grantees to carry out the projects which have been funded through the foundation without constant questioning and criticism."

After mulling the results alone for a few days, Vallier-Kaplan began sharing them with staff in small groups and sometimes individually. Like her, many of her colleagues needed to take a few days to sort out the disheartening results. "It was hard for me to get some people over that hurdle of feeling like they hadn't done a good job," she said. "We had done a good job. We just needed to do a better job." And that's what they did.

Three years later, after repeating the GPR, the results were almost the inverse of the first time around. On many of the dimensions where the Endowment had lagged behind most other funders, it was now among the leaders. One of the Endowment's grantees said, "I had experience with [the Endowment] during its infancy and can confidently say the focus on personal relationships and interactions between staff and grantees is wonderful! The changes put into place—and consistent self-evaluation by [the Endowment]—have made a tremendous difference."

Looking back in 2011, the foundation's leaders saw the feedback they received as crucial to helping them chart a better path. Karen Horsch, an evaluation consultant working with the Endowment, described the period after the first GPR as difficult but said the changes the Endowment undertook since then "made us a better foundation." For Vallier-Kaplan, hearing from grantees was important because she and the staff relied on grantees to carry out the foundation's mission. "All the money in the world isn't going to accomplish the outcomes if the relationship and partnership [with grantees] doesn't work," she said.[23]

The GPR has shifted the dynamics between funders and the funded at many foundations, just as it did at Endowment for Health. It won't tell you everything you want to know about your impact—no single data source will. But it can help you understand how effectively you're working with those you depend on to pursue your shared goals: the nonprofits you fund.

If you're an individual giver interacting with nonprofits, you can bring a self-awareness that those organizations want your support and that this affects the way they interact with you. As a general rule, givers should significantly discount the praise that those they support have lavished on them. I recommend that you seek satisfaction instead from the knowledge that you're supporting effective organizations achieving results for communities and people.

Listening to Those Who Should Matter Most

The GPR brings the perspectives of grantees to givers. But what about the people who should matter most: those whose lives you seek to improve?[24] That was the question Fay Twersky put to me in the fall of 2007, when she called me from her office at the Bill & Melinda Gates Foundation in Seattle as I walked off a plane in Boston.

Hearing from intended beneficiaries is something that nonprofits routinely seek to do, but it's more difficult for givers because they're not the ones doing the work on the ground. Yet, it is absolutely crucial for givers to understand the perspectives of those you seek to help. It's the right thing to do, but, as Twersky—now of the William and Flora Hewlett Foundation—often says, it's also the smart thing to do.

Twersky felt that the staff of the Gates Foundation were too isolated from those their work was intended to benefit, and she wanted to test ways of changing that. She received interest at Gates from those working in education and asked CEP to explore the possibility of creating a comparative student survey to provide feedback to schools, school districts, and education funders. That effort led to the creation of YouthTruth, an initiative run out of CEP that has brought the perspectives of one million students to education leaders and givers.

The YouthTruth student surveys cover a range of issues, from perspectives on academic rigor and college and career readiness to bullying and other aspects of school culture. YouthTruth now surveys high school, middle school, and upper elementary school students, as well as families and school staff. The Gates Foundation stopped supporting the effort several years after it launched, but a number of other foundations have stepped in to support districts and schools in their use of YouthTruth, as well as to learn from the data themselves. And most of the participating districts and charter networks have set aside money in their own budgets for surveys because they see how important it is to hear, in a comprehensive, comparative, and candid way, from students in their schools.

High Tech High, a network of thirteen charter schools in San Diego County, is among the thousands of schools that have used YouthTruth. Much of the feedback they heard from students affirmed their approach, but they have also used the data to get better. "Most recently, while looking at our college and career readiness component, we identified that students in 11th and 12th grades were saying, 'Yes, we understand about the college process,'" Nikki Hinostro, director of High Tech Middle, explained. "And our 9th and 10th grade students told us, 'No, we don't—we don't feel as ready for the college experience or ready to make the decisions around college.'" This discrepancy was causing needless worry and anxiety, so the school took steps to address it.[25]

Elementary school students have valuable insights on their experience, too. Evergreen School District in San Jose, California, serves nearly 11,000 students across eighteen schools. Its use of YouthTruth led to a recognition that the district needed to prioritize school culture and student engagement. At one of the district's elementary schools, the steps school leaders took in response to what they learned—including implementing a new behavior management and support approach—led to a decline in discipline cases by more than half in a single year.[26] YouthTruth, whose founding executive director was Valerie Threlfall and which is currently led by Jen Vorse Wilka, has demonstrated the power of capturing the unvarnished perspectives of those you seek to help.

The Fund for Shared Insight is a funder's collaborative working on this issue—feedback from those you seek to help—that includes the William and Flora Hewlett Foundation, Ford Foundation, Gates Foundation, and Einhorn Family Charitable Trust. More than ninety funders have been involved since its inception five years ago, and the fund is working to support nonprofits in collecting feedback through simple but rigorous surveys through an initiative called Listen for Good.

Cathy Moore and the staff of ECHOs gained an understanding of clients' frustrations with long lines through participation in Listen for Good.

This understanding led them to identify bottlenecks and, with the work of an outside efficiency expert, rework their processes. "When you're in the thick of it, you don't see it," Moore explained. Now, everything the staff does is focused on "client hospitality" and "getting clients to know they're valued and respected." For example, staff decided that they would come in at 7:00 a.m. every day to unlock the office, so people didn't have to wait outside. The staff worked hard to respond to the feedback because everyone "really cares about the people we serve," said Moore.

We can't be effective in helping people when we don't understand their views. Given the strong evidence of a link between perceptual data and desired outcomes, perceptual data can be a vital leading indicator of outcomes.[27] Most nonprofits do try to hear from those they seek to help.[28] But they struggle to find the time and resources.

As a giver, you should try to understand whether the organizations you support get feedback from those they seek to help, how they do it, and how they use what they hear to improve. Those involved in the Fund for Shared Insight told me it can be a struggle. One said it can be difficult "to figure out how to truly listen, to be vulnerable and comfortable not knowing and really listening to people who are the experts on their own lives and experiences and dreams." Another noted the challenge of hearing from those they seek to help without going around the nonprofits they support.

But it's crucial to find ways to have personal interactions and, if possible, build relationships with those whose lives your philanthropy seeks to affect. That's what Mark and Leslie Sillcox, the couple we met in Chapter 3 who focus on helping low-income students succeed academically, did with the young students they sought to help in New York. After all, who knows better what will help than those we seek to help?

So, we need to listen to them.

Metric Dangers

The push for more-rigorous measurement of social programs has sometimes been compared to the "moneyball" approach in baseball, in which statistical analysis is used to determine the best rosters and lineups. But those pushing the analogy to sports, where statistics are generally reliable and where victories and defeats are easy to judge, should be cautious not to make it all sound a whole lot easier than it is.

So, too, should those like Sean Parker, who analogized philanthropy to technology, writing that new, young donors, "want metrics and analytic tools comparable to the dashboards, like Mixpanel, that power their software products."[29] I'm familiar with Mixpanel because CEP uses it. It's a helpful tool to measure use of websites and apps. However, the notion that measuring how someone uses a website is comparable to measuring progress on, say, efforts to improve life outcomes for foster youth, is beyond naïve.

Similarly, the many calls for philanthropy to use "big data" in the way business does also tends to simplify matters or to downplay the difficulty of execution. Yes, Netflix can predict the shows and movies I might be interested in. But predicting complex social phenomena isn't as easy.

For example, foundations have sought to support the use of software to predict the likelihood of recidivism in order to inform sentencing of convicted criminals. The CEO of one of the foundations behind this effort told me a major benefit of putting this kind of tool in the hands of judges is that it would eliminate racial bias. "Software is just better than humans at certain things," he told me, "because it's not biased."

But, of course, it's humans who create the software. Moreover, the algorithms that seek to predict future behavior are based on data about people living amid, and affected by, racism. So perhaps it shouldn't have been surprising that an investigation by ProPublica found just the opposite of what was intended: The software was biased against black people.[30] We're beginning to understand more about the ways in which "big data" can perpetuate inequality.

It isn't just that measurement and the use of data when working on the toughest societal challenges is especially difficult; it's also that the cost of mistakes is especially high. After all, if Netflix suggests I might like a particular movie and then I don't, I might be frustrated or bored—or my wife might be annoyed at me for making her sit through it with me—but no one gets hurt. No one spends extra time in prison. No one dies. No one goes hungry.

Are there ways to mine data to inform better decision-making in philanthropy and the nonprofit sector? Absolutely, and it's being done in areas from health care to education. But we need to be realistic about what's possible and sober about the unique challenges of assessing philanthropic effectiveness.

It's dangerous to simplify the measurement challenge. Too often, well-intentioned leaders have put all their measurement eggs in one basket, focusing on a single metric. This is what happened in education in recent years, as funders and both the Bush and Obama administrations emphasized test scores as the high-stakes metric by which students, schools, and school districts would be judged. In retrospect, it looks predictable that the result would include cheating scandals in multiple American cities, teaching to the test, and less emphasis on subjects like music and the arts that weren't the focus of standardized tests.

By the final months of the Obama administration, the Department of Education had essentially reversed itself, calling for a decreased emphasis on testing and a more holistic approach to measuring results.[31] Measurement of progress on complicated, stubborn social problems isn't easy.

A Challenge Worth Embracing

Assessment is uniquely challenging in philanthropy, but the payoff is worth it. It's the only way to learn and then to clarify goals and strategies as a result. After all, you can't assess progress against goals and strategies unless you know what your goals and strategies are. Moreover, a commitment to performance assessment, and to developing a set of indicators, often leads to a realization that goals are unclear, or that there are too many, or that strategies aren't explicitly articulated. This realization prompts a clarification of goals and strategies that makes the giver's philanthropy better for the long term.

In addition, making clear the measures or indicators by which progress will be judged helps in building a shared sense of how success will be determined. Donors, staff, and board members are all too often on different pages about what success will look like. This is a recipe for problematic decision-making and poor performance. Making explicit what data will inform judgments about giving, and ensuring that all relevant parties—spouses or families or foundation board and staff—have input into the process, reduces the odds of major misunderstandings. It also gets everyone rowing in the same direction.

Specifying measures also instills a sense of reality. It leads to the question, "Can we really affect that?" This question leads to conversations about the logic of how giving is connected to the ultimate outcomes the giver seeks. It often deepens the recognition that, to be effective, the giver will need to work in alignment with others—not just grantees, but also other funders, as well as, sometimes, actors in business or government.

Most importantly, assessment fuels learning. It may not be easy, but without it, you're flying blind.

⊹⊱⊰⊹⊰⊰⊹

Chapter 6 Review: Giving Guidance

1. **There is no universal metric to gauge giving.** The right metrics depend on your goals and strategy, and focusing on only one measure can have harmful unintended consequences (such as an overemphasis on testing leading to cheating scandals). Beware of simplistic, dumbed-down measures, such as administrative cost or "cost-per-life-touched" ratios.

2. **There's a lot of readily available information about what works.** Find out what's available in the areas in which you're doing your giving and ensure that your giving is aligned with existing knowledge about what's effective. There are clearinghouse websites and resources about which approaches have been shown to work in many areas. There are also organizations that rigorously evaluate specific nonprofits. Individual givers can also look to their community foundations for guidance.

3. **Nonprofits care about assessment, but they need support to do this work well.** Rather than placing your demands for assessment data on nonprofits, ask them what would be helpful for them to do their work better. Ask them about the range of data that's needed, including understanding the perspectives of the people the nonprofit seeks to help.

7

DEPLOYING ALL THE TOOLS

"WE'RE ABOUT SO much more than just giving," donors and foundation staff frequently say. "We want to use all the tools available to make a difference."

That makes sense, of course. But I must confess, I've seen too many who aspire to "do more than give," in the words of one philanthropy how-to book, but aren't even doing the giving very well.[1]

That's partly why, so far, we've been primarily discussing what it takes to be effective in your giving: clarifying goals; finding and supporting sound strategies; making good choices about what organizations to support and then building strong, supportive relationships with those organizations; and assessing performance. We've also discussed volunteering, how givers can use their unique ability to see across fields and communities and share knowledge, and efforts beyond the grant that can help strengthen organizations.

So, what else is there?

Turns out, a lot. It's true that giving and the highly related activities discussed thus far are sometimes necessary but insufficient. Beyond the direct work with nonprofits that givers support, there are also other important ways that givers can maximize their impact. Four, in particular, should be considered by every giver:

⬦ Influence on policy

⬦ Communications

⬦ Alternative investing approaches

⬦ Influence on business

In each case, there's no single right answer as to whether a particular approach makes sense for you. The right answer is almost invariably, "it depends"—on your goals and strategies, the resources available to you, and the context in which you're operating.

Some of the tactics I'll discuss in this chapter are more relevant to big givers, whether individuals or foundations, than those of more modest means. But I'll discuss each of the four approaches and then raise some guiding questions to help you determine whether any or all of these are right for you.

Influencing Policy: A Long Tradition

Every citizen who cares about communities or social or environmental issues cares about policy. Givers can seek to influence policy both through their giving and in ways that go beyond giving. The election of Donald J. Trump as president in 2016 led to a wave of individual giving to policy-oriented national organizations such as the American Civil Liberties Union (ACLU) and Planned Parenthood. Many citizens also took to the streets to protest the new president's priorities; for example, in the Women's March in January 2017. But policy influence also takes place on the local level, as citizens mobilize to persuade their town governments to add more bike lanes or ban plastic bags.

While private foundations and operating nonprofits with the 501(c)(3) designation (the vast majority) face restrictions on what they can do in the political arena, they can seek to affect policy broadly. Environmental organizations can raise awareness and educate lawmakers about the importance of clean water or conservation. Children's advocacy organizations can argue for policies that protect children from abuse. Some organizations, such as the ACLU, have both a 501(c)(3) and a 501(c)(4) arm because the latter designation allows for less-fettered lobbying and political activity. As an individual giver, you'll want to pay attention because contributions to the former are tax-deductible for itemizers, whereas contributions to the latter aren't.

Policy influence is often necessary for major givers to make a difference in pursuit of their goals. Indeed, the desire to influence policy was widely cited among the reasons big givers like eBay founder Pierre Omidyar and Facebook's Mark Zuckerberg didn't just establish large foundations through which to do their giving. Omidyar created a 501(c)(4), as well as an LLC. Zuckerberg is, so far, intent on using an LLC—the Chan Zuckerberg Initiative (CZI)—for much of his giving. CZI describes itself as "a new kind of philanthropic organization that brings together world-class engineering, grantmaking, impact investing, policy, and advocacy work. Our initial areas of focus include supporting science through basic biomedical research and education through personalized learning."[2]

Why an LLC? Although private foundations offer tax benefits, they face disclosure requirements and are limited from directly advocating for legislation or political candidates, and some say that's the appeal of the LLC. An LLC structure allows donors to avoid regulatory and transparency requirements and maximize control, and many predict these features will be increasingly attractive to big givers.[3] While some see benefits, others see LLCs as offering nothing more than a bank account does—and see their establishment for philanthropic purposes as publicity stunts by givers to delay making real decisions about their philanthropy. I'm concerned about the potential use of LLCs as an alternative to foundations, in particular because of the lack of transparency.

Regardless, many in the philanthropy world have predicted we will see a rise in the use of LLCs for giving as donors follow Zuckerberg's lead, seeking both the freedom to work more directly on policy matters and the desire to retain tight control of information about them and their philanthropy. Whether or not the predicted shift in legal vehicles comes to fruition, the desire to influence policy is hardly new. Big givers have sought to influence policy in this country for a century. The appropriateness of their role in policy debates has been a subject of discussion—and often, considerable controversy—for just as long. That criticism has intensified again in the past few years, with questions raised about philanthropists' influence on policy and whether it is at some level antidemocratic.

Historian Olivier Zunz observed:

> It is remarkable how much effort lawmakers, regulators, and philanthropists alike have invested throughout the twentieth century in the nearly impossible task of maintaining a solid distinction between philanthropy and politics. Promoting the common good often leads to political advocacy. All the same, the prevailing view was that philanthropy should educate but it could not advocate, a distinction that depended on an artificial boundary between communication and lobbying.[4]

Zunz argued that major individual and institutional givers' participation in the policy process has "enlarged democracy," and I agree. I'm glad that foundations including the Stern Family Fund, Ford Foundation, and the Carnegie Corporation, among others, "threw themselves wholeheartedly into the national campaign to end racial segregation" during the civil rights movement, rather than sitting on the sidelines for fear of having an undue or undemocratic influence on policy.[5]

I'm also glad that the funders involved in the Civil Marriage Collaborative undertook influencing policy with respect to LGBT rights. And that foundations with disparate goals but an overlapping interest in fixing a dysfunctional approach to education funding in California came together and helped support research and advocacy that led to an overhaul in public education funding.[6] And that givers across the political spectrum, such as the Public Welfare Foundation, Open Society Foundations, Ford Foundation, the Koch brothers, Laura and John Arnold Foundation, and California Endowment, have been seeking—with some success—to shift our approach to criminal justice to reduce the number of our citizens who are counterproductively jailed for nonviolent crimes.

It's true that some givers have used their money and power to influence policy in ways that I, personally, see as less positive. But I agree with Zunz that this is part of the democratic give and take. To be sure, there should be greater transparency about giving that seeks to influence policy, so we can clearly understand who is seeking to affect what. However, I don't think that greater government regulation is warranted beyond the requirement for disclosure, nor do I think givers should shy away from the policy arena.

Today, in a post–*Citizens United* world, in which the potential for individuals and corporations to influence policy and politics is essentially unchecked, the answer is surely not for givers to unilaterally take themselves out of the game. We need actors in our society who are seeking to influence the public debate that have motivations other than, say, gaining profit for themselves or their shareholders or preserving public office for themselves.

Although some have suggested that philanthropy can be a threat to our democratic principles because they worry that big givers have an outside influence on policy, I'm optimistic that the opposite is true: that philanthropy can serve as a ballast against the ever-encroaching influence of big companies on public policy.

Responsible Policy Influence

Can you really contribute to change in an area such as global warming without influencing public policy? Federal and state laws, after all, govern harmful emissions from factories and cars that contribute to climate change—and can create incentives or disincentives for behaviors that increase those emissions. Or consider childhood obesity, a program area of many health-focused foundations. The problem requires a policy focus because it's affected by factors that government controls—from the number of parks and play areas to the lunch options at elementary schools to the ingredient labeling requirements on food and beverages.

Policy influence is a crucial lever for change. A giver who seeks to influence policy should, as with all aspects of strategy, work to do so in alignment and coordination with others rather than going it alone. And givers need to be mindful of the growing public distrust of institutions and aware of their responsibility to ensure the solutions for which they advocate have support from those they're intended to help. The most effective givers open themselves to the possibility that others are in a better position to identify solutions, rather than simply assuming that, once they've identified a solution, they need to gain buy-in. As executive director of the Libra Foundation, Crystal Hayling, put it when reflecting on her career as a foundation executive, "I learned, in those early years, that folks did not take kindly to the notion that their communities or their lives were problems to be solved."[7]

Yes, givers will need to operate in the policy arena if they seek to make a difference in certain areas, but they should do so with self-awareness and care—and in a way that amplifies, rather than crowds out, the voices of regular citizens. That may sound obvious or platitudinous, but recent experience suggests it's harder than it looks to get the balance right. In a deep examination of four foundations' roles in education reform, University of Michigan's Megan Tompkins-Stange contrasted the more top-down approaches of the Eli and Edythe Broad and the Gates Foundations with the more participatory approaches of the Ford and W. K. Kellogg Foundations. Her excellent analysis, based on dozens of interviews with those inside those foundations as well as other observers, shows the promise and pitfalls of a focus on influencing policy. "Given the power that foundations have to shape policies through not only their financial capital but also their social and political legitimacy, questions of democratic governance come into sharp relief," she wrote.[8] Her concerns extend to big givers doing their giving through LLCs or donor-advised funds, too; the lessons she draws are applicable well beyond foundations.[9]

Tompkins-Stange's research suggests there may be a growing concern among at least some big givers about how they use their policy influence responsibly. Years after external critiques of what some saw as an undue and antidemocratic influence on educational policy by Gates and other funders, some staff within the Gates Foundation are now voicing concerns that are strikingly similar. "We have this enormous power to sway the public conversations about things like effective teaching or standards and mobilizing lots of resources in their favor without real robust data," one Gates official told Tompkins-Stange, adding, "I mean, it's striking to me, actually."

Tompkins-Stange reported that a number of Gates officials worry privately about the power they wield. There has even been some public acknowledgment of this concern, as we discussed earlier. Referencing the foundation's push for so-called common core standards, Gates CEO Sue Desmond-Hellmann observed, "Unfortunately, our foundation underestimated the level of resources and support required for our public education systems to be well-equipped to implement the standards. We missed an early opportunity to sufficiently engage educators—particularly teachers—but also parents and communities so that the benefits of the standards could take flight from the beginning."[10]

Humility is especially crucial in policy work because influencing policy is perhaps the most powerful tool a big giver can employ; it has had a role in almost every great historical example of philanthropy making an important and lasting contribution to progress. Think again of the reduction in smoking in this country. Or of the expansion of civil rights. Or of the environmental policies that have protected our air and water. Policy influence is crucial to change and has lasting repercussions, although, as we're seeing, it can also be undone quickly. So, givers shouldn't undertake it lightly, and they should do so with humility about the limits of the influence that any single person or institution should attempt to wield in a democracy.

Questions to answer before you decide policy influence should be part of your strategy:

◊ Is policy change needed for you to achieve your goals?
  ○ Is the needed policy change at the local, state, or federal level, or all of the above?
  ○ Are you in a position to act on any or all of those levels? If not, are there others in such a position with whom you can work?
◊ Is there a coalition of others who support your policy goals and, if not, can you build one?
  ○ Does the coalition include those who are closest to the action—those working directly with the people, communities, or fields that are most affected by the policies in question—and, when relevant, the intended beneficiaries themselves?
◊ How will you seek to influence policy through your giving and/or position?
  ○ Through funding research?

- ○ Through direct interactions with policymakers?
- ○ Through public leadership (such as speaking and writing)?
- ◊ Do you have the capacity, skills, and knowledge to do this?

Communications: A Means to an End

Efforts to make change often require a significant investment in communications. The Civil Marriage Collaborative used communications strategies to change public perceptions of same-sex marriage. Atlantic Philanthropies has successfully used smart communications and advocacy to help increase the number of US states banning capital punishment.[11]

Givers can also support efforts to document injustices as a way to build interest in an issue and mobilize action. In recent years, documentary films have chronicled issues from the treatment of illegal immigrants to climate change to rape on college campuses. Philanthropic support allowed these films to be made and promoted. Vince Stehle, executive director of Media Impact Funders, has argued that documentaries can be a counterweight to corporate voices in shaping public opinion. "Instead of just wringing their hands about the edge that companies now have in the political sphere," he suggested, givers "should realize that a small investment in documentaries and creative digital activism campaigns could help to bring some balance back into public policy debates."[12]

Givers might also seek to communicate in ways that don't relate directly to policy. For example, they might seek to raise awareness of an issue or problem without a clear point of view on the potential solutions. They might invest in communications to support dissemination of research findings they've supported—whether by seeking media coverage, writing op-eds, or other means. They might seek to raise awareness about an effective approach to addressing a problem. And givers might support grantees' communication efforts—through their financial contributions or assistance beyond the grant.

One CEO of a large foundation told me that she and her colleagues have recognized that they can't make the difference they aspire to make in one of their grantmaking areas—addressing a disease—without a significant communications effort. The CEO, whom I'll call Sarah, described what she sees as a typical evolution among big givers toward an appreciation of the role of communications.

"People start wanting to focus on the root cause. 'Let's cure the disease,'" she said. When that doesn't happen as quickly as hoped, there's often a recognition that "we need to do more to help those with the disease deal with living with it."

The foundation she leads is aware of some promising new treatments to help alleviate suffering. But the challenge then becomes to educate both medical professionals and patients about the promise of this new approach.

"That's where communication comes in," Sarah explained. Her foundation is still determining the best way to raise awareness, whether through grantmaking to nonprofits that can get the word out, through its own communications efforts, or, most likely, through a mix of the two. But one thing is clear: Communications are going to be key.

"People often undervalue communications in grantmaking," Sarah argued, and I agree.

It's always important, however, to see communications as a means to an end—to be clear on how it contributes to goal achievement. Don't just assume that a high profile for yourself is desirable, as some foundations and individual givers do. Sometimes, in these cases, attention is diverted away from grantees, robbing them of opportunities to build support and gain more funders. Or communications focused on a single giver's role can end up diminishing chances for collaboration because other givers don't know how they'll fit in. Too often, communications efforts aren't strategic; they don't engage the question of how communications are helpful to goal achievement.

Focusing narrowly on media mentions, reputation, and brand as ends in themselves may hinder rather than help a giver's programmatic causes. It's crucial to ask, as Sarah is doing, whom are we trying to influence, and to what end? From there, it becomes easier to see what the role of communications will be in your approach.

When used wisely, a foundation's or big giver's media profile and reputation can be powerful levers for influence and change. Ford Foundation president Darren Walker has effectively used his bully pulpit position to raise awareness and shape debates on crucial issues such as poverty and race. Bill and Melinda Gates and their foundation have drawn attention to people dying needlessly of diseases in ways that have mobilized interest, action, and giving. These examples illustrate the smart use of "brand" to achieve goals.

But most givers don't have the profile or history of Ford or Gates and will never be able to exert direct influence as effectively. In some cases, a giver's aims will be better served by being a low-key partner— supporting grantees in *their* efforts to get messages out rather than being the messenger.

Even givers with big names are sometimes wise to step out of the spotlight. The president of one of the most recognized foundations in the world told me a compelling story about when his foundation did just that so it could put the focus on grantees and other funders. In this case, stepping aside allowed the foundation to achieve more than it ever would have if it had sought to burnish its reputation by claiming credit for its work. Indeed, many of what that CEO considers the foundation's greatest achievements will never be widely seen as resulting from the foundation's work. And that's fine with him.

The point is impact, not celebrity.

Anonymity and Voice

While it's sometimes effective to step out of the spotlight, complete anonymity is usually not helpful to givers' ability to achieve their goals. I've seen givers who start out wanting to maintain anonymity, often because of genuine humility, but realize that this, too, can limit impact.

That was the case for Boston's Amos and Barbara Hostetter, whose multibillion-dollar net worth led them to establish the Barr Foundation, which, in its early years, did its giving anonymously. But the foundation was so large relative to its area of geographic focus that its giving was, essentially, an open secret. Today, the foundation has nearly $2 billion in assets and plays a significant role in shaping local debate and discussion related to climate and transportation, education, and the arts—as well as supporting organizations working in these areas directly through its giving.

"We began to realize that we don't have the privilege of stepping back and doing the work anonymously," Barbara Hostetter told *Boston* magazine. "We need to stand behind the work to leverage it and make it better."[13]

It's difficult to coordinate your work with others, make introductions, or build relationships while standing in the shadows of anonymity. Big givers and foundations, whether locally or nationally focused, have an opportunity to use their voices. The Barr Foundation's current president, Jim Canales, has a high profile in the Boston area by design: He uses his influence and relationships to push for sound policies related to climate change and the enhancement of the Boston waterfront, for example.

Speaking out can be powerful for givers with this kind of high profile. In the wake of videos of fatal police shootings of African American men surfacing on two consecutive days in July 2016—one in Louisiana and one in Minnesota—Heinz Endowments' Grant Oliphant decided he had to say something. He understood that with his position of privilege and influence (a local business journal named him the most influential person in Pittsburgh, where the foundation, with $2 billion in assets, is located and does much of its grantmaking) comes responsibility. He wrote a powerful blog post on the foundation's website:

> In my view of the field and institution I am privileged to serve, we have a special responsibility in our work and in our roles sometimes simply to bear witness. . . . Here in Pittsburgh efforts by our police chief to adopt community policing techniques and train officers in implicit bias have been ridiculed by some as "hug a thug." Think about the words. Please, just think about the words. In one terse little phrase they criminalize anyone the police encounter and make them less than the rest of us, less than human, an enemy deserving of whatever happens to them.[14]

Although the incidents didn't occur in Pittsburgh, Oliphant recognized the opportunity to weigh in and perhaps influence a debate—and give support to a local police chief trying to make change. Hours after his post went live, a man targeted and assassinated policemen in Dallas, but Oliphant didn't take the post down. He wrote another one, grieving over the violence, honoring the police who were killed doing their job that night, and making a plea for peace.

While Oliphant wasn't alone among philanthropic leaders in speaking out, many have stayed strangely silent as the nation endures a significant struggle related to race and policing. In an interview following his posts, he said, "The willingness of the field to say, 'This is a crisis and an emergency and we need to act on it'—that's not something that foundations have historically been good at." Philanthropy has to be "braver than we have been," he argued. "We are often silent."[15] A year and a half later, Oliphant and the Pittsburgh Community Foundation CEO Maxwell King wrote an op-ed taking on their local newspaper, the *Pittsburgh Post-Gazette*, for an editorial that Oliphant and King thought was excusing racism. Their decision to speak out sent a powerful message to the citizens of their city that racism had no place there.

Oliphant noted that too often, big givers remain quiet or issue carefully worded, hedging statements when difficult issues confront our nation or the world. But while they can't speak out about everything—and surely need to be humble about their role and about the degree to which their work is even known outside its grantee community—givers are uniquely positioned to take difficult stands. With access to charitable dollars comes the potential for influence, at least for those that are well-known in their communities. Such influence can be exerted as a powerful form of moral leadership, which can help create an environment in which others feel empowered to speak out, too.

Everyday citizens can also use their voices in ways that powerfully influence public debate, especially in an era of viral videos and tweets. In the wake of the mass shooting at the Marjory Stoneman Douglas High School in Florida in 2018, students spoke out as powerful advocates for gun law reform. Within a few days of opening a Twitter account, eighteen-year-old Emma Gonzáles had more followers than the National Rifle Association.[16] Think of your own community and the regular citizens who have influenced others' thinking on local issues, from what time school should start to where a traffic light should be added to reduce accidents. It's easy for givers to forget the power citizens have to use their voices, and not just their wallets, to effect change.

Questions to answer before you decide whether communications should be part of your strategy:

◊ Given your goals and strategy, what is the communications need and whom, exactly, are you trying to influence?

◊ Who is best positioned to get messages across, to which audiences, and for what purposes?

◊ What is the giver's role, and how does that relate to the role other donors, as well as grantees, are playing?

◊ How will you ensure coordination of communications efforts across relevant organizations working toward common goals?

◊ What are the opportunities for you to exert moral leadership by taking a stand publicly?

Alternative Investing Approaches

For the past century, big givers establishing foundations have tended to default to an identical approach to managing their assets: one that sees the investing and philanthropic sides as separate, with endowments invested to maximize returns to support the foundation's existence in perpetuity. Individuals, too, have tended to view their wealth creation and management as separate from their giving. They invest to maximize returns, and they often limit their giving to a fixed proportion of their total assets.

That all may be changing now. Three practices, in particular, seem to be on the uptick among individual and institutional givers alike:

◊ Giving earlier in life

◊ Seeking impact through investments in for-profit companies

◊ Avoiding investments that conflict with the individual's or institution's values and giving goals

Increasingly, givers are looking at their investments with an eye to greater impact, and there's a concerted push toward more "giving while living." The traditional model of discrete life stages—learn, earn, serve—has been upended by millennials who don't want to wait to make a difference. This is, in my view, all to the good because the more energy we spend trying to make an impact on tough challenges, the better our chances of success—especially when we do our work effectively. Furthermore, the more capital we can deploy in ways that support positive change, the better. True, there's nothing new about "giving while living" or limited life foundations. Sears, Roebuck leader Julius Rosenwald did all his giving in his lifetime in the 1920s and early 1930s. Rosenwald's giving focused on providing education for African Americans, which, along with other giving including that of the Peabody Education Fund, helped set the stage for the 1954 *Brown v. Board of Education* US Supreme Court decision and the desegregation of schools.[17]

Today, we see examples of other major givers following Rosenwald's lead. Chuck Feeney and his foundation, the Atlantic Philanthropies, are in the final years of spending all their wealth and are actively attempting to influence other givers to make the same choice they have made. More than 175 billionaires have taken the Giving Pledge, spearheaded by Bill Gates and Warren Buffett, and have pledged to dedicate at least half of their wealth to philanthropy. The aims of the pledge are "to help shift the social norms of philanthropy toward giving more, giving sooner, and giving smarter."[18]

It's said that "perpetuity is a very long time," and indeed it is. Yet, most givers to foundations have designated that their foundations should be established to exist forever, with spending on grantmaking and related administrative costs hovering around the legally mandated minimum of 5 percent. Among forty-nine of the largest US foundations that responded to a 2015 CEP survey, for example, just six are committed to a limited life.[19]

What this means, from a macro perspective, is that more and more foundation resources are sitting, untapped, in endowments. Meanwhile, there are pressing social challenges that require attention today. That fact, along with concerns about whether future staff and board can be relied upon to be faithful to donor intent, are the chief arguments against perpetuity. On the other hand, advocates for perpetuity argue that society benefits from institutions with a long-term view.

The arguments are well-trod. From my perspective, this is a pointless debate in the abstract. Like nearly all the choices a donor faces, this one should be considered in the context of goals and strategies.

◊ If you're focused on the arts in Baltimore, for example, you may well want your foundation to exist in perpetuity to ensure that your grant-making can provide support for key institutions for the long term.

◊ If, however, you're focused on eradicating a disease, you may be best served to spend down in the short term to find a cure and prevent future suffering.

The mistake donors make is to decide too early what their giving timetable will be—in the absence of this context. While the giver can always revisit the decision to spend out by a specific date, the decision to establish a foundation to exist in perpetuity, if communicated clearly in founding documents, lives long after the giver is dead. Givers would be wise to allow future generations to decide to spend down their foundations.

On the flip side, Duke University's Joel Fleishman has argued that pressure on megagivers who commit to spending all their resources in a given time can lead to less than effective philanthropy. He noted that even Andrew Carnegie, perhaps the most prominent early advocate of giving while living, ultimately left behind endowed institutions that still exist today because he recognized that this would be more effective than rushing to disburse all his assets in his lifetime. Fleishman's hope is that some of those who have committed to giving all of their charitable assets away by a set time, such as Gates and Zuckerberg, might rethink their choices, too.[20]

The point, again, is to decide how much to give in light of what you're trying to achieve. Foundations shouldn't just default to the mandated minimum 5 percent payout. Many observers have noted that the payout requirement floor has become the ceiling for many foundations. Debate about what is a reasonable spending level to maintain an endowment's real purchasing power is vigorous.

Endowed foundations especially should be mindful of their potential to be a countercyclical force, providing support for grantees during economic downturns to help offset reductions in individual contributions, government funding, or other earned revenue. Some, such as the Rockefeller Brothers Fund and the MacArthur Foundation, did this during the Great Recession, confident that they'd be able to grow their endowments later. Similarly, the

Rockefeller Brothers Fund and other foundations, such as the Nathan Cummings and David and Lucile Packard Foundations, increased their payout rates after Trump was elected president, believing progress toward their goals was imperiled by the new administration and that the nonprofits they supported needed additional funds in a suddenly more challenging context. Rose Letwin, the living donor behind the Wilburforce Foundation, similarly stepped up her foundation's giving toward environmental conservation by 15 percent in response to the changing political environments in both the United States and Canada, to build and engage new constituencies, address immediate threats, and seize conservation opportunities.

Unfortunately, this is more the exception than the rule. Givers tend to retrench when nonprofits retrench, essentially forfeiting one of their most powerful potential roles out of worry that they won't be able to claw their way back to the same endowment or asset levels afterward. In putting the preservation of their assets above all else—often, in the case of foundations, mistakenly believing that it's their fiduciary responsibility to do so—they simply exacerbate challenges for nonprofits during an already difficult time.

Foundations' relentless focus on endowment size is misguided. The goal should not be to have the largest endowment or always to be at peak real purchasing power relative to the past. The goal should be to balance the need to steward resources wisely with the mission of the foundation, which requires supporting nonprofits working today to address shared goals. Nonprofits must concern themselves with meeting payroll, and few have significant reserves. Foundations don't have this worry, and they can serve as a buffer for key grantees by taking a less rigid approach and flexing their grant spending in reaction to changes in context.

Individuals, too, can challenge themselves to be countercyclical forces—stepping up their giving in times when it's needed most and taking the long view of their assets and wealth. They can also carefully consider how much they really need for retirement and how much of their wealth they hope to pass along to their children—and from there, push themselves to give as much as they can. They can be inspired by the examples of givers like Jason Hackmann and the Sillcoxes, who have found a deep sense of purpose in their giving. If that's not enough to convince you to give more, check the research, which shows a correlation between giving and happiness.[21]

Impact Investing

Impact investing, in which givers seek social returns alongside financial ones, isn't new. The Ford Foundation was doing it decades ago through investments, for example, in inner-city businesses. Still, impact investing has recently morphed from a little-discussed practice among a few givers to seemingly being all the rage today, both for institutions and individuals. Multibillion-dollar foundations like Ford as well as the McKnight Foundation in Minneapolis have committed to investing 10 percent of their endowments in ways that align with their programmatic goals. Major investment and financial institutions such as BlackRock, Goldman Sachs, and Bain Capital now offer impact investing funds for wealthy individual donors.[22]

In early 2016, the F. B. Heron Foundation in New York, which seeks to use "every dollar" at its disposal for impact, took the unusual step of issuing a press release urging its peer foundations to follow its lead and "jettison outdated operating models that leave resources untapped in the face of systemic social ills." Clara Miller, then president of Heron, argued in her essay, "Building a Foundation for the 21st Century," that "money and mission were never meant to be apart."[23]

Heron, with nearly $300 million in assets, is a radical experiment in impact investing by foundations, in that the foundation is seeking to align all of its endowment with mission. The Nathan Cummings Foundation, also based in New York and with $500 million in assets, followed suit with a similar pledge in 2018. For the majority of foundations, however, grant-making and endowment management remain separate—with the possible exception of a small allocation for program- or mission-related investments. Miller described typical foundation operations as a "hedge fund with a small giving program attached to it."[24] She maintains that all foundations are doing impact investing—they just don't know whether the impact is positive or negative.

Heron's and now Nathan Cummings's efforts are perhaps the most significant experiments in contemporary philanthropy. It remains to be seen how they will play out. Implementation of a model like this is tough, and even more so for larger foundations. More than one foundation CEO has described to me these "all-in for impact" announcements as "B.S."—impossible to do while invested in public equities. Indeed, there are many questions.

One question is, *are there even sufficient investment opportunities that both align with a foundation's mission and generate financial returns?* While impact investing seems to be a crucial tool for givers focused on fostering economic development in a specific community, it's more difficult to figure out what opportunities might exist for, say, a child welfare–focused giver. Furthermore, impact investing opportunities have to be assessed with open eyes about the trade-offs in financial returns relative to other options. (In cases when there aren't trade-offs, a fair assumption would be that no special effort to invest is needed; capital will presumably find the investing options that have high returns.)

Another question is, *how do you gauge the impact of companies?* As a practical matter, it's often tough, if not impossible, even to know who is a good guy and who isn't among the major corporations in which foundation endowments are invested. For example, together with FSG, with which he is affiliated, Michael Porter of HBS has promoted companies such as Nestlé, Coca-Cola, and General Electric (GE) as exemplars of "shared value"— doing social good and making a profit (arguing there is no tension between the two). University of Essex sociologist Linsey McGoey is among those who raised questions about the concept of shared value's purported exemplars— and about what she sees as a dangerous blending of profit and philanthropy. "Admiration for Nestlé is not universally held," she wrote in her book *No Such Thing as a Free Gift*, adding that the company "has faced considerable criticism for allegedly encouraging intimidating and lethal union-busting tactics in Colombia, and for aggressively patenting tactics that restrict access to affordable medical procedures and food substances." She made similar critiques of Coca-Cola, which, along with Nestlé, has been criticized for contributing to an epidemic of obesity in developing countries, and GE, which has been called "one of the top ten 'greenwashers'"—accused of using disinformation to appear to be more environmentally conscious than it really is.[25]

The point is this: It isn't always easy to determine which companies are doing good work that could align with a foundation's mission, which ones are having a negative impact that runs counter to mission, and which are doing what is probably most common: a mix of both. Moreover, the number of investment opportunities that align with a foundation's programmatic goals is typically limited. So, especially for larger foundations, aligning everything—going "all-in for impact" with every dollar—is easier said than done.[26]

Individual and institutional givers alike should be wary of the impact investing hype. While more than 40 percent of large foundations say they do "impact investing" (and definitions of what exactly qualifies as such remain fuzzy), they are doing so with small dollars: 2.0 percent of endowment and 0.5 percent of program budget at the median.[27] Similarly, for individual givers, impact investing remains just a drop in the bucket. So far, impact investing isn't going to replace giving, as some overzealous proponents have suggested. Several leaders of foundations that have made significant recent commitments to impact investing have confessed to me privately that the jury is out. Still, there are opportunities where investing and social good align. In the words of Antony Bugg-Levine, CEO of the Nonprofit Finance Fund and a thoughtful and measured advocate of impact investing, the question should be, "What are the social issues we want to address, and how can impact investment be one part of an integrated solution?"[28]

Negative Screening and Other Tools

Like giving while living and impact investing, negative screening to avoid egregious conflict with values or goals isn't new. See, for example, the South Africa divestment movement of the 1980s or the tobacco divestment movement in the 1990s. Individuals and institutions have for decades sought ways to ensure they aren't supporting industries that are at odds with their values or religious beliefs through their investment portfolio.

Although negative screening remains rare among large foundations—just 17 percent of large foundations CEP surveyed in 2015 do any negative screening at all—the past several years have seen a number of significant examples of major foundations pledging to divest from entire industries.[29] There was, for example, the much-publicized decision of the Rockefeller Brothers Fund to divest from fossil fuels (which was especially noteworthy given the origins of the Rockefeller family's wealth).[30] Others, such as the Los Angeles–based California Endowment, with $4 billion in assets, have divested from for-profit prisons.[31] The effects of divestment from particular industries is much debated, with some arguing that it accomplishes nothing because there's no shortage of investors eager to maximize their returns in so-called vice industries. But others point, for example, to South Africa in the 1980s as an example in which divestment put pressure on that country's oppressive apartheid government.

The McKnight Foundation, as we've discussed, is a leader among large foundations in impact investing, putting 10 percent of its endowment to work in this way. But the other 90 percent isn't simply invested to maximize returns without regard to the foundation's mission and goals. The foundation seeks to exert influence through its investments in other ways, too.

> Our [investment] approach is organized around four points of leverage: our role as a customer of financial services, as a shareholder, as a market participant, and as an owner of assets. It provides a practical framework that we can scale up or down depending on financial and human resources, and it can assist experienced impact investors in flexing the muscle of their entire endowment.[32]

Given the size of its endowment, McKnight has been able to influence investment managers to offer new products and persuade companies to do more-accurate reporting of environmental impact.[33] Other foundations, too, have sought to use their roles as shareholders to influence corporate decisions; for example, by introducing resolutions on specific practices. McKnight's approach strikes me as a model other foundations and big givers should study, in part because the foundation and its leaders acknowledge the complexity of alignment between endowment and impact and are realistic about the limits.

Questions to answer as you consider how investing approaches will fit into your strategy:

◊ How do your investments relate to your giving?

◊ Are there certain industries or businesses in which you won't invest because doing so is counter to your giving goals?

◊ Will you seek to actively pursue your programmatic goals through investments in for-profit companies? What are the costs, benefits, and potential challenges?

◊ How do you define "impact investments," and, if you choose to pursue them, how will you measure their impact?

◊ What is your view on the time frame of your giving in light of your goals and strategies?

Influencing Business

Clarity about the roles the different sectors play is important not just in approaching impact investing but also in considering how givers will interact with business. After all, businesses play a crucial role in facilitating or impeding progress in many of the key areas in which givers do their work.

Some examples:

◊ For givers and nonprofits working to help at-risk youth in a community, raising awareness and building strong relationships with local businesses that are looking to hire will likely be crucial.

◊ For givers and nonprofits seeking to make progress on environmental issues, the need to challenge companies to do better, sometimes even to call out offenders—as well as an opportunity to highlight and work with exemplars—will likely be imperative.

◊ For givers and nonprofits working on childhood obesity, an essential part of their strategy might be to challenge companies producing and marketing products that contribute to obesity while also pursuing opportunities to highlight (and even invest in) businesses seeking to provide healthy foods to school cafeterias.

Just as givers often need to influence government to achieve their goals, they also need to influence business. Sometimes, business can be a crucial ally to givers, as was the case in the tuberculosis epidemic in the United States a century ago. Insurers like Metropolitan Life joined forces with foundations and nonprofits in supporting both research and education efforts. Metropolitan Life obviously had a vested interest in fewer deaths of its customers (and therefore fewer payouts to beneficiaries), but that shouldn't take anything away from the important role the company played.[34] At other times, givers will need to stand up to business or call on the government to do more to rein in corporate behavior, as is frequently the case in environmental work.

Pointing out that companies often have a role in givers' efforts to achieve their programmatic goals is not to suggest that philanthropy and business should somehow happily merge, with no distinctions to be drawn. Unfortunately, however, this seems to be what many hope to see happen.

As an MBA student at HBS almost two decades ago, I heard many people make gleeful predictions about blurring sector boundaries. James Austin, my professor in a second-year elective, predicted hopefully, "We'll see the stark differences between [nonprofit organizations] and business diminish, revealing a new world of integrated, rather than independent, sectors."[35] More recently, in 2016, Mark Kramer, of FSG and also now at HBS, declared in an interview that the "the lines between what is . . . a nonprofit versus a for-profit . . . is [sic] beginning to dissolve," and that "I hope that will really begin to break down some of the barriers between the sectors so they can start to work more effectively together."[36] It has become an article of faith that the boundaries are blurring between nonprofits and companies and that this is an inarguably positive development.

Neither of these assertions is true.

The growth in numbers of L3Cs or B Corps—"hybrid" companies seeking profit and impact—is often cited as evidence of boundary-blurring, despite the fact that their numbers relative to the number of existing non-profits literally round to zero. Those prophesying the happy merging of business and nonprofits into one sector-agnostic orgy of good-doing are often, as we've seen, faculty at business schools. But they have more in common with the guy on the street holding signs reading "The End Is Near"—as though some other guy hadn't held a similar sign two decades before—than they do with real scholars studying the actual facts.

The sectors remain distinct, playing distinct roles, and—contrary to the B-school hype—this is a good thing. My wife is a therapist and often notes that, in personal relationships, boundaries matter. We don't want our neighbor showing up unannounced every day, even if she's holding a casserole. So, too, do boundaries matter between the sectors.

What we need today is a further clarifying—not a blurring—of the boundaries between the sectors. Each sector plays a distinct role. We live in a market economy, but markets have limits—and markets fail—and that's why the nonprofit sector is so crucial.

Each sector needs the others to play its distinct role and play it well.

- Business needs government to set the rules of the game and to help ensure a strong infrastructure and the political stability required for market economies to thrive.
- Business needs nonprofits to pursue goals that can't be pursued while also generating profit and to call attention to issues that need to be addressed.
- Government needs a thriving business sector to create jobs and opportunities for citizens and to ensure enough tax revenue to allow it to take care of crucial infrastructure needs, as well as defense and a safety net for vulnerable citizens.
- Government also needs nonprofits to help deliver crucial services, strengthen civil society, build and sustain arts and culture organizations, and spur debate and discussion of important issues.
- And nonprofits, of course, depend on effective government and strong business in the ways we've been discussing.

No sector is superior, and it's time to stop engaging in the kind of "sector war" rhetoric that suggests otherwise. I hear it all too often. The hype about new hybrid forms replacing nonprofits as the primary means of addressing our vexing social problems is just that: hype.

The pursuit of profit and that of social impact goals may not always conflict, but they frequently do. Nonprofits are often working to address the very problems markets have failed to address. So, it makes little sense to maintain that "market approaches" are the answer to every problem.

Questions to answer as you consider the role of business in your strategy:

- What is the relationship of businesses—and which ones, specifically—to the achievement of your goals and the implementation of your strategies?
- Are businesses primarily allies or opponents to your giving goals—or a mix of both?
- Who is best positioned to build the relationships with businesses needed for success—you or your grantees?

All the Tools

Achieving your goals requires sound strategies. You'll pursue those strategies through grantmaking, but you'll also face choices about the other tools you can use: influence on policy, communications, alternate investing approaches, and interaction with business.

There is no one approach that cuts across contexts. What is right for you will depend on a deep understanding of the issues you care about, the roles others are playing, and how you can best contribute given the assets—financial and otherwise—that you bring to the table.

⋧⋞⋧⋞⋧⋞

Chapter 7 Review: Giving Guidance

1. **Giving is central to how givers can most make a difference, but there are other tools they should consider employing.** Big givers

especially have other means at their disposal through which they can make progress toward their goals, including policy influence, communications, investing approaches, and influencing business.

2. **Policy influence is a powerful lever that is crucial to achieving many objectives but should also be deployed with caution and sensitivity.** Much progress that giving has contributed to has involved policy influence, but there are also legitimate concerns about the influence of big givers on policy in a democratic society. Givers should approach policy influence with a sense of responsibility to ensure that the positions they're advocating are based in evidence and shared by those who will be most affected—and with a commitment to transparency and openness about what they're doing.

3. **Communications can likewise be crucial to achieving impact.** The role of communications, and the degree to which the giver should be visible, varies depending on the giver's context, goals, and strategies. Givers shouldn't chase publicity for its own sake but should recognize that they are sometimes in a unique position to raise awareness or speak out about crucial moral issues.

4. **Givers should consider the time frame for their philanthropy as well as whether to integrate their approaches to investing and giving.** Increasingly, givers are seeking to have positive influence through their investing or at least to avoid investment approaches that run counter to their giving goals. Those establishing foundations shouldn't default to perpetuity; they should consider the timetable for their giving in light of what they are seeking to achieve.

5. **Business is a crucial player affecting many issues givers care about, but the sectors play distinct roles, and boundaries are helpful.** Sometimes, alliances between givers and businesses are crucial; other times, givers serve as a critical check on and counterweight to business. Beware of hype regarding boundary-blurring and working across sectors, and chart a course that's sober and rooted in the particular context of your giving efforts.

Conclusion

A VIRTUOUS CYCLE OF GOOD

WHEN I MET Andre (a name he asked me to use instead of his real one) at the UTEC café in downtown Lowell, Massachusetts, in June 2018, he was twenty-five, with a bouncy walk and long dreadlocks, greeting everyone he knew with a hug. Gregg Croteau, UTEC's CEO, had introduced me to him, so I could hear directly from a young person typical of the kind UTEC serves. Andre told me that his "big mistake" had haunted him for the better part of a decade.

It had all started because he didn't enjoy being at home with a demanding father who argued frequently, and loudly, with Andre's stepmother. He had begun spending more and more time on the streets, hanging out with older guys—anything to get out of the house and to find community and connection. One of them, whom Andre had particularly wanted to impress, asked him to join him one night in a "stickup, to rob some white guys."

Andre knew he should say no, but he said yes, "to prove myself." No one was hurt. But he knew that night that he had made a terrible mistake.

He hoped he and his friends wouldn't be caught. A few weeks later, Andre was preparing for a big test in his high school geometry class. He wanted to do well, to learn the material and bring up his grade, so he studied hard and it paid off. He felt good about the test when it was over—like he had nailed it.

But when the bell rang, his high school principal came into the classroom. The police were at the school to talk with him. That night, he was arrested for robbery and assault with a deadly weapon. He would serve eighteen months in prison for the crimes. His life trajectory had changed in an instant.

In prison, "I thought all the time of all the heartache I gave my mom, all the tears she let go because one night I was so recklessly selfish," he told me. He learned how to survive in prison. But he also wondered what would happen when he'd done his time. "I acted tough inside because I had to. But I was scared," he told me. "What was I going to do? Where was I going to go when I got out?"

It wasn't easy when he finally did get out. "The drugs were starting to grab me," resulting in parole violations that landed him back in jail several times. He called a UTEC street worker he knew from UTEC's frequent visits to prison to see Andre and other incarcerated youth.

"I need help," Andre told him. The UTEC staff member told him to show up at UTEC's building the next day at 9:00 a.m.

"They Fathered Me"

At UTEC, Andre went to work—first in the mattress-recycling facility, and then, after just two weeks, he was "moved up" to the woodworking shop. Finally, he was promoted into the café kitchen, which he eventually managed. It wasn't a straight path as Andre worked to turn his life around. But he knew UTEC had his back. "People here understand that people make mistakes," Andre explained. "A lot of people look at me and my long dreads, and they think I am guilty until proven innocent. Here, it really is innocent until proven guilty."

For Andre, UTEC became a home, a source of unconditional love of a kind he had never experienced. "Everyone here gives you a hug when they see you. When I'd walk in, I'd feel like I was home. Like I was someone's kid. They fathered me, mothered me, brothered me, 'cousined' me. This place represents love."

UTEC also made him feel responsible and trusted. Andre talked to me about what he learned about "the importance of feeling important" and about his own growth as a person. He became involved in UTEC's advocacy efforts, helping to make the case to state legislators to allow for expungement of juvenile arrest records.

Now a father to a two-year-old about to enter UTEC's just-opened preschool, Andre has recognized his many strengths, including a gift for public speaking. He was a month away from being off probation, once and for all, when we talked. Having aged out of the program, he had moved on from UTEC to other jobs, but he came back frequently to see people. On this day, he gave hugs to his former coworkers in the café and to Croteau. He even greeted warmly the juvenile judge who crossed the street from the courthouse most days to have lunch at the UTEC café.

Andre's dream job? To come back to UTEC, or a place like it, as a counselor or street worker, helping young people get their lives on the right track.[1]

Andre's story is just one of millions.

It is a story of a life changed—transformed, even—by effective philanthropy supporting amazing nonprofits doing the work no one else is doing: helping those who need it most.

Effective giving to strong organizations like UTEC makes a difference. Don't let anyone tell you otherwise. Don't let anyone tell you that charitable giving isn't helping or that nonprofits in general aren't effective. It's not true.

There are stellar organizations like UTEC or ECHOS or countless others in your community—in every community. Many others work nationally, from ones you know, like the YMCA, to ones you may not know, like BELL. The same is true of givers.

You'll find effective individual givers working nationally and globally. You'll also find effective individual givers working locally. The same is true of institutional givers, from the many community foundations and regionally focused private foundations working in local communities to foundations that are working to address issues from poverty to climate change globally.

Great giving is all around us, often unseen.

Making It Count

Regardless of your focus, effective philanthropy requires both an understanding of the unique challenge of running a nonprofit and an awareness of the interdependent nature of problems. It necessitates specific goals, coherent strategies, strong relationships with those you're supporting, and smart performance indicators to help you understand whether you're on the right track. Sometimes, it requires tools beyond giving, from policy advocacy to impact investing. Most fundamentally, it requires a deep humility and a rejection of the prevailing conventional wisdom that analogizes nonprofits to businesses or giving to investing.

The subtitle of this book is *Effective Philanthropy and Making Every Dollar Count*. Ironically, the best way to make every dollar count is not to try to count every dollar by obsessing over exactly how the dollars you provide to a nonprofit are used.

Instead, get clear on your goals, which is no easy task. Find strategies that are likely to lead to progress against your goals—no cakewalk, either. Identify strong organizations doing effective work that aligns with your goals and strategies—also not easy. Then, give those organizations the kind of flexible support they desperately need.

Effective givers don't obsess about the different line items in a budget. They focus on understanding the issues, the context in which they're working, and finding organizations whose goals and strategies align with their own.

Effective givers, like the ones I've discussed in these pages, will reject the simplistic business analogies peddled by consultants, business school faculty, and countless others who claim to have good advice for aspiring philanthropists. It's tough to do. We live, after all, in an era in which markets seem to know no bounds.

But we need institutions whose primary purpose is mission, not profit. We need a nonprofit sector. And we need philanthropy to support it. This is a belief that has historically been shared among the wealthiest individuals and greatest successes in business—going back to the days of Andrew Carnegie.

But Princeton University historian Stanley Katz has observed a worrisome shift:

The current foundation rhetoric also makes use of a wide range of business metaphors, none more important than the notion that philanthropy is best thought of as "investment" in change, and frequently characterized, using the language of hedge funds, as "bets" on successfully producing change. Much of the current language of philanthropy is drawn from venture capital activity, and the new philanthropy can also be thought of as "venture" philanthropy. This is a new attitude.

The original philanthropists knew they were adapting the then-modern techniques of business organization and management to their grantmaking, but they thought of philanthropy as different from business. That distinction seems to have eluded much of the current generation of philanthropists.[2]

However, as I hope I have made clear in the preceding chapters, this distinction matters greatly. The lack of appreciation for it trips up givers in all kinds of ways.

- ❏ A failure to appreciate the distinct challenge of running a nonprofit contributes to giving that is more focused on where the money was spent than what the organization achieved.
- ❏ A lack of understanding that, in giving, there aren't the same competitive dynamics as in business leads givers to choose goals without sufficient attention to what other funders are doing, resulting in missed opportunities.
- ❏ A similar problem occurs with respect to strategy, where a focus on uniqueness that would serve a business well actually undermines givers.
- ❏ Ill-fitting analogies—to customers, contractors, or "investees"— lead givers to not appreciate the unique dynamics between the givers and the nonprofits they fund, undermining this crucially important relationship.
- ❏ A desire for a simple, universal performance measure—an analog to return on investment or profit—gets in the way of the kind of thoughtful assessment of progress that will yield real improvement.

The analogy to business undermines effective giving at every step of the way.

Who Needs Giving?

Some go further still, suggesting not just that philanthropy and nonprofits should emulate business, but that philanthropy may be irrelevant—that, perhaps, philanthropy isn't necessary. But, as I hope this book has helped to persuade you, the US philanthropic and nonprofit sector stands as an important example of the good that can be done, and indeed that has been done, by institutions that put mission above all else. Giving in the United States is the envy of many other countries—even as we too often take it for granted. Sure, we can lament that nonprofits in the United States are asked to do work that governments do in other countries. But in our country, with the choices we've made in our democracy about the role of government, nonprofits doing the wide range of work they do—supported by philanthropy—are essential. Without them, our country wouldn't be nearly what it is today, nor would we have seen the kind of striking progress we've witnessed in so many aspects of our lives.

Many would have you believe otherwise, and they point to the persistent problems we have in this country or globally as evidence of the "failure" of philanthropy. In recent decades, some business school faculty and consultants employing this argument have sought to essentially colonize the nonprofit sector, taking it over and applying their principles and values forcibly. The locus of study of the sector is now on business school campuses.

But "study" is not the right word because much of what occurs on these campuses includes little rigorous analysis of the sector, its history, or its role. Instead, the focus is on prognostication, on the assumption that what is useful in a business context will be useful in a philanthropic one. While exceptions exist, the bulk of those teaching and writing about the nonprofit sector and philanthropy at leading business schools know precious little about the subjects.

The same is true for media. Mainstream newspapers from the *New York Times* to the *Mercury News* in San Jose, California, have phased out their "philanthropy" or "nonprofit" beats, which means reporting on philanthropy and nonprofits is increasingly the domain of the business press—from the *Economist* to *Bloomberg* to *Forbes*. Story after story is written about the "new" donors who are bringing their "business smarts" to philanthropy, as though this were a new idea or a good one—when neither is the case. It is amazing how shallow much of the work is.

This trend needs to change. Thoughtful givers and nonprofit leaders need to stand up and make clear that their work is uniquely challenging and requires its own approach and discipline. It's no more logical to argue that running a successful business prepares you to run a nonprofit than it is to argue that running a real estate empire prepares you to be president of the United States.

Today, the philanthropic and nonprofit sectors tend to organize around perceived threats but aren't as good at articulating a strong, positive vision for themselves. Community foundations seek to defend themselves against charges that donor-advised funders should be regulated more aggressively. Associations like the Council on Foundations and Independent Sector have largely concentrated their efforts on opposing changes in regulations concerning the charitable deduction for contributions to nonprofits or foundations' minimum mandated payouts. That said, the current, recently appointed CEOs of both these organizations seem to understand the need for a more positive and assertive stance, which gives me hope.

What's been lacking is a positive and forceful case for the distinctiveness of philanthropy and the nonprofit sector as essential parts of what has made America, even with all its flaws, the successful, vibrant democracy it historically has been—and what will make it still more successful tomorrow.

Exemplifying Effectiveness

The best argument against the critics, finally, is even more—and more effective—giving. What it takes to be effective is often not new or different from what has characterized the most effective funders for the past century. The issue is that effective giving is not well enough understood and is exceedingly difficult to do. What it takes to be effective runs counter to current conventional wisdom.

It's important to remember that none of the givers I've discussed in these pages saw results quickly or easily. Success takes diligence and patience. Jason Hackmann has devoted countless hours, not to mention significant resources, to the effort to end childhood slavery in Ghana. The Gill Foundation and Haas, Jr. Fund spent years, and were willing to question assumptions and shift strategies, in their quest for marriage equality. Leslie and Mark Sillcox recognized that they couldn't achieve their goals of helping young people get a college education without also addressing the fact that many of them were undocumented and needed legal help.

There are no magic apps, secret formulas, quick fixes, or one-size-fits-all frameworks. But effective giving can produce extraordinary results.

On balance, I'm an optimist. I am fundamentally positive in my outlook about the role that givers and nonprofits have played, do play, and will play. Yes, there are also too many ineffective givers. But it is possible to believe both that givers are a crucial part of the social fabric of this country and have done much good *and* that they can, and must, do better. Just as all our institutions must do better.

So, let's focus on doing better. The payoff is worth it, after all.

Cycle of Good

The good you do through your giving doesn't just affect the recipients. It affects you, too. In a rigorous, five-year research effort called the Science of Generosity initiative, University of Notre Dame researchers studied the effects of generosity on those who give. "Those who give their resources away, receive back in turn," wrote Christian Smith and Hilary Davidson in their book on the study, *The Paradox of Generosity*. "In offering our time, money, and energy in service of others' well-being, we enhance our own well-being as well. In letting go of some of what we own for the good of others, we better secure our own lives, too. This paradox of generosity is a sociological fact, confirmed by evidence from quantitative surveys and qualitative interviews."[3]

Giving ripples inward and outward. Giving begets giving.

Tiffany Cooper Gueye hadn't worked at BELL long when she met Crisamar Martinez. Martinez was in the first grade and had just started in BELL's program, which, you'll remember, helps low-income students succeed. "Her first words to me when we met were, 'My name is Crisamar, and my sister is a genius,'" Gueye told me, remarking that she was struck by the way Crisamar admired her sister's intelligence.

Today, Martinez is twenty-five and works as a pharmaceutical sales rep. She credits much of her success in life to BELL.

"BELL helped form every single part of me," she told me. Her family came from the Dominican Republic when she was a baby and struggled financially. The support she received at BELL "brought so much life to my life," she explained. BELL, she said, gave her the confidence to pursue her passion for dance and become a leader. It also gave her academic confidence.

"I didn't love math. Now, I love math. I didn't love science. Now, I love science," Martinez said. Bell also "shaped my education and my moral values." She is grateful to all who helped her and is passionate about giving back. Witnessing her mother's battles with breast cancer inspired her to raise awareness about the issue while competing in beauty pageants in high school. She has also worked as a volunteer in Morocco, helping to establish health clinics. And she serves on the Advisory Council of the Red Sox Foundation.

"BELL taught us the importance of the little people who have a big impact in the world."[4]

BELL has been rigorously evaluated and shown to be effective in counteracting so-called summer learning loss. But formal evaluations can only capture so much. The ripple effects of giving to nonprofits like BELL or UTEC or ECHOS, the way they affect the lives of people like Martinez, who then commit themselves to affecting the lives of others, cannot be measured. It's what compels Andre to want to give back, and it's what inspired Yuri Valenzuela and Janice Guirola to want to work at ECHOS in Houston, the very organization that had helped them in their times of greatest need.

It's a virtuous cycle of good.

I hope you are inspired to give as much as you can give—and to do the hard work necessary to give effectively.

Giving, after all, is about the best of what this country is and what it can be, providing hope and opportunity and inspiration. Giving is a central part of what it means to be American. It is an element of who we are that is separate and distinct from our market economy or our government. It brings out the best in us. It has contributed to tremendous progress, domestically and globally. And we're just getting started.

It's time to double down on giving done right.

GIVING DONE RIGHT:
10 Differences Between
Ineffective and **Effective** Givers

INEFFECTIVE GIVERS	EFFECTIVE GIVERS
Think most nonprofits are poorly run and staff are overpaid	Understand that leading a nonprofit is uniquely challenging, requiring exceptional talent
Believe in need to find a unique goal or niche	Recognize that joining others in pursuit of shared goals is the best recipe for success
Think of strategy as if in a competitive context, with an emphasis on uniqueness, and believe strategy is static	Realize strategies in philanthropy should be broadly shared and will need to iterate based on continual feedback and learning
Believe there will be a quick-fix "innovation" that will solve complicated social problems	Recognize that there are multiple causes of our toughest problems and that progress can take decades and require many actors
See market-based solutions and "hybrid" organizations or "social enterprises" as the best way to address social problems	Recognize that many problems can't be solved by markets, or they'd be solved by now, and that philanthropy and the nonprofit sector play a crucial role in our society
See nonprofit grantees as implementers of their vision and seek to track how grantees spend every dollar	See nonprofit grantees as essential partners in achieving shared goals and provide consistent, unrestricted support
Look for one-size-fits-all performance measures, like administrative cost ratios or "cost per life touched"	Understand that assessment in giving is uniquely complex and crucially important and tailor their approaches to goals and strategies
Believe in reinventing philanthropy with a new approach	Recognize that good giving has accomplished a great deal and seek to learn from history
Seek credit and attention for its own sake	Focus on results, not credit
Hold a clear and fixed idea of what is best for those they seek to help without incorporating their views	Listen and learn from those who are most directly affected by problems and by the nonprofits working closely with them

GIVING RESOURCES

This is a noncomprehensive list of additional resources that can be helpful to givers. Also, for more about this book, go to givingdoneright.org.

Resources to Help You Choose Nonprofits to Support

- Your local community foundation
  - see cof.org/community-foundation-locator
- GuideStar
  - guidestar.org
- BBB Wise Giving Alliance
  - give.org
- Givewell
  - givewell.org
- Leap of Reason
  - leapofreason.org
- The Life You Can Save
  - thelifeyoucansave.org
- Social Programs That Work
  - evidencebasedprograms.org

Resources on Giving for Individual Givers

- The Center for Effective Philanthropy (CEP)
  - cep.org
- The Center for High Impact Philanthropy
  - impact.upenn.edu

- Giving Compass
  - givingcompass.org
- The Philanthropy Workshop
  - tpw.org
- National Center for Family Philanthropy
  - ncfp.org

Resources on Giving for Institutional Givers

- The Center for Effective Philanthropy (CEP)
  - cep.org
- Grantmakers for Effective Organizations
  - geofunders.org
- Council on Foundations
  - cof.org
- Foundation Center
  - foundationcenter.org
- National Committee for Responsive Philanthropy
  - ncrp.org
- Philanthropy Roundtable
  - philanthropyroundtable.org
- Exponent Philanthropy
  - exponentphilanthropy.org
- The Johnson Center at Grand Valley State University
  - johnsoncenter.org
- National Center for Family Philanthropy
  - ncfp.org
- Your regional association of grantmakers
  - For a listing, see United Philanthropy Forum: www.unitedphil forum.org/find-your-regional-philanthropy-serving-organization
- Issue-based associations of grantmakers
  - For a listing, see United Philanthropy Forum: unitedphilforum .org/national-philanthropy-serving-organizations
- CFLeads (for community foundation staff)
  - cfleads.org

Information on Volunteering

◊ VolunteerMatch
  ○ volunteermatch.org

Further Reading

How-To Books for Individual Givers

◊ *Give Smart: Philanthropy That Gets Results*, by Thomas J. Tierney and Joel L. Fleishman
◊ *Doing Good Better—Effective Altruism and a Radical New Way to Make a Difference*, by Will MacAskill
◊ *It Ain't What You Give, It's the Way You Give It: Making Charitable Donations That Get Results*, by Caroline Fiennes

How-To Books for Large-Scale and Institutional Givers

◊ *Money Well Spent: A Strategic Plan for Smart Philanthropy*, by Paul Brest and Hal Harvey
◊ *The Insider's Guide to Grantmaking: How Foundations Find, Fund, and Manage Effective Programs*, by Joel Orosz
◊ *Effective Foundation Management: 14 Challenges of Philanthropic Leadership—And How to Outfox Them*, by Joel Orosz

ACKNOWLEDGMENTS

Thanks especially are due to my wife, Lara—who provided much advice and counsel as I wrote this book and throughout my time at CEP (and before)—for all her love, humor, support, belief in me, and companionship. I am grateful also to her for her editorial suggestions, ideas, and encouragement to take on this project. Lara, my life changed for the better when you showed up in Dupont Circle in August 1992.

Thanks also to my daughters, Ava and Margo, who inspire me and who have encouraged me through the ups and downs of this project and life more generally. You each amaze me every day.

I am extremely grateful to my agent, Leah Spiro, who believed in me and in this project and helped me to reconceive of this book in a different and more useful way than I had been able to do on my own. Leah served as more than an agent, coaching me and editing chapter drafts. Special thanks go to my editor at PublicAffairs, Colleen Lawrie, who is a total pro and whose work—and spot-on and very direct critiques—greatly strengthened this book as well as the team of other staff there. I also owe thanks to her and to Peter Osnos for taking a chance on this project in the first place.

Nan Stone helped me organize and then improve very early versions of this book for no other reason than her generosity and belief in this project and in me. She then carefully edited a near-final draft; I am beyond grateful for her help. Lowell Weiss also provided detailed editorial suggestions that strengthened this book, and he has influenced my thinking about philanthropy.

The CEP Board of Directors has encouraged me patiently throughout the past two-plus years, granting me a sabbatical in the summer of 2016 that allowed me to begin work on this project. I am deeply grateful to each of them and especially to our board chair, Grant Oliphant, who has been an incredibly supportive coach and colleague throughout the entire process. A number of other current and former CEP board members have helped me to clarify my thinking on the issues discussed in this book, including Michael Bailin, Paul Beaudet, Kathleen Cravero, Alexa Cortes Culwell, Christine DeVita, Mark Edwards, Joel Fleishman, Phil Giudice, Tiffany Cooper Gueye, Crystal Hayling, Stephen Heintz, Christine James-Brown, Barbara Kibbe, Jim Knickman, Pat Kozu, Ricardo Millett, Richard (Dick) Ober, Hilary Pennington, Christy Pichel, Nadya Shmavonian, Kelvin Taketa, Fay Twersky, Anne Warhover, and Lynn Perry Wooten. Grant, Paul, Kathleen, Mark, Joel, Phil, Tiffany, Stephen, Dick, Hilary, Christy, Fay, and Vince in particular helped me by providing feedback, in some cases very detailed feedback, on earlier drafts of this book. Joel deserves special thanks for his roles as an early funder (when at Atlantic Philanthropies) of CEP, a CEP board member, a mentor to me, and as someone who helped behind the scenes to make this book possible (in ways others will never see and for which I am immensely grateful).

Others, beyond those I've already mentioned, have reviewed chapters, sections, or a full manuscript and provided me encouragement, editorial suggestions, and counsel, including Paul Brest, Joanne Creighton, Larry Kramer, Lindsay Louie, Mario Morino, Tony Richardson, Lorie Slutsky, and Henry Timms.

Ethan McCoy and Amy Monaghan provided crucial editing support. This book reads better because of them. I am also grateful to Stacy Palmer, editor of the *Chronicle of Philanthropy*, who has helped me over the years to clarify and improve my writing in pieces I have submitted as a columnist for her publication; some of the ideas I first floated in those columns are discussed in this book.

Nearly every member of the CEP staff—present and past—has contributed in some way to what I have written about here, and I'm grateful to each one, though I can't list them all here by name.

Alyse d'Amico helped me think through the structure of this book and its ideas (as she has done for much of my writing over the past fifteen years), edited early drafts, and took on additional work at CEP to allow me to focus on the book, as did my other close colleagues. She helped me get this project over the finish line, and I am deeply indebted to her for that.

CEP's Kevin Bolduc and Ellie Buteau, PhD, have done much work related to what I have written about and have provided significant advice and counsel as I wrote this book. Ellie has overseen the research and authored or coauthored many of the reports that inform my statements about what we know about giving practice. Kevin has either personally led or overseen the client engagements that inform many of the examples I discuss and also has worked on our research over the years.

Kevin, Ellie, and Alyse have been partners since almost day one in the creation of CEP and have been invaluable colleagues and friends. I am also grateful to the other members of the senior team at CEP. Grace Nicolette has encouraged me throughout this effort and provided advice and feedback on drafts, introductions to people I interviewed for the book, and crucial insights about how to write in a way that would be useful to individual as well as institutional givers. Jen Vorse Wilka, who leads CEP's YouthTruth initiative, and Alex Ocasio, who ensures CEP's financial health, are also invaluable close colleagues at CEP.

An informal "book club" of CEP staff reviewed early chapter drafts and provided great ideas and feedback, including some mentioned above and also Hannah Bartlebaugh, Mena Boyadzhiev, Hayden Couvillion, Jenny Goff, Tayo Ilegbusi, Sohail Kamdar, Della Menhaj, Naomi Orensten, Emma Poole, Emily Radwin, and Cathy Zhang.

Hannah Martin also provided feedback, as well as invaluable research support.

Jay Kustka helped create the "10 differences" table and various materials and resources associated with the promotion of this book. Tamara Gildengers Connolly created the images that accompany the four types of givers (charitable banker, perpetual adjuster, partial strategist, total strategist) I describe in Chapter 4. Ying Tao has helped plan (and execute) the marketing and outreach associated with this book.

I am especially grateful to my incredibly able assistant of well over a decade, Tia King-Fontánez, who supported me in doing much of the work I reference in this book. She also arranged many of the dozens of interviews I conducted specifically for this project—as well as the thousands of meetings and hundreds of trips that I have undertaken in my role at CEP and that inform my writing here.

Former CEP staffer Judy Huang and former board member Crystal Hayling were the first people to suggest I write a book about philanthropy, more than a decade ago, and I am grateful to them for their persistent encouragement.

A number of foundation leaders and philanthropy experts (beyond those already mentioned above) have influenced my thinking over the years through conversations and their writing, including Ed Cain, Chris Cardona, Marilyn Darling, Pam David, Pam Foster, Cynthia Gibson, Bob Hughes, Lucy Knight, Carol Larson, Risa Lavizzo-Mourey, Lindsay Louie, John Mullaney, Joel Orosz, Patti Patrizi, Ed Pauly, Hilary Pearson, Brian Quinn, Ann Stern, Darren Walker, and Kate Wolford, among numerous others. Enormous, special thanks to Darren for writing the foreword for this book and for all his encouragement and support. I am particularly grateful to Jim Canales, who has not only discussed effective giving with me for many years but who also, along with his Barr Foundation colleague Trevor Pollack, supported CEP in ways that allowed me to take my 2016 sabbatical.

Leaders of other "philanthropy-serving" organizations have also been great colleagues and sounding boards over the years. Friendly discussions and the occasional debate with colleagues such as Diana Aviv, David Biemesderfer, Jeff Bradach, Ronna Brown, Antony Bugg-Levine, Dan Cardinali, Tim Delaney, Aaron Dorfman, Deborah Ellwood, Kathleen Enright, Jacob Harold, Ellen LaPointe, Janine Lee, Tracy Palandjian, Hilary Pearson, Jeff Poulos, Brad Smith, and Anne Wallestad have influenced my thoughts on effective philanthropy and the nonprofit sector.

I am grateful to those who allowed me to interview them, tell their stories, or quote them in these pages, including some already mentioned above and also "Andre," Greg Baldwin, Gregg Croteau, Jason Hackmann, Steve Hilton, Rich Leimsider, Crisamar Martinez, Mary McClymont, Cathy Moore and the ECHOS staff, Robert Ottenhoff, Pat Reynolds-Hubbard, Patrick Rooney, Leslie and Mark Sillcox, and Ben Smilowitz. I draw on the stories and cases of numerous others from work that my colleagues and I have undertaken over the years and that has been previously published by CEP in reports or on our blog.

This book would not have come together were it not for the support and coaching that Doug Stone and Sheila Heen provided at their amazing, week-long "business book boot camp" in Newport, Rhode Island, in early 2017. I learned much from them and the other attendees at that session, whose friendship and encouragement has been so meaningful: Marsha Acker, Peter Hiddema, Sarah Hill, Diana Patton, and Kathryn Stanley.

I am deeply grateful to all the foundations that have provided grant support to CEP over the years or have been clients of CEP's—or both. The Robert Wood Johnson Foundation, William and Flora Hewlett Foundation, Barr Foundation, the David and Lucile Packard Foundation, Ford Foundation, S.D. Bechtel, Jr. Foundation, and Fund for Shared Insight have been especially generous and consistent supporters of CEP and the work that has informed this book.

A final thank you to my middle school history teacher, Robin Schauffler, who believed in me, called B.S. on me, and helped me to believe in myself in ways I have carried forward into adulthood. I know from experience that a single teacher can make an enormous difference in a person's life. Robin was that teacher for me.

NOTES

Introduction: It's Not Your Business

1. Ellie Buteau, Naomi Orensten, and Charis Loh, "The Future of Foundation Philanthropy: The CEO Perspective" (Cambridge, MA: The Center for Effective Philanthropy, 2016), 10, http://research.cep.org/the-future-of-foundation-philanthropy.

2. Jim Collins, *Good to Great and the Social Sectors: Why Business Thinking Is Not the Answer* (New York: HarperCollins, 2005), 1.

3. Mario Morino, interview by Phil Buchanan, January 21, 2018.

4. Nicholas Kristof, "Why 2017 Was the Best Year in Human History," *New York Times,* January 6, 2018, Opinion, https://www.nytimes.com/2018/01/06/opinion/sunday/2017-progress-illiteracy-poverty.html. Kristof cites research by Max Roser of Oxford and Steven Pinker of Harvard in this column.

5. Olivier Zunz, *Philanthropy in America: A History,* rev. ed. (Princeton, NJ: Princeton University Press, 2011).

6. "The Tobacco Campaigns of the Robert Wood Johnson Foundation and Collaborators, 1991–2010," RWJF Tobacco Retrospective Series (Purcellville, VA: Center for Public Program Evaluation, 2011), https://nebula.wsimg.com/bf3f972327b1a243101f5d3c3e88535e?AccessKeyId=BA4086636C5AC5631912&disposition=0&alloworigin=1.

7. "Hearts and Minds: The Untold Story of How Philanthropy and the Civil Marriage Collaborative Helped America Embrace Marriage Equality" (Amherst, MA: Proteus Fund, 2015), https://philanthropynewyork.org/sites/default/files/resources/heartsandminds-proteus-fund.pdf.

8. Andrew Carnegie, *The Autobiography of Andrew Carnegie and His Essay: The Gospel of Wealth,* reissue (London: Signet, 2006), 277–287.

Chapter 1: Nonprofits and Their Unsung American Heroes

1. Tiffany Cooper Gueye, "Remarks to CEP Staff," July 9, 2015. This description of Tiffany is based on the stories she told in this talk at a CEP staff retreat as well as subsequent interactions and email exchanges.

2. Ryan Seashore, "Run a Nonprofit Like a Startup to Move Fast and Help Things," *TechCrunch* (blog), January 6, 2015, http://social.techcrunch.com/2015/01/06/run-a-nonprofit-like-a-startup-to-move-fast-and-help-things/.

3. Alexis Ohanian, "The Startup Ethic and the Charitable Impulse," *Wired,* March 27, 2012, Opinion, https://www.wired.com/2012/03/startup-ethic-charity-impulse/.

4. Tiffany Cooper Gueye, email to Phil Buchanan, November 17, 2017.

5. Alexis de Tocqueville, *Democracy in America*, 13th ed. (London: Penguin Classics, 2003).

6. John W. Gardner, *Living, Leading, and the American Dream* (San Francisco: Jossey-Bass, 2003), 206.

7. Claire Gaudiani, *The Greater Good: How Philanthropy Drives the American Economy and Can Save Capitalism*, reprint (New York: Henry Holt, 2004), 1–2, 128–130.

8. Joel Fleishman, *The Foundation: A Great American Secret; How Private Wealth Is Changing the World* (New York: PublicAffairs, 2007), 11.

9. Fleishman, *The Foundation*, 13.

10. Fleishman, *The Foundation*, 15.

11. Nicole Wallace, "Where Are My Donors? With Fewer Americans Giving to Charity, Some Nonprofits Are Planning for an Uncertain Future," *Chronicle of Philanthropy*, June 5, 2018, https://www.philanthropy.com/article/Nonprofits-Plan-for-an/243573.

12. Patrick Rooney, interview by Phil Buchanan, September 10, 2018.

13. Olivier Zunz, *Philanthropy in America: A History*, rev. ed. (Princeton, NJ: Princeton University Press, 2011), 3.

14. Vu Le, "So, You Don't Think You Directly Benefit from Nonprofits," *Nonprofit AF* (blog), May 16, 2016, http://nonprofitaf.com/2016/05/so-you-dont-think-you-directly-benefit-from-nonprofits/.

15. Ariella Phillips, "Trust in Charities and Other Institutions Has Declined, Says a Report," *Chronicle of Philanthropy*, January 29, 2018, https://www.philanthropy.com/article/Trust-in-CharitiesOther/242360; Edelmen Trust Barometer, "2018 Executive Summary," http://cms.edelman.com/sites/default/files/2018-02/2018_Edelman_TrustBarometer_Executive_Summary_Jan.pdf.

16. Geraldine Fabrikant, "Harvard's Endowment Grew 10% Last Year, but Some Rivals Did Better," *New York Times*, September 28, 2018, https://www.nytimes.com/2018/09/28/business/harvard-endowment-gains.html.

17. "The Charitable Sector," Independent Sector, accessed July 9, 2018, https://independentsector.org/about/the-charitable-sector/.

18. Paul Beaudet, interview by Phil Buchanan, January 8, 2018.

19. Lester M. Salamon, *The State of Nonprofit America*, 2nd ed. (Washington, DC: Brookings Institution Press, 2012), 10.

20. Phil Buchanan, "Don't Believe the Hype, Believe the Data," *CEP Blog* (blog), April 5, 2011, http://cep.org/dont-believe-the-hype-believe-the-data/.

21. Indiana University Lilly Family School of Philanthropy, "Giving USA 2018" (Chicago: Giving USA Foundation, 2018), https://givingusa.org/giving-usa-2018-americans-gave-410-02-billion-to-charity-in-2017-crossing-the-400-billion-mark-for-the-first-time/.

22. "CAF World Giving Index 2017: A Global View of Giving Trends" (Kent, UK: Charities Aid Foundation, 2017), https://www.cafonline.org/docs/default-source/about-us-publications/cafworldgivingindex2017_2167a_web_210917.pdf.

23. Caroline Fiennes, *It Ain't What You Give, It's the Way That You Give It: Making Charitable Donations That Get Results* (Giving Evidence, 2012).

24. Tampa Bay Times, CIR, and CNN, "America's Worst Charities," *Tampa Bay Times*, accessed July 5, 2018, https://www.tampabay.com/resources/topics/specials/worst-charities/worst-charities.pdf.

25. Ken Berger, Jacob Harold, and Art Taylor, "Letter to the Donors of America," *The Overhead Myth* (blog), accessed July 5, 2018, http://overheadmyth.com/letter-to-the-donors-of-america/.

26. Paul Shoemaker, "Reconstructing Philanthropy from the Outside In" (Philanthropy Northwest, February 11, 2015), https://philanthropynw.org/news/reconstructing-philanthropy-outside.

27. David Wolcheck, email to Phil Buchanan, July 7, 2016.

28. Antoine Didienne, "Social Enterprises: The Fourth Sector," *Triple Pundit: People, Planet, Profit* (blog), March 3, 2016, http://www.triplepundit.com/2016/03/social-enterprises-fourth-sector/.

29. Heerad Sabeti, "The For-Benefit Enterprise," *Harvard Business Review*, November 2011, https://hbr.org/2011/11/the-for-benefit-enterprise.

30. "InterSector Partners, L3C," interSector Partners, L3C, accessed July 5, 2018, https://www.intersectorl3c.com; "B Corporation," B Lab, accessed July 5, 2018, http://www.bcorporation.net/.

31. Brice McKeever, "The Nonprofit Sector in Brief 2015: Public Charities, Giving, and Volunteering" (Washington, DC: Urban Institute, October 2015), https://www.urban.org/sites/default/files/publication/72536/2000497-The-Nonprofit-Sector-in-Brief-2015-Public-Charities-Giving-and-Volunteering.pdf.

32. Valerie Strauss, "Where Private Foundations Award Education Cash," *Answer Sheet—The Washington Post* (blog), July 25, 2011, https://www.washingtonpost.com/blogs/answer-sheet/post/where-private-foundations-award-education-cash/2011/07/24/gIQA0M0mYI_blog.html.

33. Stephen Sawchuck, "At 25, Teach for America Enters Period of Change," *Education Week*, January 15, 2016, https://www.edweek.org/ew/articles/2016/01/15/at-25-teach-for-america-enters-period.html.

34. Andrea Brock, Ellie Buteau, and An-Li Herring, "Room for Improvement: Foundations' Support of Nonprofit Performance Assessment" (Cambridge, MA: Center for Effective Philanthropy, 2012), http://research.cep.org/room-for-improvement-foundation-support-performance-assessment.

35. Ellie Buteau, Ramya Gopal, and Jennifer Glickman, "Assessing to Achieve High Performance: What Nonprofits Are Doing and How Foundations Can Help" (Cambridge, MA: Center for Effective Philanthropy, 2015), http://research.cep.org/assessing-to-achieve-high-performance-what-nonprofits-are-doing-and-how-foundations-can-help.

36. Gregg Croteau, several interviews by Phil Buchanan, including one at UTEC on December 20, 2017.

Chapter 2: So Many Ways to Give

1. Christine W. Letts, William P. Ryan, and Allen S. Grossman, "Virtuous Capital: What Foundations Can Learn from Venture Capitalists," *Harvard Business Review*, April 1997, https://hbr.org/1997/03/virtuous-capital-what-foundations-can-learn-from-venture-capitalists.

2. "The New Powers in Giving," *Economist*, June 29, 2006, Philanthropy, https://www.economist.com/special-report/2006/06/29/the-new-powers-in-giving.

3. Andrew Carnegie, *The Autobiography of Andrew Carnegie and His Essay: The Gospel of Wealth*, reissue (London: Signet, 2006).

4. Indiana University Lilly Family School of Philanthropy, "Giving USA 2018" (Chicago: Giving USA Foundation, 2018), https://givingusa.org/giving-usa-2018-americans-gave-410-02-billion-to-charity-in-2017-crossing-the-400-billion-mark-for-the-first-time/.

5. Arlyn Tobias Gajilan, "Something Had to Give: Dan Pallotta's Fundraising Business Was, as He Put It, 'Trying to Save the World.' So How Come It Couldn't Save Itself?" *CNN Money*, December 1, 2002, Small Business, http://money.cnn.com/magazines/fsb/fsb_archive/2002/12/01/333874/index.htm.

6. Dianne Chipps Bailey, "The Power of Giving Circles: Rocket Fuel for the Future of Philanthropy," *Huffpost*, November 21, 2017, https://www.huffingtonpost.com/entry/the-power-of-giving-circles-rocket-fuel-for-the-future_us_5a142c24e4b05ec0ae844589.

7. Jessica Bearman. Julia Carboni, Angela Eikenberry, and Jason Franklin, "The State of Giving Circles Today: Overview of New Research Findings from a Three-Part Study" (Cambridge, MA: Collective Giving Research Group, 2016), http://johnsoncenter.org/wp-content/uploads/2017/11/Giving-Circles-Research-Executive-Summary-WEB.pdf.

8. Bearman et al., "The State of Giving Circles Today."

9. "African American Women's Giving Circle," Washington Area Women's Foundation, accessed July 9, 2018, https://thewomensfoundation.org/african-american-womens-giving-circle/.

10. "Our Approach," Everychild Foundation, accessed July 5, 2018, https://everychildfoundation.org/about-us/our-approach/.

11. "2018 Donor-Advised Fund Report" (Jenkintown, PA: National Philanthropic Trust, 2018), https://www.nptrust.org/daf-report/index.html.

12. "100 Key Achievements," The Cleveland Foundation Centennial, accessed July 5, 2018, https://www.clevelandfoundation100.org/foundation-of-change/impact/100-key-achievements/.

13. Phil Buchanan, Ellie Buteau, and Mark Chaffin, "What Donors Value: How Community Foundations Can Increase Donor Satisfaction, Referrals, and Future Giving" (Cambridge, MA: Center for Effective Philanthropy, 2014), http://research.cep.org/what-donors-value-how-community-foundations-can-increase-donor-satisfaction-referrals-and-future-giving.

14. "New Hampshire Tomorrow," New Hampshire Charitable Foundation, accessed July 5, 2018, https://www.nhcf.org/what-were-up-to/focus-on/new-hampshire-tomorrow/.

15. Buchanan, Buteau, Chaffin, "What Donors Value."

16. Gary Quackenbush, "Community Foundation Sonoma County," *North Bay Business Journal*, March 27, 2018, http://www.northbaybusinessjournal.com/northbay/sonomacounty/8086040-181/community-foundation-sonoma-county.

17. "Hurricane Harvey Relief Fund," Greater Houston Community Foundation, accessed July 5, 2018, https://ghcf.org/learn/.

18. Heather Joslyn and Peter Olsen-Phillips, "Fidelity Charitable Tops United Way for 2nd Year in a Row in the Philanthropy 400," *Chronicle of Philanthropy*, November 1, 2017, https://www.philanthropy.com/article/Fidelity-Charitable-Tops/241612/.

19. Rebecca Morphis, email to Phil Buchanan, July 27, 2018.

20. David Gelles, "How Tech Billionaires Hack Their Taxes with a Philanthropic Loophole," *New York Times*, August 3, 2018, https://www.nytimes.com/2018/08/03/business/donor-advised-funds-tech-tax.html.

21. Ray D. Madoff, "Congress's Assault on Charities," *New York Times*, January 20, 2018, Opinion, https://www.nytimes.com/2017/11/26/opinion/congress-charities-giving .html.

22. Lewis B. Cullman and Ray Madoff, "The Undermining of American Charity," *New York Review of Books*, July 14, 2016, http://www.nybooks.com/articles/2016/07/14/the -undermining-of-american-charity/.

23. Patrick Rooney, "Have Donor-Advised Funds and Other Philanthropic Innova-tions Changed the Flow of Giving in the United States?" *Nonprofit Quarterly*, November 7, 2017, https://nonprofitquarterly.org/2017/11/07/have-donor-advised-funds-and-other -philanthropic-innovations-changed-the-flow-of-giving-in-the-united-states/.

24. "2018 Donor-Advised Fund Report."

25. Indiana University Lilly Family School of Philanthropy, "Giving USA 2018."

26. Joel Fleishman, *The Foundation: A Great American Secret; How Private Wealth Is Changing the World* (New York: PublicAffairs, 2017), xv.

27. Joel J. Orosz, *Effective Foundation Management: 14 Challenges of Philanthropic Leadership—and How to Outfox Them* (Lanham, MD: AltaMira Press, 2007), 27–36.

28. Benjamin Soskis, "The Importance of Criticizing Philanthropy," *The Atlan-tic*, May 12, 2014, https://www.theatlantic.com/business/archive/2014/05/the-case-for -philanthropy-criticism/361951/.

29. Megan Tompkins-Stange, "Through a Glass Darkly: How Transparent Should Foundations Be?" *CEP Blog* (blog), July 12, 2016, http://cep.org/glass-darkly-transparent -foundations/.

30. Michael Edwards, "Will Zuckerberg and Chan End the Philanthropic Oligar-chy?" *Chronicle of Philanthropy*, December 4, 2015, https://www.philanthropy.com/article /Opinion-Will-Zuckerberg-and/234477/.

31. Anand Giridharadas, "Beware Rich People Who Say They Want to Change the World," *New York Times*, August 24, 2018, https://www.nytimes.com/2018/08/24/opinion /sunday/wealth-philanthropy-fake-change.html.

32. Diane Ravitch, *The Death and Life of the Great American School System: How Test-ing and Choice Are Undermining Education* (New York: Basic Books, 2010).

33. Sean Parker, "Philanthropy for Hackers," *Wall Street Journal*, June 26, 2015, Life, https://www.wsj.com/articles/sean-parker-philanthropy-for-hackers-1435345787.

34. Christopher Hayes, *Twilight of the Elites: America after Meritocracy* (New York: Crown, 2012), 13.

35. Ellie Buteau, Ramya Gopal, and Phil Buchanan, "Hearing from Those We Seek to Help: Nonprofit Practices and Perspectives in Beneficiary Feedback" (Cambridge, MA: Center for Effective Philanthropy, October 2014), http://research.effectivephilanthropy.org /hearing-from-those-we-seek-to-help-nonprofit-practices-and-perspectives-in-beneficiary -feedback.

36. Jeremy Heimans and Henry Timms, "New Power: How Power Works in Our Hyper-connected World—and How to Make It Work for You" (New York: Doubleday 2018).

37. Joyce Gannon, "Heinz Endowments Refocuses Its Grantmaking Strategy," *Pitts-burgh Post-Gazette*, February 28, 2016, Business, http://www.post-gazette.com/business /pittsburgh-company-news/2016/02/28/Heinz-Endowments-refocuses-its-grantmaking -strategy/stories/201602210078.

38. Several paragraphs in this section are drawn from a 2016 essay I wrote and that CEP published entitled "Big Issues, Many Questions."

39. Ellie Buteau, Naomi Orensten, and Charis Loh, "The Future of Foundation Philanthropy: The CEO Perspective" (Cambridge, MA: Center for Effective Philanthropy, 2016), 10, http://research.cep.org/the-future-of-foundation-philanthropy.

40. Stephen Heintz, email to Phil Buchanan, August 2, 2018.

41. Rose Letwin, "Deepening Commitment in a Moment of Change," *CEP Blog* (blog), May 17, 2018. http://cep.org/deepening-commitment-in-a-moment-of-change/.

42. Paul Beaudet, interview by Phil Buchanan, January 8, 2018.

43. Andrea Brock, Phil Buchanan, and Ellie Buteau, "Essentials of Foundation Strategy" (Cambridge, MA: Center for Effective Philanthropy, 2009), http://research.cep.org/essentials-of-foundation-strategy.

44. Jennifer Glickman, Matthew Leiwant, and Ellie Buteau, "Staying Connected: How Five Foundations Understand Those They Seek to Help" (Cambridge, MA: Center for Effective Philanthropy, 2017), http://research.cep.org/staying-connected-how-five-foundations-understand-those-they-seek-to-help.

45. Jason Hackmann, interview by Phil Buchanan, June 18, 2018.

46. Keosha Varela, "Death Row Attorney Bryan Stevenson on 4 Ways to Fight Against Injustice" (The Aspen Institute, 2016), https://www.aspeninstitute.org/blog-posts/death-row-attorney-bryan-stevenson-4-ways-fight-injustice/.

47. Bryan Stevenson, "Against the Odds: Finding Mercy and Justice for the Most Vulnerable" (April 4, 2017).

48. Henry Gass, "Juvenile Incarceration Rate Has Dropped in Half. Is Trend Sustainable?" *Christian Science Monitor*, November 10, 2015, USA | Justice, https://www.csmonitor.com/USA/Justice/2015/1110/Juvenile-incarceration-rate-has-dropped-in-half.-Is-trend-sustainable?utm_content=bufferd8ed0&utm_medium=social&utm_source=twitter.com&utm_campaign=buffer.

49. Trita Parsi, *Losing an Enemy: Obama, Iran, and the Triumph of Diplomacy* (New Haven, CT: Yale University Press, 2017), 330.

Chapter 3: A Tough Balance

1. Mark and Leslie Sillcox, interview by Phil Buchanan, May 30, 2018.

2. Paul Brest and Hal Harvey, *Money Well Spent: A Strategic Plan for Smart Philanthropy* (New York: Bloomberg Press, 2008), 22–23.

3. "Finding Your Focus in Philanthropy: What Challenges Will You Tackle, and What Do You Want to Achieve?" (Rockefeller Philanthropy Advisors, August 2018), https://www.rockpa.org/wp-content/uploads/2017/08/Finding-Your-Focus.pdf.

4. Peter Singer, *The Most Good You Can Do: How Effective Altruism Is Changing Ideas About Living Ethically* (New Haven, CT: Yale University Press, 2015), 117.

5. Singer, *The Most Good You Can Do*, 117.

6. Singer, *The Most Good You Can Do*, 117–136.

7. Phil Buchanan et al., "New Models of Philanthropy: What's Promising, What's Not" (May 21, 2015), https://www.youtube.com/watch?v=hWbJPeY_tDo.

8. "Dustin Moskovitz," *Forbes*, accessed July 6, 2018, https://www.forbes.com/profile/dustin-moskovitz/.

9. Mario Morino, interview by Phil Buchanan, January 21, 2018.

10. Kasia Moreno, "The Top Five Most Promising Trends in Philanthropy," *Forbes*, March 2, 2015, Forbes Insights, http://www.forbes.com/sites/forbesinsights/2015/03/02 /the-top-five-most-promising-trends-in-philanthropy.

11. Daniel Coit Gilman, "Five Great Gifts," *The Outlook*, 1907.

12. "Eradicating Hookworm," The Rockefeller Foundation: A Digital History, https:// rockfound.rockarch.org/eradicating-hookworm.

13. William Schambra, "Root Causes vs. Reality," *Philanthropy Magazine*, 2004.

14. Joel L. Fleishman and Thomas J. Tierney, *Give Smart: Philanthropy That Gets Results*, (New York: PublicAffairs, 2011), 26–27.

15. Shawn Reifsteck, email to Phil Buchanan, August 6, 2018.

16. Mark R. Kramer and Michael E. Porter, "Philanthropy's New Agenda: Creating Value," *Harvard Business Review*, December 1999, https://hbr.org/1999/11/philanthropys -new-agenda-creating-value.

17. Ellie Buteau, Phil Buchanan, and Ramya Gopal, "How Far Have We Come? Foundation CEOs on Progress and Impact" (Cambridge, MA: Center for Effective Philanthropy, 2013), http://research.effectivephilanthropy.org/how_far_have_we_come.

18. Jim Collins, "CEP 2009 Conference Highlights" (April 31, 2009), http://cep.org /programming/national-conferences/2009-conference/.

19. Bill Gates, "A Conversation with Bill Gates: Making a Healthier World for Children and Future Generations," interview by Bill Moyers, May 9, 2003, https://billmoyers .com/content/conversation-bill-gates-making-healthier-world-children-future-generations -transcript/.

20. "What We Do," Bill & Melinda Gates Foundation, accessed July 6, 2018, https:// www.gatesfoundation.org/What-We-Do.

21. Rich Leimsider, interview by Phil Buchanan, June 8, 2018.

22. Dale Russakoff, *The Prize: Who's in Charge of America's Schools?* (Boston, MA: Houghton Mifflin Harcourt, 2015).

23. Russakoff, *The Prize*, 27–28.

24. Russakoff, *The Prize*, 212–213.

25. Steven Hilton, interview by Phil Buchanan, January 31, 2018.

26. Hilton, interview.

27. Nick Wingfield, "Jeff Bezos Wants Ideas for Philanthropy, So He Asked Twitter," *New York Times*, December 22, 2017, Technology, https://www.nytimes.com/2017/06/15 /technology/jeff-bezos-amazon-twitter-charity.html.

Chapter 4: Strategy Done Right

1. Pat Reynolds-Hubbard, interview by Phil Buchanan, August 8, 2018.

2. Reynolds-Hubbard, interview.

3. Judith A. Ross, "Striving for Transformative Change at the Stuart Foundation," case study, Lessons from the Field (Cambridge, MA: Center for Effective Philanthropy, December 2009), http://www.effectivephilanthropy.org/wp-content/uploads/2014/01 /TransformativeChange_Stuart.pdf.

4. Ross, "Striving for Transformative Change at the Stuart Foundation."

5. Reynolds-Hubbard, interview.

6. Sharon Van Epps, "New Attitudes Toward Adoption from Foster Care Offer Hope," *Washington Post*, July 24, 2017, Perspective, https://www.washingtonpost.com/news/parenting/wp/2017/07/24/new-attitudes-toward-adoption-from-foster-care-offer-hope/.

7. Ross, "Striving for Transformative Change at the Stuart Foundation."

8. Kevin Bolduc et al., "Beyond the Rhetoric: Foundation Strategy" (Cambridge, MA: Center for Effective Philanthropy, 2007).

9. Paul Brest and Hal Harvey, *Money Well Spent: A Strategic Plan for Smart Philanthropy*, 2nd ed. (Stanford, CA: Stanford Business Press, 2018), 46–47.

10. Jason Beaubien, "The New Debate over Bed Nets and Malaria Prevention," *NPR*, November 22, 2016, Health, https://www.npr.org/sections/goatsandsoda/2016/11/22/503036774/the-new-debate-over-bed-nets.

11. Bill Gates, "Why I Would Raise Chickens," *GatesNotes* (blog), June 7, 2016, https://www.gatesnotes.com/Development/Why-I-Would-Raise-Chickens.

12. "Cluck You: Bolivia Rejects Bill Gates' Donation of Hens," *Guardian*, June 15, 2016, World news, http://www.theguardian.com/world/2016/jun/15/bolivia-rejects-bill-gates-hens-donation.

13. Andres Schipani, "Bill Gates's Hen Donation Plan Ruffles Feathers in Bolivia," *Financial Times*, June 16, 2016, Americas Society, https://www.ft.com/content/06d25074-335b-11e6-bda0-04585c31b153.

14. Bill and Melinda Gates, "The 10 Toughest Questions We Get," February 13, 2018, https://www.gatesnotes.com/2018-Annual-Letter.

15. William MacAskill, *Doing Good Better: How Effective Altruism Can Help You Help Others, Do Work That Matters, and Make Smarter Choices About Giving Back*, reprint (New York: Avery, 2016), 1–4.

16. Phil Buchanan and Aaron Dorfman, "'Strategy' Is Essential to Grass-Roots Movements," *Chronicle of Philanthropy*, June 16, 2013, https://www.philanthropy.com/article/Strategy-Is-Essential-to/154705/.

17. Phil Buchanan, "Philanthropic Strategy," *Stanford Social Innovation Review*, February 12, 2014, https://ssir.org/articles/entry/five_myths_that_perpetuate_poor_philanthropic_strategy.

18. David Segal, "In Letter, Warren Buffett Concedes a Tough Year," *New York Times*, February 28, 2009, Business, https://www.nytimes.com/2009/03/01/business/01buffett.html.

19. Patricia Patrizi and Elizabeth Heid Thompson, "Beyond the Veneer of Strategic Philanthropy," *The Foundation Review* 2, no. 3 (January 1, 2011): 52–60, https://doi.org/10.4087/FOUNDATIONREVIEW-D-10-00022.

20. Patrizi and Thompson, "Beyond the Veneer of Strategic Philanthropy."

21. Paul Brest has been immensely supportive of CEP (Hewlett has been among CEP's largest, and sometimes the largest, grant funders for a number of years).

22. Paul Brest, "Strategic Philanthropy and Its Discontents," *Stanford Social Innovation Review*, April 27, 2015, https://ssir.org/articles/entry/strategic_philanthropy_and_its_discontents.

23. Paul Brest, "A Decade of Outcome-Oriented Philanthropy," *Stanford Social Innovation Review*, Spring 2012.

24. Hal Harvey, "Why I Regret Pushing Strategic Philanthropy," *Chronicle of Philanthropy*, April 4, 2016, https://www.philanthropy.com/article/Opinion-Why-I-Regret-Pushing/235924.

25. Chris Addy et al., "Making Big Bets for Social Change," *Stanford Social Innovation Review*, Winter 2016.

26. Larry Kramer, "Against 'Big Bets,'" *Stanford Social Innovation Review*, Summer 2017, https://ssir.org/articles/entry/against_big_bets.

27. Larry Kramer, "Stop Disrupting for Disruption's Sake," *BRIGHT Magazine*, March 7, 2018, https://brightthemag.com/philanthropy-disruption-big-bet-moonshots-9c6c3639644d.

28. Peter Sims, *Little Bets: How Breakthrough Ideas Emerge from Small Discoveries*, reprint (New York: Simon and Schuster, 2013).

29. Thomas J. Kane, "Develop and Validate, then Scale," *Education Next*, October 15, 2018, https://www.educationnext.org/develop-validate-scale-lessons-gates-foundation-effective-teaching-strategy/.

30. Addy et al., "Making Big Bets for Social Change."

31. Felix Salmon, "Elon Musk, Mark Zuckerberg, Jeff Bezos, and Ethically Iffy 'Philanthropy,'" *Wired*, May 15, 2018, https://www.wired.com/story/musk-zuckerberg-bezos-and-ethically-iffy-philanthropy/?mbid=social_twitter_onsiteshare.

32. "Against Malaria Foundation," GiveWell, November 2017, https://www.givewell.org/charities/amf.

33. Andrea Brock, Phil Buchanan, and Ellie Buteau, "Essentials of Foundation Strategy" (Cambridge, MA: Center for Effective Philanthropy, 2009), http://research.cep.org/essentials-of-foundation strategy.

34. Brock, Buchanan, and Buteau, "Essentials of Foundation Strategy."

35. Ben Smilowitz, interview by Phil Buchanan, March 16, 2018.

36. Robert Ottenhoff, interview by Phil Buchanan, March 22, 2018.

37. Phil Buchanan et al., "New Models of Philanthropy: What's Promising, What's Not" (May 21, 2015), https://www.youtube.com/watch?v=hWbJPeY_tDo.

38. Sylvia Yee, "Equal Effort," *Stanford Social Innovation Review*, Fall 2014.

39. Yee, "Equal Effort."

40. Yee, "Equal Effort."

Chapter 5: Essential Partners

1. Dave Peery, "Grantees as Customers," *Stanford Social Innovation Review*, November 26, 2013, https://ssir.org/articles/entry/grantees_as_customers.

2. "Best Charities for Highly Effective Giving," The Life You Can Save, accessed July 6, 2018, https://www.thelifeyoucansave.org/best-charities.

3. "The Performance Imperative: A Framework for Social-Sector Excellence" (Leap of Reason, April 2018), https://leapambassadors.org/products/performance-imperative/.

4. Mario Morino, interview by Phil Buchanan, January 21, 2018.

5. Cathy Moore, interview by Phil Buchanan, June 5, 2018; Epiphany Community Health Outreach Services staff and volunteers, interview by Phil Buchanan, June 5, 2018.

6. Sacha Pfeiffer, "Corporate Volunteers Can Be a Burden for Nonprofits," *Boston Globe*, March 25, 2015, Business, https://www.bostonglobe.com/business/2015/03/24/unwanted -volunteers/SNJQGGMQUUcIhYFh6M6k4M/story.html.

7. Greg Baldwin, interview by Phil Buchanan, March 8, 2018.

8. Paul Brest and Hal Harvey, *Money Well Spent: A Strategic Plan for Smart Philanthropy* (New York: Bloomberg Press, 2008), 22–23.

9. Gregg Croteau, interview by Phil Buchanan, December 20, 2017.

10. Ellie Buteau, Jennifer Glickman, and Matthew Leiwant, "Relationships Matter: Program Officers, Grantees, and the Keys to Success" (Cambridge, MA: Center for Effective Philanthropy, 2017), http://research.cep.org/relationships-matter_program-officers _grantees_keys-to-success.

11. John Esterle, Malka Kopell, and Palma Strand, "From the Kids' Table to the Adults' Table: Taking Relationships Seriously in a World of Networks" (San Francisco: The Whitman Institute, n.d.), https://thewhitmaninstitute.org/wp-content/uploads /FromTheKidsTabletoAdultsTable.pdf.

12. "Trust-Based Philanthropy," The Whitman Institute, accessed July 6, 2018, https:// thewhitmaninstitute.org/grantmaking/trust-based-philanthropy/.

13. "Grantmaking Strategies," Einhorn Family Charitable Trust, accessed July 6, 2018, https://www.efct.org/grantmaking-strategies.

14. Ethan McCoy, "High-Engagement Funders & Strong Funder-Grantee Relationships: Are They Mutually Exclusive? (Hint: No.)," *CEP Blog* (blog), June 2, 2016, http:// cep.org/high-engagement-funders-strong-funder-grantee-relationships-are-they-mutually -exclusive-hint-no/.

15. McCoy, "High-Engagement Funders & Strong Funder-Grantee Relationships."

16. Phil Buchanan, Margot Rogers, and Jennifer Hoos Rothberg, "A Fresh Take on the Funder-Grantee Power Dynamic: A Conversation on Supporting High Performance," (January 30, 2018), https://www.youtube.com/watch?v=SY1KsuO9I0k.

17. Ellie Buteau, Charis Loh, and Temitayo Ilegbusi, "Strengthening Grantees: Foundation and Nonprofit Perspectives," (Cambridge, MA: Center for Effective Philanthropy, 2018), https://cep.org/portfolio/strengthening-grantees-foundation-and-nonprofit-perspective/.

18. "Our Portfolio," RippleWorks Foundation, accessed July 6, 2018, http://www .rippleworks.org/portfolio/.

19. Andrew Jacobs, "A Simple Way to Improve a Billion Lives: Eyeglasses," *New York Times*, May 5, 2018, Health, https://www.nytimes.com/2018/05/05/health/glasses -developing-world-global-health.html.

20. Buteau, Loh, and Ilegbusi, "Strengthening Grantees."

21. Jeri Eckhart-Queenan, Michael Etzel, and Sridhar Prasad, "Pay-What-It-Takes Philanthropy," *Stanford Social Innovation Review*, Summer 2016.

22. "Grantee Experience," The David and Lucile Packard Foundation, accessed July 6, 2018, https://www.packard.org/grants-and-investments/for-our-current-grantees /grantee-experience/.

23. Paul Beaudet, "Putting Grantees in the Center of Your Map," *CEP Blog* (blog), January 24, 2012, http://cep.org/putting-grantees-in-the-center-of-your-map/.

24. Tony Richardson on a CEP webinar (February 13, 2018).

Chapter 6: No Easy Answers

1. Peter F. Drucker, *Managing the Non-Profit Organization: Principles and Practices* (New York: HarperCollins, 1992), 107.

2. "Toward a Common Language: Listening to Foundation CEOs and Other Experts Talk About Performance Measurement in Philanthropy" (Cambridge, MA: Center for Effective Philanthropy, 2002); "Indicators of Effectiveness: Understanding and Improving Foundation Performance" (Cambridge, MA: Center for Effective Philanthropy, 2002).

3. Jim Collins, *Good to Great and the Social Sectors: Why Business Thinking Is Not the Answer* (New York: HarperCollins, 2005), 7.

4. Matthew Bishop and Michael Green, *Philanthrocapitalism: How the Rich Can Save the World* (London: Bloomsbury Press, 2008), 219.

5. Ellie Buteau, Ramya Gopal, and Jennifer Glickman, "Assessing to Achieve High Performance: What Nonprofits Are Doing and How Foundations Can Help" (Cambridge, MA: Center for Effective Philanthropy, 2015), http://research.cep.org/assessing-to-achieve-high -performance-what-nonprofits-are-doing-and-how-foundations-can-help.

6. Ellie Buteau, Ramya Gopal, and Phil Buchanan, "Hearing from Those We Seek to Help: Nonprofit Practices and Perspectives in Beneficiary Feedback" (Cambridge, MA: Center for Effective Philanthropy, October 2014), http://research.effectivephilanthropy.org /hearing-from-those-we-seek-to-help-nonprofit-practices-and-perspectives-in-beneficiary -feedback.

7. Buteau, Gopal, and Buchanan, "Hearing from Those We Seek to Help."

8. Tanya Beer et al., "Benchmarking Foundation Evaluation Practices" (Cambridge, MA: Center for Effective Philanthropy and Center for Evaluation Innovation, 2016), http:// research.cep.org/benchmarking-foundation-evaluation-practices.

9. This is the actual mission statement of the Seattle Children's Museum, but the rest of the example is fictional.

10. "Roca Inc.," Strategic Grant Partners, accessed July 6, 2018, http://www.strategic grantpartners.org/project/roca-inc/.

11. Srik Gopal and Lisbeth B. Schorr, "Getting 'Moneyball' Right in the Social Sector," *Stanford Social Innovation Review*, June 2, 2016, https://ssir.org/articles/entry/getting _moneyball_right_in_the_social_sector.

12. Patrick Lester, "Defining Evidence Down," *Stanford Social Innovation Review*, July 14, 2016, https://ssir.org/articles/entry/defining_evidence_down.

13. Anthony Petrosino, Carolyn Turpin-Petrosino, Meghan E. Hollis-Peel, Julia G. Lavenberg, "Scared Straight and Other Juvenile Awareness Programs for Preventing Juvenile Delinquency: A Systematic Review," The Campbell Collaboration, June 2012.

14. Beer et al., "Benchmarking Foundation Evaluation Practices."

15. "The Center for Evidence-Based Mentoring," The National Mentoring Partnership, accessed July 6, 2018, https://www.mentoring.org/program-resources/the-center-for -evidence-based-mentoring/.

16. Ellie Buteau, Phil Buchanan, and Ramya Gopal, "How Far Have We Come? Foundation CEOs on Progress and Impact" (Cambridge, MA: Center for Effective Philanthropy, 2013), http://research.effectivephilanthropy.org/how_far_have_we_come.

17. Beer et al., "Benchmarking Foundation Evaluation Practices."

18. Andrea Brock, Ellie Buteau, and An-Li Herring, "Room for Improvement: Foundations' Support of Nonprofit Performance Assessment" (Cambridge, MA: Center for Effective Philanthropy, 2012), http://research.cep.org/room-for-improvement-foundation-support-performance-assessment.

19. Brock, Buteau, and Herring, "Room for Improvement," 21.

20. Ellie Buteau and Phil Buchanan, "The State of Foundation Performance Assessment: A Survey of Foundation CEOs" (Cambridge, MA: Center for Effective Philanthropy, September 2011), http://research.cep.org/state-of-foundation-performance-assessment.

21. Buteau and Buchanan, "The State of Foundation Performance Assessment."

22. Beer et al., "Benchmarking Foundation Evaluation Practices."

23. Phil Buchanan, Ellie Buteau, and Shahryar Minhas, "Can Feedback Fuel Change at Foundations? An Analysis of the Grantee Perception Report" (Cambridge, MA: Center for Effective Philanthropy, 2011), http://research.cep.org/can-feedback-fuel-change-at-foundations.

24. Fay Twersky, Phil Buchanan, and Valerie Threlfall, "Listening to Those Who Matter Most, the Beneficiaries," *Stanford Social Innovation Review*, Spring 2013.

25. "How One Innovative School Network Uses Student Perception Data for Continuous Improvement" (San Francisco, CA: YouthTruth, August 15, 2014), http://youthtruthsurvey.org/charter-network-uses-data-continuous-improvement/.

26. "Putting the Pieces Together: Student Feedback in Evergreen Elementary School District" (San Francisco, CA: YouthTruth, May 2018), http://youthtruthsurvey.org/wp-content/uploads/2018/05/Evergreen-School-District-YouthTruth-Case-Study.pdf.

27. Twersky, Buchanan, and Threlfall, "Listening to Those Who Matter Most, the Beneficiaries."

28. Beer et al., "Benchmarking Foundation Evaluation Practices."

29. Sean Parker, "Philanthropy for Hackers," *Wall Street Journal*, June 26, 2015, Life, https://www.wsj.com/articles/sean-parker-philanthropy-for-hackers-1435345787.

30. Julia Angwin, Jeff Larson, Surya Mattu, and Lauren Kirchner, "Machine Bias," *ProPublica*, May 23, 2016, https://www.propublica.org/article/machine-bias-risk-assessments-in-criminal-sentencing.

31. Kate Zernike, "Obama Administration Calls for Limits on Testing in Schools," *New York Times*, October 24, 2015, US, https://www.nytimes.com/2015/10/25/us/obama-administration-calls-for-limits-on-testing-in-schools.html.

Chapter 7: Deploying All the Tools

1. Leslie R. Crutchfield, John V. Kania, and Mark R. Kramer, *Do More than Give: The Six Practices of Donors Who Change the World*, (Hoboken, NJ: John Wiley & Sons, 2011).

2. www.chanzuckerberg.com/about, accessed September 7, 2018.

3. Dana Brakman Reiser, "Is the Chan Zuckerberg Initiative the Future of Philanthropy?" *Stanford Social Innovation Review*, Summer 2018, https://ssir.org/articles/entry/the_rise_of_philanthropy_llcs.

4. Olivier Zunz, *Philanthropy in America: A History*, rev. ed. (Princeton, NJ: Princeton University Press, 2011), 77.

5. Zunz, *Philanthropy in America*, 201.

6. Kris Putnam-Walkerly and Elizabeth Russell, "Many Voices, One Goal: How an Informal Foundation Collaborative Helped Make California History" (San Francisco: Stuart Foundation, December 10, 2014), http://stuartfoundation.org/wp-content/uploads/2016/05/Many-Voices-One-Goal-Stuart-LCFF-FINAL_12-10-20141.pdf.

7. Crystal Hayling, "Where Does Good Strategy Start? Listen Up," *CEP Blog* (blog), September 17, 2015, http://cep.org/where-does-good-strategy-start-listen-up/.

8. Megan E. Tompkins-Stange, *Policy Patrons: Philanthropy, Education Reform, and the Politics of Influence*, (Cambridge, MA: Harvard Education Press, 2016), 145.

9. Tompkins-Stange, *Policy Patrons*, 145.

10. Sue Desmond-Hellmann, "What If . . . A Letter from the CEO of the Bill & Melinda Gates Foundation," 2016, https://www.gatesfoundation.org/2016/ceo-letter.

11. Annmarie Benedict and Eric Brown, "Advocating an End to the Death Penalty," The Case for Communications (Stanford, CA: Stanford Social Innovation Review, July 20, 2016), https://ssir.org/articles/entry/advocating_an_end_to_the_death_penalty.

12. Vincent Stehle, "A Revolution in Documentaries as Advocacy Tools," *Chronicle of Philanthropy*, October 2, 2011, https://www.philanthropy.com/article/A-Revolution-in-Documentaries/157757/.

13. Patti Hartigan, "Who's Behind the Barr Foundation?" *Boston*, January 31, 2016, News, https://www.bostonmagazine.com/news/2016/01/31/barr-foundation-boston/.

14. Grant Oliphant, "Enough," *The Point* (blog), July 7, 2016, http://www.heinz.org/blog-the-point/blog-detail?id=33.

15. Grant Oliphant, *Heinz Endowments Chief: Philanthropy Faces Critical Test on Racial Equity* (Tiny Spark, 2016), https://html5-player.libsyn.com/embed/episode/id/4518500/height/90/width/640/theme/custom/autonext/no/thumbnail/no/autoplay/no/preload/no/no_addthis/no/direction/backward/no-cache/true/render-playlist/no/custom-color/a93a3a/.

16. Mary Bowerman, "Parkland Student Emma Gonzalez Has More Followers than NRA Days After Joining Twitter," *USA Today*, February 26, 2018, News, https://www.usatoday.com/story/news/nation-now/2018/02/26/parkland-student-emma-gonzalez-has-more-followers-than-nra-days/372757002/.

17. Pamela Barnhouse Walters and Emily A. Bowman, "Foundations and the Making of Public Education," in *American Foundations: Roles and Contributions* (Washington, DC: The Brookings Institution, 2010), 31–50.

18. "The Giving Pledge," Giving Pledge, accessed July 6, 2018, https://givingpledge.org/About.aspx.

19. Phil Buchanan, Ellie Buteau, and Jennifer Glickman, "Investing and Social Impact: Practices of Private Foundations" (Cambridge, MA: Center for Effective Philanthropy, 2015), http://research.cep.org/investing_and_social_impact.

20. Joel L. Fleishman, *Putting Wealth to Work: Philanthropy for Today or Investing for Tomorrow?* (London: Hachette UK, 2017).

21. Christian Smith and Hilary Davidson, *The Paradox of Generosity: Giving We Receive, Grasping We Lose* (New York: Oxford University Press, 2014).

22. Jay Coen Gilbert, "Putting the Impact in Impact Investing: 28 Funds Building a Credible, Transparent Marketplace," *Forbes*, October 9, 2017, https://www.forbes.com

/sites/jaycoengilbert/2017/10/09/putting-the-impact-in-impact-investing-28-funds -building-a-credible-transparent-marketplace/.

23. Clara Miller, "Building a Foundation for the 21st Century" (New York: Heron Foundation, January 25, 2016), http://www.heron.org/sites/default/files/Clara%20Miller --Building%20a%20Foundation%20for%20the%2021st%20Century--FINAL_0.pdf.

24. Phil Buchanan et al., "New Models of Philanthropy: What's Promising, What's Not" (May 21, 2015), https://www.youtube.com/watch?v=hWbJPeY_tDo.

25. Linsey McGoey, *No Such Thing as a Free Gift: The Gates Foundation and the Price of Philanthropy* (New York: Verso, 2015), 96–97.

26. Several paragraphs in this discussion of impact investing are drawn from a 2016 essay I wrote and that CEP published entitled "Big Issues, Many Questions."

27. Buchanan, Buteau, and Glickman, "Investing and Social Impact."

28. Willy Foote, "Impact Investing Headwinds: A Conversation with Antony Bugg-Levine," *Forbes*, August 1, 2013, https://www.forbes.com/sites/willyfoote/2013/08/01 /impact-investing-headwinds-a-conversation-with-antony-bugg-levine/2/#2e6ab04b7fe6.

29. Buchanan, Buteau, and Glickman, "Investing and Social Impact."

30. John Schwartz, "Rockefellers, Heirs to an Oil Fortune, Will Divest Charity of Fossil Fuels," *New York Times*, December 21, 2017, US, https://www.nytimes.com/2014/09/22/us /heirs-to-an-oil-fortune-join-the-divestment-drive.html.

31. Nicole Wallace, "California Endowment Spurns Investment in Private Prisons," *Chronicle of Philanthropy*, December 9, 2015, https://www.philanthropy.com/article /California-Endowment-Spurns/234533/.

32. Kate Wolford and Ted Staryk, "Looking Beyond Impact Investing to Support Climate Solutions," *Stanford Social Innovation Review*, November 30, 2015, https://ssir.org /articles/entry/looking_beyond_impact_investing_to_support_climate_solutions.

33. Wolford and Staryk, "Looking Beyond Impact Investing to Support Climate Solutions."

34. Zunz, *Philanthropy in America*, 50–52.

35. Nancy O. Perry, "Strategic Alliances," *Working Knowledge*, January 25, 2000, Research & Ideas, http://hbswk.hbs.edu/item/strategic-alliances.

36. Mark Kramer, "Mark Kramer on Collective Impact," interview by Greg Cherry, June 28, 2016, http://www.philanthropyhour.com/blog/2016/6/10/mark-kramer-on-shared -value.

Conclusion: A Virtuous Cycle of Good

1. "Andre," interview by Phil Buchanan, June 11, 2018.

2. Stanley Katz, Maribel Morey, and Benjamin Soskis, "Learning from Philanthropy's Past: An Interview with the HistPhil Blog," interview by Neil Edgington, November 10, 2015, http://www.socialvelocity.net/2015/11/learning-from-philanthropys-past-an -interview-with-the-histphil-blog/.

3. Christian Smith and Hilary Davidson, *The Paradox of Generosity: Giving We Receive, Grasping We Lose* (New York: Oxford University Press, 2014), 224.

4. Crismar Martinez, interview by Phil Buchanan, June 22, 2018.

INDEX

Affiliations, giving related to, 41–43, 61
African American Women's Giving Circle,
    42
Against Malaria Foundation, 99
Agriculture production, support for
    advances in, 48–49
Alma mater, giving to, 41–42
Amazon, 80
Ambition, and effective giving, 54–57, 61,
    76–81, 96–98, 105, 188
American Civil Liberties Union (ACLU),
    160–161
American Red Cross, 17, 100–102
Andre, UTEC beneficiary, 185–187
Anonymity in philanthropy, 168–169
Arnold Foundation, 162
Astaire, Fred, 14
Atlantic Philanthropies, 16, 166, 172
At-risk youth, organization to alter life
    trajectories of, 142, 185–187
Austin, James, 180

B corps, 25–27, 180–182
Bailin, Michael, 150
Bain Capital, 175
Baldwin, Greg, 116
Ballmer, Steve, 47
Barr Foundation, 168–169
BBB Wise Giving Alliance, 24
Beaudet, Paul, 19, 55–56, 132
BELL (Building Educated Leaders for Life),
    11–14, 18, 28, 31, 32, 143, 146,
    187, 192–193
Bennett, Bob, 116

Berger, Ken, 24
Berkshire Hathaway, 37–38
Bezos, Jeff, 80
Big bets on proven strategies, 97–99
Bill & Melinda Gates Foundation
    assets of, 75
    Buffett stock gift to, 37–38, 51
    communications and raising awareness
        about goals of, 168
    education goals of, 51, 75, 90–91, 98,
        153, 164–165
    Fund for Shared Insight role of, 154
    global health and global development
        goals of, 75–76, 98, 168
    grants made by, 45
    overhead of nonprofits, changing views
        on, 24
    polio eradication efforts of, 69
    vaccine and immunization initiative,
        98
Bishop, Matthew, 51, 139
BlackRock, 175
Bolduc, Kevin, 8, 86, 103, 118
Bolivia, chickens for, 90
Booker, Cory, 77
Brest, Paul, 95–97, 119
Bridgespan Group, The, 130
Broad, Eli, 51, 164–165
Brown v. Board of Education, 172
Buffett, Warren, 37–38, 51, 94, 172
Bugg-Levine, Antony, 177
Building Educated Leaders for Life (BELL),
    11–14, 18, 28, 31, 32, 143, 146,
    187, 192–193

Business
    blurring boundaries between
        nonprofits and, 25–27, 180–182,
        183
    business strategy and strategy in
        philanthropy, 92–95, 105–106,
        188–191
    business thinking for nonprofits and
        effectiveness of giving, 3–5,
        71–73, 138–139, 146, 188–191
    interaction with and influence on,
        179–183
    shared value exemplars, 176–177
Buteau, Ellie, 8, 86, 103, 140
Butterfly effect, 7

Cain, Edmund, 79
California Endowment, 162, 178
Canales, Jim, 169
Capacity building, 119, 126–127, 128–129
Capital projects, 119, 129
Carnation Company, 84
Carnegie, Andrew, 16, 38, 47, 67, 173
Carnegie Corporation, 162
Carter Center, Global Development
    Initiative, The, 79
Center for Disaster Philanthropy, 102
Center for Effective Philanthropy (CEP)
    benchmarking study by, 145, 150
    board of directors of, 8
    funding research by, 119
    grant support for, 8, 108
    offices of, 8
    research and surveys conducted by,
        1–2, 6–7, 8
    research on goals of foundations, 72
    research on strategy use at
        foundations, 86–88
    research on understanding needs of
        beneficiaries by foundations, 53,
        54
    staff at, 8
    YouthTruth initiative, 153–154
    See also Grantee Perception Report
        (GPR)

Center for Evaluation Innovation, 145, 150
Chan Zuckerberg Initiative (CZI), 161
Charitable bankers, 87–88
Charity Navigator, 24, 99
Chicago Community Trust, 24
Child Welfare Program, 83–86
Children's museum, performance
    assessment of, 140–142
Children/youth
    Building Educated Leaders for Life
        (BELL), 11–14, 18, 28, 31, 32,
        143, 146, 187, 192–193
    drug, crime, and delinquency
        prevention programs, 144
    foster care, efforts to help children in,
        83–86, 105, 119, 131
    gang members, efforts to improve lives
        of, 29–32, 120, 185–187
    Ghana, child slavery in, 57–59, 191
    incarceration of and juvenile justice
        reform, 59–60
    mentoring programs, 27, 63–64, 145,
        192
    obesity problems, efforts to address,
        163, 179–180
    at-risk youth, organization to alter life
        trajectories of, 142, 185–187
    See also Education
Choices, for giving
    how to channel giving, 38, 41–50, 61
    who to give to, 109–117, 128–134,
        195–196
Citi Foundation, 24
Civil Marriage Collaborative, 5–6,
    103–104, 162, 166
Civil rights
    desegregation of schools, 162, 172
    LGBT people, civil rights for,
        102–105, 131, 137, 162
    policy on, influence of philanthropy
        on, 162, 165
    See also Race issues
Cleveland Foundation, 43
Climate change, 70–71, 163, 168–169
ClimateWorks Foundation, 70–71, 96

Coca-Cola, 176

Cocarico, César, 90

Cochrane Library, 146

CodeNow, 13

Collins, Jim, 4, 74–75, 137

Common Cause, 15

Commonwealth Fund, 150

Communications strategy, 160, 166–171, 182–183

Community Foundation Boulder County, 44

Community Foundation of Greater Birmingham, 43

Community Foundation Sonoma County, 44

Community foundations, 43–45, 46, 61, 110, 121, 191

Conrad N. Hilton Foundation, 78–81, 105

Contractor analogy, 189

Cope, Pam, 57

Corporate volunteer projects, 116

Corporation for Supportive Housing, 80

Council on Foundations, 191

CrimeSolutions.gov, 146

Criminal justice
    data use for sentencing decisions, 156
    for-profit prisons, divestment from, 178
    reform initiatives, 59–60, 137, 162
    resources on existing knowledge and best practices, 146

Croteau, Gregg, 29–32, 120, 143, 185, 187

Cullman, Lewis, 46

Customer analogy, 108–109, 117, 189

Cycle of giving resulting from giving done right, 7, 192–193

DAFs (donor-advised funds), 43, 44–47

D.A.R.E., 144

Data and statistical analysis for decision-making, 155–158

David and Lucile Packard Foundation, 70–71, 130–131, 174

Davidson, Hilary, 192

de Tocqueville, Alexis, 14, 38

Dependency, concerns about, 21–22

Desegregation of schools, 162, 172

Desmond-Hellmann, Sue, 165

Diabetes care initiative, 145, 149

Didienne, Antoine, 26

Disaster Accountability Project, 101

Disaster preparedness, relief, and recovery, 44, 79, 100–102, 106

Distance, proximity, and problem-solving, 57–59

Diversity, of givers, 38–39

Documentaries, 166

Donor-advised funds (DAFs), 43, 44–47

Dorr, John V. N., 68–69

Dorr, Nell, 68–69

Dorr Foundation, 68–69

Drucker, Peter, 136

eBay, 161

ECHOS (Epiphany Community Health Outreach Services), 113–116, 154–155, 187, 193

Edelman Trust Barometer, 17

Edna McConnell Clark Foundation, 18, 146, 150

Education
    African Americans, education for, 172
    big bets on strategies for, 97–98
    Building Educated Leaders for Life (BELL), 11–14, 18, 28, 31, 32, 143, 187, 192–193
    challenge of solutions for, 97–98
    community foundation goals, 43–44
    data and statistical analysis for decision-making about, 157
    desegregation of schools, 162, 172
    funding for, initiatives to overhaul, 162
    Gates Foundation goals, 51, 75, 90–91, 98, 153, 164–165
    Horizons for Homeless Children, 21–22
    Newark initiative on, 77–78, 91, 97–98
    policy on, influence of philanthropy on, 51, 164–165

Education *(continued)*
　realistic goals about interventions
　　related to, 69–70
　resources on existing knowledge and
　　best practices, 146
　Sillcox foundation goals, 63–64, 76
　Teach for America (TFA), 28
　test scores as basis for performance,
　　157
　undocumented students, assistance
　　for, 76
　Washington, DC, initiative on, 78,
　　97–98
　YouthTruth initiative, 153–154
Edwards, Michael, 51
Effective altruism movement, 65–67
Effective giving/philanthropy
　essential ingredients for, 2–3, 6–7,
　　8–9, 191–192, 194
　giving to nonprofits as most important
　　and effective tool, 26, 32,
　　185–189
　importance of, 191–192
　ineffective givers compared to
　　effective givers, 194
　negative effects of ineffective giving,
　　7
　results from, 59–61
　skills and techniques for, 9, 60–61
　tools to maximize impact, 159–160,
　　182–183
Einhorn, David, 124
Einhorn Family Charitable Trust (EFCT),
　124–126, 154
Eli and Edythe Broad Foundation, The, 51,
　164–165
Elites, faith and trust in, 50–54, 163–165
Empire Blue Cross Blue Shield, 145
Endowment for Health, 151–152
Energy Foundation, 96
Enron, 52
Environmental Defense Fund, 15
Environmental issues
　challenging companies on and calling
　　out offenders, 179, 180

policy on, influence of philanthropy
　on, 160, 165, 168–169
protection initiatives, 18
Wilburforce Foundation initiatives, 19,
　54–56, 59, 132, 174
Epiphany Community Health Outreach
　Services (ECHOS), 113–116,
　154–155, 187, 193
Episcopal Health Foundation, 115
Equal Justice Initiative, 59–60
Esterle, John, 123
Eugenics movement, 68
Evelyn and Walter Haas, Jr. Fund,
　103–104, 131, 191–192
Evergreen School District, 154
Everychild Foundation, 42
evidencebasedprograms.org, 144, 146
Eye glasses, for poor people, 126–127

F. B. Heron Foundation, 175–176
Facebook, 25, 47, 52, 66, 77, 161
Family office, 38, 47
Feeney, Chuck, 172
Fidelity Charitable, 45, 46
Fires, support following, 44
501(c)(3) organizations, 18, 160–161
501(c)(4) organizations, 160–161
Fleishman, Joel, 16, 48, 68, 173
Flooding, support following, 44
Ford Foundation
　communications strategy of,
　　167–168
　Fund for Shared Insight role of, 154
　Green Revolution support from,
　　48–49
　impact investing by, 175
　influence on policy by, 162, 164,
　　167–168
　overhead restrictions policy of, 24
For-profit hybrid companies (social purpose
　for-profits), 25–27, 180–182
Fossil fuels, divestment from, 178
Foster care, efforts to help children in,
　83–86, 105, 119, 131
Foundation Center, 119

Foundations
    accreditation of community
        foundations, 46
    communications strategy for, 166–171
    community foundations, 43–45, 46,
        61, 110, 121, 191
    contributions to progress and
        improvements made by, 2, 48–49
    elitist attitudes of, 117
    freedom and responsibilities of,
        48–50
    giving more and sooner instead of
        existing in perpetuity, 172–173
    grants made by, 48
    health conversion foundations, 145
    investing approaches, alternative, 160,
        171–179, 182–183
    number of and assets of, 48
    payout requirements, 172, 173
    power dynamics between nonprofits
        and, 117–121, 128, 133–134
    private foundations, 46, 47–50, 61,
        161
    program staff for, 130–131, 132
    trust in, 50–54, 163–165
FSG, 71–72, 176, 180
Fund for Shared Insight, 154–155
Funding and revenue streams
    DAFs, availability of and impact of
        funding from, 47
    fees charges by nonprofits (earned
        revenue), 17–18, 19–21
    flexible, unrestricted funding, 24–25,
        31, 33, 119–121, 124, 129–130,
        133–134, 188
    listening to intended beneficiaries and
        staying grounded and humble,
        120–121, 122–126, 128–130
    overhead and program spending
        allocations, 22–25, 33, 121, 130
    performance assessment to qualify for
        funding, 31
    program-restricted funding, 119, 130
    time spent raising money, 31
    See also Grants

Gang members, initiative to improve lives
        of, 29–32, 120, 185–187
Gardner, John, 15
Gates, Bill
    chickens for Bolivia and strategic
        thinking of, 89–90
    example of American tradition of
        giving, 16
    giving all assets away by set time, 173
    Giving Pledge and dedication to
        philanthropy, 172
    goals of foundation, 51, 75–76, 91
    lessons from giving of, 7
    private foundation of, 47
Gates, Melinda
    goals of foundation, 51, 75–76, 91
Gates Foundation. See Bill & Melinda
        Gates Foundation
Gaudiani, Claire, 15
Gavi, the Vaccine Alliance, 98
Gay rights, 102–105
General Atlantic, 37
General Electric (GE), 176–177
Generosity, effects of on those who give,
        192–193
Ghana, child slavery in, 57–59, 191
Gill, Tim, 103–104
Gill Foundation, 103–104, 131, 191–192
Gilman, Daniel, 67
Giridharadas, Anand, 51
Girl Scouts, 20
Giudice, Phil, 118
Give Smart (Tierney and Fleishman), 68
givedirectly.org, 110
GiveWell, 99, 109–110, 146
Giving circles, 42–43, 61, 70, 76
Giving Compass, 151
Giving Pledge, 172
Giving while living, 171–179, 183
Giving/philanthropy
    American tradition of, 16, 38, 193
    concern about impact of, 1–3, 26–27
    importance of progress and
        improvements made by, 3, 5–6, 8,
        32, 37–38, 48–49

Giving/philanthropy *(continued)*
    motivations for, 50–54, 57–59
    optimism about, 191–192
    relevance of, opinions about,
        190–191
    US ranking among charitable nations,
        20, 39
    See also Effective giving/philanthropy
Global Rights, 59–60
Goal agnostic philanthropy, 64–66
Goals
    clarity and realism of, 63–64, 69–81,
        82, 159, 188
    collaboration and partnerships for
        achievements of, 70–72, 76, 82,
        105–106
    communications strategy for
        achievement of, 166–171
    data-driven approach to, 65–66
    diligence and patience for
        achievement of, 191–192
    focus, drift, and number of goals, 71,
        72–76, 82
    listening to intended beneficiaries and
        staying grounded and humble,
        76–81
    root-cause approach to selection of,
        67–69, 80, 81–82, 167
    short-term needs focus of, 80, 81–82,
        102
    thoughtful selection of, 6, 64–67,
        80–81
    unique positioning and competition,
        70–72, 82
Goldman Sachs, 175
Gonzáles, Emma, 170
Good Ventures, 66
Goodwill, 20
GrantAdvisor, 117
Grantee Perception Report (GPR)
    administration of, 122
    background and development of,
        117–118, 121–122
    benefit of data from, 118, 122–123,
        128, 149–150, 152

Einhorn Family Charitable Trust
    example, 124–126
Endowment for Health example,
    151–152
Hilton Foundation example, 79
response to results by foundations,
    94–95, 151–152
Whitman Institute example, 123–124
Wilburforce example, 55–56
Grants
    CEP support from, 8, 108
    communications in grantmaking, 167
    community foundation grants, 43–44
    DAF grants, 45–47
    declining applications, 132
    EFCT grants, 125–126
    flexible, unrestricted grants, 24–25,
        33, 119–121, 124, 129–130,
        133–134, 188
    foundation grants, 48
    Gill grants, 103
    Public Welfare grants, 59
    restricted grants, 31, 119, 130
    selection and evaluation process,
        129–130
    Stuart grants, 84
    targeted grant support, 127
    UTEC support from, 31
    Wilburforce grants, 19, 55–56
Grateful patient giving, 41–42
Greater Houston Community Foundation,
    44
Green, Michael, 139
Green Revolution, 48–49
Greenlight Capital, 124
Gueye, Tiffany Cooper, 11–14, 32, 192–193
GuideStar, 24, 110
Guirola, Janice, 115, 193
Gun law reform, 170

Haas, Jr. Fund, Evelyn and Walter,
    103–104, 131, 191–192
Hackmann, Jason, 57–59, 60, 174–175,
    191
Hackmann, Jennifer, 57–58

Harold, Jacob, 24

Harvard Business Review articles, 26, 35, 71–72, 94

Harvard Business School, 35–36, 136, 138, 176, 180

Harvard Square restaurant story, 107–108

Harvard University, 17

Harvey, Hal, 96–97, 119

Hate crime legislation, 103

Hayes, Christopher, 53

Hayling, Crystal, 164

Health conversion foundations, 145

Health issues and initiatives
    childhood obesity problems, initiative to address, 163, 179–180
    community health promoters, 109–110
    curing physical diseases, 97, 166–167
    diabetes care initiative, 145, 149
    Epiphany Community Health Outreach Services (ECHOS), 113–116, 154–155, 187, 193
    global health goals of Gates Foundation, 75–76, 98, 168
    resources on existing knowledge and best practices, 146
    school-based deworming initiative, 110
    vaccine and immunization initiative, 98

Heifer International, 90

Heintz, Stephen, 15, 54

Heinz Endowments, 54, 169–170

Henderson, Kaya, 78

Hewlett Foundation, 70–71, 95–96, 97, 120, 154

High Tech High, 154

High Tech Middle, 154

Hilton, Barron, 78–79

Hilton, Conrad, Sr., 78–79

Hilton, Steven, 79–81

Hilton Foundation, 78–81, 105

Hinostro, Nikki, 154

Homeless, initiative to help, 21–22, 79, 80, 135–136

Horizons for Homeless Children, 21–22

Horsch, Karen, 152

Hostetter, Amos, 168

Hostetter, Barbara, 168–169

Huang, Judy, 118

Humility, and effective giving, 54–57, 61, 76–81, 96–98, 105, 124–125, 164–165, 170, 188

Hurricane Harvey, 102, 116

Hurricane Katrina, 100–101

Hurricane Sandy, 101

Hybrid social purpose for-profit companies, 25–27, 180–182

Impact investing, 171–172, 175–177, 178–179

Independent Sector, 191

Ineffective givers compared to effective givers, 194

Institute of Education Sciences, What Works Clearinghouse, 146

Institutions, trust in, 50–54, 163–165

InterAction, 59–60

International Justice Mission, 58

Investing analogies, 35–38, 61, 71–72, 188–189

Investing approaches, alternative, 160, 171–179, 182–183

Iran, 60

Jantsen's Gift (Cope), 57

Jill and Nicholas Woodman Foundation, 45, 46, 47

John D. and Catherine T. MacArthur Foundation, 70–71, 173–174

Just Mercy (Stevenson), 59–60

Katz, Stanley, 188–189

Kids Wish Network, 24

King, Maxwell, 170

Knickman, James, 149

Koch, Charles, 52, 162

Koch, David, 162

Kopp, Wendy, 28

Kramer, Larry, 97–98

Kramer, Mark, 180
Kristof, Nicholas, 5

L3Cs (low-profit liability companies),
 25–27, 180–182
Laugharn, Peter, 79
Laura and John Arnold Foundation, 162
Le, Vu, 16–17
Leimsider, Rich, 76
Lester, Patrick, 143
Letwin, Rose, 19, 54–55, 60, 174
Levi Strauss, 103
LGBT people, civil rights for, 102–105,
 131, 137, 162
Libra Foundation, The, 164
Life You Can Save, The (Singer), 66
LightRails, 43
Limited liability company (LLC), 38, 47,
 161
Listen for Good initiative, 154–155
Living, giving while, 171–179, 183
Living Goods, 109
Lowell, Massachusetts, 29–32
Low-profit liability companies (L3Cs),
 25–27, 180–182

MacArthur Foundation, 70–71, 173–174
MacAskill, William, 91
Madoff, Ray, 46
Malaria, prevention of deaths from, 89, 99,
 105
Marguerite Casey Foundation, 120
Marjory Stoneman Douglas High School
 shooting, 170
Marriage equality, 103–104, 131, 162, 166,
 191–192
Marsh, Charles Edward, 59
Martinez, Crisamar, 192–193
Mary Reynolds Babcock Foundation, 147
McClymont, Mary, 59–60
McCoy, Ethan, 125
McDonald's, 72–73, 75
McFarlane, Rodger, 103
McGoey, Linsey, 176
McKinsey, 25, 77

McKnight Foundation, 70–71, 175,
 178–179
Media Impact Funders, 166
Mentoring programs, 27, 63–64, 145, 192
Merry-go-round–powered water pumps,
 91–92
Metropolitan Life, 180
Miller, Clara, 175
Mixpanel, 156
Money Well Spent (Brest and Harvey),
 96–97
Moore, Cathy, 113–115, 154–155
Moral imperative to do the most possible
 good, 50, 65–67, 80–81
Morino, Mario, 4–5, 37, 66, 111, 112
Moskovitz, Dustin, 66
Most Good You Can Do, The (Singer), 66

Napster, 52
Nathan Cummings Foundation, 174,
 175–176
National gift funds, 45, 46
National Iranian American Council, 60
National Registry of Evidence-based
 Programs and Practices, 146
National Rifle Association, 170
National Standards for US Community
 Foundations, 46
Natural habitats, protection of, 19, 54–56,
 59, 174
Negative screening, 177–179
Nestlé, 176
New Hampshire Charitable Foundation,
 43–44
New York State Health Foundation,
 145–146, 149
Newark, New Jersey, 77–78, 91, 97–98
No Such Thing as a Free Gift (McGoey),
 176
Nonprofit AF blog, 17
Nonprofit Finance Fund, 177
Nonprofits
 blurring boundaries between business
 and, 25–27, 180–182, 183
 budget of, 18–19

business thinking for and businesses
compared to, 3–5, 71–73,
138–139, 146, 188–191
challenges addressed by, 5, 14–15, 26,
32–33, 37–38
challenges of running, 14, 187–191
collaborative dynamics in, 37
diversity of, 17–18
economic impact and revenue from, 16
faith and trust in, 17, 50–54
fees charged by, 17–18
generalizations about, 18
leadership of, 12–14, 29–32
missions and roles of, 14–18, 26
model for, 12
optimism about, 191–192
overhead and program spending
allocations, 22–25, 33, 121, 130
passion of leaders of, 13, 29–32
power dynamics between givers and,
117–121, 128, 133–134
for-profit solicitors for, 23–24, 39–40
questions to ask and choosing who to
give to, 110
respect and understanding of leaders
of, 13–14, 32–33
role as counterweight to business and
government, 15, 183
salaries for personnel, 25, 31, 120
size of, 18–19, 33
sustainability and dependency, 20–22
tax-exempt status of, 18
as a tool for effective giving, 26, 32,
185–189
See also Performance
Nord Family Foundation, 132–133
Nurse-Family Partnership, 146

Oak Foundation, 70–71, 120
Occupy movement, 52–53
Ohanian, Alexis, 13
Oligarchs, 53–54
Oliphant, Grant, 54, 169–170
Omidyar, Pierre, 161
Omidyar Network, 120

Open Society Foundations, 52, 162
Oregon Fair Share, 40
Orosz, Joel, 49
Ottenhoff, Bob, 102

Pallotta, Dan, 39
Paradox of Generosity, The (Smith and
Davidson), 192
Parker, Sean, 52, 156
Parsi, Trita, 60
Partial strategists, 87–88
Partners and partnerships
assistance other than financial
support, 126–127, 128–129,
134
building relationships with nonprofits,
6, 117–126, 127–134, 159
capacity building, 119, 126–127,
128–129
choosing who to give to, 109–117,
128–134
collaboration and partnerships for
achievements of goals, 70–72,
76, 82, 105–106
contractor analogy, 118–121
ending relationships with nonprofits,
131
giver control over strategy instead of
grantees as partners, 94–97
grantees as customers analogy,
108–109, 117, 189
listening to intended beneficiaries and
staying grounded and humble,
120–121, 122–126, 128–130
nonprofit grantee views on
relationships with foundations,
121–126
Performance Imperative seven pillars
of excellence, 111–112, 126
power dynamics between givers
and nonprofits, 117–121, 128,
133–134
rules for working with grantees,
127–132
small organizations, 113–116

Partners and partnerships *(continued)*
    understanding, transparency, and
        trust in relationships, 122–126,
        128–134, 147–148, 151–152,
        163–165
    volunteers and volunteering, 16, 116,
        126, 159, 197
Patagonia, 25–27
Patrizi, Patricia, 94, 95
Peabody Education Fund, 172
Peery, Dave, 109
Peery Foundation, 109
Performance
    assessment of, challenge of, 2, 5, 6,
        27–29, 112, 135–145, 155–158,
        189
    cost-per-life-touched ratio, 135–136,
        158
    data and statistical analysis for
        decision-making about,
        155–158
    data system to track indicators, 85
    existing knowledge and knowing what
        works, 145–147, 158
    external evaluations, 149–150
    feedback for givers, 55–56, 128,
        151–153
    feedback from beneficiaries, 140,
        153–155
    giver assessment, challenge of,
        135–138
    impact as measure of, 35, 137–138,
        140–145
    indicators and measures to track,
        27–28, 135–136, 137, 140, 142,
        148–151, 158
    individual giver assessment of,
        150–151, 152–153
    learning opportunities from
        assessment process, 147, 158
    nonprofit assessment, challenge of,
        138–145
    overhead, program spending
        allocations, and impact of
        nonprofits, 23–25, 33, 121

    performance management system,
        27–28
    randomized control trials (RCTs) to
        assess, 12, 28, 31, 143–145
    scaling what works, 146
    seven pillars of excellence
        (Performance Imperative),
        111–112, 126
    sharing what works, 146–147
    subjectivity in judgment of, 137–138
    support for assessment of, 140,
        144–145, 147–148, 158
Performance Imperative seven pillars of
    excellence, 111–112, 126
Perpetual adjusters, 87–88
Pfeiffer, Sacha, 116
Philanthrocapitalism (Bishop and Green),
    139
Phone requests for donations, 39–41, 61
Pichel, Christy, 85
Pilot flying a plane analogy, 95–96
Pittsburgh Community Foundation, 170
Pittsburgh community policing techniques,
    169–170
Planned Parenthood, 160
PlayPumps International, 91–92
Police shootings, 169–170
Policy and politics, influence of
        philanthropy on, 50–53,
        160–166, 182–183
Polio, 69
Porter, Michael, 176
Poverty
    alleviation of, role of nonprofits in,
        15–16
    at-risk youth, organization to alter life
        trajectories of, 142, 185–187
    challenge of solutions for, 97
    communications and raising awareness
        about, 168
    disrupting poverty goal, 70
    focus of goals related to, 73
    goals for reduction of, 42, 77
    initiatives to help people living in, 110
    UTEC goals related to, 30

Preschool for homeless children, 21–22
Pride Foundation, 44
Private foundations, 46, 47–50, 61, 161
ProPublica, 156
Public opinion and communications
    strategy, 166–171
Public Welfare Foundation, 59–60, 162

Race issues
    BELL founding and, 11–12
    communications and raising awareness
        about, 168
    policing and, 169–170
Raghavendra, Vijay, 126
Railroad Park, 43
Rainier Valley Corps, 16–17
Randomized control trials (RCTs), 12, 28,
    31, 143–145
Ravitch, Diane, 51
Red Cross, 17, 100–102
Red Sox Foundation, 193
Reddit, 13
Relationships, giving related to, 41–43,
    56–57, 61
Religious beliefs, giving related to,
    57–58
Religious-based foundations, 44
Requests for donations, saying no to,
    39–41, 61
Reynolds-Hubbard, Pat, 83–85, 105
Rhee, Michelle, 78
Richardson, Anthony, 132–133
RippleWorks, 126
Robert Wood Johnson Foundation, 5, 48,
    137, 149
Roca, 142
Rockefeller, John D., 7, 67
Rockefeller Brothers Fund, 15, 54, 60, 150,
    173–174, 178
Rockefeller Foundation, 48–49, 68
Rockefeller Philanthropy Advisors (RPA),
    64–65
Rockefeller Sanitary Commission for
    the Eradication of Hookworm
    Disease, 67

Rogers, Ginger, 14
Rooney, Patrick, 16, 46
Rosenwald, Julius, 172
Rotary Foundation, 69
Rothberg, Jennifer Hoos, 125, 126
Russakoff, Dale, 77–78

Sabeti, Heerad, 26
Safe Passage Project, 76
Same-sex marriage, 5–6
Scared Straight, 144
Schambra, William, 68
Schistosomiasis Control Initiative, 110
Schwab, 45
Science of Generosity initiative, 192
Sears, Roebuck, 172
Seashore, Ryan, 13
Shared value exemplars, 176–177
Shoemaker, Paul, 24–25
Silicon Valley Community Foundation, 45
Silicon Valley philanthropists, 52, 66, 97
Sillcox, Leslie, 63–64, 76, 105, 155,
    174–175, 192
Sillcox, Mark, 63–64, 76, 105, 155,
    174–175, 192
Singer, Peter, 65–67, 80, 109–110
Sitka Conservation Society, 19
Slocum Sage, Margaret Olivia, 67
SmartResponse website, 101
Smilowitz, Ben, 100–101
Smith, Christian, 192
Smoking, reduction in rates of, 5, 48, 137,
    165
Social Innovation Research Center, 143
Social programs
    challenge of solutions for social issues,
        97
    data and statistical analysis for
        decision-making about,
        155–158
    social justice promotion of by
        nonprofits, 16–17
Social purpose for-profits (for-profit hybrid
    companies), 25–27, 180–182
Social Venture Partners, 24–25

Soros, George, 52
Soskis, Benjamin, 50
South Africa divestment movement, 177, 178
Stehle, Vince, 166
Stern Family Fund, 162
Stevenson, Bryan, 59–60
Strategy
    bad strategy, 92
    big bets on proven strategies, 97–99
    business strategy and strategy in philanthropy, 92–95, 105–106, 188–191
    collaboration and support for existing, effective strategies, 102–106
    data-driven approach to, 65, 85, 103–104
    decision-making and logic of, 86–87, 100, 105
    dynamic nature and revision of, 102–105, 106
    emotional desire to have impact and strategic decisions, 86, 88–92
    giver control over strategy instead of grantees as partners, 94–97, 105–106
    individual giver strategies, 99–100
    listening to intended beneficiaries and staying grounded and humble, 92–102, 106
    sound strategies to achieve goals, 6, 159, 182, 188
    strategic philanthropy, backlash against, 91–92
    Stuart Foundation example, 83–86
    total strategists, 86, 88–89
    types of givers, 87–89
    unique positioning and competition, 94
Stuart, E. A., 84
Stuart Foundation, 83–86, 99, 119, 131
Substance abuse resources, 146
Summer programs for inner-city kids, 12–14
Systems change, 37

Tax code and charitable deductions, 4, 38, 45, 50, 191
Taylor, Art, 24
Tea Party movement, 52–53
Teach for America (TFA), 28
thelifeyoucansave.org, 109–110, 146
Thompson, Elizabeth Heid, 94, 95
Threlfall, Valerie, 154
Tierney, Thomas, 68
Tobacco divestment movement, 177
Tompkins-Stange, Megan, 50–51, 164–165
Tools to maximize impact, 159–160, 182–183
Total strategists, 88–89
Traffic safety, and Dorr Foundation, 68–69
Trump, Donald J., 160, 174
Trust
    elites and institutions, faith and trust in, 50–54, 163–165
    nonprofits, faith and trust in, 17, 50–54
    understanding, transparency, and trust in relationships, 122–126, 128–134, 147–148, 151–152, 163–165
Tuna, Cari, 66
Twersky, Fay, 153
Twitter, philanthropy advice on, 80
Types of givers, 87–89

Undocumented students, assistance for, 76
United Nations Children's Fund (UNICEF), 69
United States (US)
    Iran interactions with, efforts to foster more-productive, 60
    US-Iran nuclear deal, 60
United Way, 45
UTEC, 29–32, 120, 143, 185–187, 193

Vaccine and immunization initiative, of Gates Foundation, 98
Valenzuela, Yuri, 115, 193
Vallier-Kaplan, Mary, 151–152
Vanguard, 45

Vavavida, 26
Venture philanthropy, 35–38, 135–136
Venture Philanthropy Partners, 37
VisionSpring, 126–127
VolunteerMatch, 116
Volunteers and volunteering, 16, 116, 126, 159, 197

W. K. Kellogg Foundation, 49, 164
Walker, Darren, 167–168
Walmart.com, 126
Walton family, 51
Warby Parker, 25–26
Washington, DC, 42, 78, 97–98
Washington, Gladys, 147
Water pumps, 91–92
Weingart Foundation, 120
Wells Fargo, 52
What Works Clearinghouse, Institute of Education Sciences, 146
White lines on roads, and Dorr Foundation, 68–69

Whitman Institute, The (TWI), 123–124
Wilburforce Foundation, 19, 54–56, 59, 132, 174
Wilka, Jen Vorse, 154
William and Flora Hewlett Foundation, 70–71, 95–96, 97, 120, 153, 154
Women's March, 160
Woodman, Nicholas, 45, 46, 47
World Health Organization, 69

Yee, Sylvia, 104, 105
Yelp, 108, 117
YMCA, 12, 187
Youth. *See* Children/youth
Youth Villages, 146
YouthTruth initiative, 153–154

Zagat, 117
Zuckerberg, Mark, 47, 77–78, 91, 161, 173
Zunz, Olivier, 16, 162

Phil Buchanan is founding chief executive of the Center for Effective Philanthropy, a seventeen-year-old nonprofit that conducts research and advises the largest foundations in the country, including the Ford Foundation, the William and Flora Hewlett Foundation, the David and Lucile Packard Foundation, the MacArthur Foundation, and the Rockefeller Foundation. He is also co-founder of YouthTruth, a national student survey provider. He is a columnist for the *Chronicle of Philanthropy*, and his op-eds and articles have appeared in the *New York Times*, *Stanford Social Innovation Review*, and *Financial Times*. In 2016, the *Nonprofit Times* named him the nonprofit "influencer of the year," and he has seven times been among the newspaper's "power & influence top 50." He speaks around the country on philanthropic issues and lives in Lexington, Massachusetts with his wife and two daughters.

PublicAffairs is a publishing house founded in 1997. It is a tribute to the standards, values, and flair of three persons who have served as mentors to countless reporters, writers, editors, and book people of all kinds, including me.

I. F. Stone, proprietor of *I. F. Stone's Weekly*, combined a commitment to the First Amendment with entrepreneurial zeal and reporting skill and became one of the great independent journalists in American history. At the age of eighty, Izzy published *The Trial of Socrates*, which was a national bestseller. He wrote the book after he taught himself ancient Greek.

Benjamin C. Bradlee was for nearly thirty years the charismatic editorial leader of *The Washington Post*. It was Ben who gave the *Post* the range and courage to pursue such historic issues as Watergate. He supported his reporters with a tenacity that made them fearless and it is no accident that so many became authors of influential, best-selling books.

Robert L. Bernstein, the chief executive of Random House for more than a quarter century, guided one of the nation's premier publishing houses. Bob was personally responsible for many books of political dissent and argument that challenged tyranny around the globe. He is also the founder and longtime chair of Human Rights Watch, one of the most respected human rights organizations in the world.

• • •

For fifty years, the banner of Public Affairs Press was carried by its owner Morris B. Schnapper, who published Gandhi, Nasser, Toynbee, Truman, and about 1,500 other authors. In 1983, Schnapper was described by *The Washington Post* as "a redoubtable gadfly." His legacy will endure in the books to come.

Peter Osnos, *Founder*